Self-Reference in Literature and Music

WORD AND
MUSIC STUDIES
11

Series Editors

Walter Bernhart
Michael Halliwell
Lawrence Kramer
Suzanne M. Lodato
Werner Wolf

The book series WORD AND MUSIC STUDIES (WMS) is the central organ of the International Association for Word and Music Studies (WMA), an association founded in 1997 to promote transdisciplinary scholarly inquiry devoted to the relations between literature/verbal texts/language and music. WMA aims to provide an international forum for musicologists and liteary scholars with an interest in interart/intermedia studies and in crossing cutural as well as disciplinary boundaries.

WORD AND MUSIC STUDIES publishes, generally on an annual basis, theme-oriented volumes, documenting and critically assessing the scope, theory, methodology, and the disciplinary and institutional dimensions and prospects of the field on an international scale: conference proceedings, collections of scholarly essays, and, occasionally, monographs on pertinent individual topics.

Self-Reference
in Literature and Music

Edited by
Walter Bernhart and Werner Wolf

Amsterdam - New York, NY 2010

The paper on which this book is printed meets the requirements of "ISO 9706: 1994, Information and documentation - Paper for documents - Requirements for permanence".

ISBN: 978-90-420-3158-6
E-Book ISBN: 978-90-420-3159-3
©Editions Rodopi B.V., Amsterdam - New York, NY 2010
Printed in The Netherlands

Contents

Preface

The essays collected in this volume are a selection of revised papers originally presented at the Sixth International Conference on Word and Music Studies, which was held at the University of Edinburgh in June 2007. It has become a custom to dedicate these biannual conferences of the International Association for Word and Music Studies (WMA) to particular topics of general interest for the field under discussion. The topic chosen for the 2007 conference and, in its wake, for the present proceedings is 'self-reference in literature and music'.

Self-reference is a general possibility open to all the arts and media. This is particularly true if one conceptualizes self-reference in a broad sense as any form of intra-systemic relationship. Relationships of this kind do not only include basic formal devices such as similarity, contrast or ordered series occurring within one and the same work or performance, but also – if one regards the 'system' within which self-reference operates as comprising music and literature or even all forms of media – a number of other devices: e. g. intertextual (or 'intermusical') and intermedial references. The well-known description of 'poetic function' in the classic structuralist exploration of 'poetry', Jakobson's 1960 essay "Linguistics and Poetics", is based precisely on such a broad concept of self-reference and has frequently been used in literary studies for the exploration of self-referential structures not only within literary texts but also in advertisements and other forms of discourse.

If self-reference is conceived of in this broad sense, it is obviously applicable to all media and hence also to music, including instrumental music, where music's medial specificity can be perceived most clearly. One may even argue that instrumental music (at least that of the past few centuries' Western tradition) is the most self-referential of the arts and media. For music without words, which is on the one hand notoriously under-privileged as far as its capability of 'hetero-referentially' pointing beyond itself is concerned, is on the other hand highly privileged when it comes to 'verbatim' repetitions of whole passages of a work or performance . Indeed, music's ease in doing so is unparalleled in any other medium: in a musical score the simple sign : ‖ or the instruction 'da capo al fine' can induce performers to repeat at length what has been already performed once, an unthinkable feat in the recital of a story or even of poetry, where at best short parts such as refrains can be repeated word for word (a device which, significantly, is often regarded as linking poetry to music).

However, a completely different picture emerges when one compares literature and music not before the backdrop of the aforementioned broad sense of self-reference but rather with a special form of self-reference in mind represented by devices such as literary 'metafiction', which elicits reflections on the mediality of fiction, or 'metadrama', which triggers an awareness of drama as a specific medium, its conventions, forms of reception, production (including theatricality). The meta-dimension occurring in these and similar cases is actually the effect of a special, cognitive kind of self-reference and in this quality differs from merely formal self-reference based on similarity, contrast and ordered series. In some contributions to the present volume this special form is termed 'metareference' (a notion that is used as a media-independent umbrella term for referring to meta-aspects in all the arts and media [see Wolf 2009]). Metareference is comparatively easy to achieve by means of words, for language can become meta-language without difficulties, and words can clearly denote metareferential content concerning various aspects of the arts and media. This includes not only self-reflexivity in terms of comments on a given text and hence on a verbal medium but also intermedial explorations of other media including music, as investigated in Joachim Grage's discussion of "Intermedial Reference as Metareference: Hans Christian Andersen's Musical Novels" in this volume. Yet it is as difficult to imagine that 'mere' instrumental music would hetero-referentially refer to extraneous reality as it is to envisage it metareferentially highlighting medial aspects of music itself (let alone of other arts and media). The very notion of 'metamusic' was therefore virtually unknown until recently, and it is still a concept which does not have a currency that would in any way be comparable to, say, the notion of 'metafiction' which has been used for over four decades. Even synonyms or paraphrases such as 'music on music', while not unknown in musicology (see, for instance, Klaus Schneider's 2004 *Lexikon 'Musik über Musik'*), are not by any means as wide-spread and well-known as their corresponding literary terms.

And yet some of the contributors to the present volume argue that music, and instrumental music in particular, nevertheless possess a potential for metareference, albeit a restricted one (see the essays by Peter Dayan on "Self-Reference between Words and Music in Erik Satie's Piano Pieces", Robert Samuels on Mahler's symphonies in

"Mahler within Mahler", and Werner Wolf on Mozart's sextet or 'serenade', *Ein musikalischer Spaß* in "Metamusic? Potentials and Limits of 'Metareference' in Instrumental Music: Theoretical Reflections and a Case Study"). The majority of contributors, however, quite understandably concentrate on forms of vocal music or the musical theatre, where the combination of music and words provides a less problematic way for metareference to enter musical compositions. This applies to the following contributions: to Frieder von Ammon's general exploration of metaopera in "Opera on Opera (on Opera): Self-Referential Negotiations of a Difficult Genre", to Walter Bernhart's interpretation of Schreker's opera *Christophorus, oder "Die Vision einer Oper"* "as a Metareferential Work", to Michael Halliwell's investigation of contemporary 'Literaturoper' in "'The Play's the Thing': Self- and Metareference in Contemporary Operatic Adaptation of Twentieth-Century Drama", to Bernhard Kuhn's approach to metareference from the particular angle of intermedial transposition (his focus is on metareference in film as a result of a filmicization of an opera, Leoncavallo's *Pagliacci*), and to Simon Williams' focus on "Robert Carsen's Production of *Les contes d'Hoffmann*" as an "Exercise in Theatrical Self-Reflection" (or meta-theatricality).

Regardless of whether the contributors to the present volume focus on instrumental music or on various instances of plurimedial combinations of words and music, it is no coincidence that the emphasis, in all of these essays except for Grage's, is not on the self- and metareferential potential of literature but rather of music, for it is this field that currently contains the most conspicuous lacunae in research. It is to be hoped that the present volume will contribute to closing these and thereby follow the example of its predecessors in shedding light on fascinating aspects of word-music relations which are as yet poorly researched.

This volume would not have come into existence without the indefatigable cooperation of co-editor Walter Bernhart whom I would therefore like to thank first and foremost for this, our fourth joint venture in the present book series. Moreover, and, of course, also on behalf of Walter Bernhart, I would like to thank the conference organizers Mary Breatnach and Peter Dayan from the University of Edinburgh for their excellent organization of the conference as well as Jutta Klobasek-Ladler for her valuable secretarial help in producing this volume and last but not least Katharina Bantleon for skilfully and expertly copy-editing and layouting the entire text.

Graz, Spring 2010   Werner Wolf

References

Jakobson, Roman (1960). "Closing Statement: Linguistics and Poetics". Thomas A. Sebeok, ed. *Style in Language*. Cambridge, MA: M. I. T. Press. 350–377.

Schneider, Klaus (2004). *Lexikon 'Musik über Musik': Variationen – Transkriptionen – Hommagen – Stilimitationen – B-A-C-H.* Kassel: Bärenreiter.

Wolf, Werner (2009). "Metareference across Media: The Concept, its Transmedial Potentials and Problems, Main Forms and Functions". Werner Wolf, ed., in collaboration with Katharina Bantleon and Jeff Thoss. *Metareference across Media: Theory and Case Studies. Dedicated to Walter Bernhart on the Occasion of his Retirement.* Studies in Intermediality 4. Amsterdam/New York, NY: Rodopi. 1–85.

Metamusic? Potentials and Limits of 'Metareference' in Instrumental Music Theoretical Reflections and a Case Study (Mozart's *Ein musikalischer Spaß*)

Werner Wolf, Graz

One of the most intriguing – as well as neglected – areas of musical self-reference is instrumental 'metamusic': that is, music which, similar to, for example, metafiction, metapainting or metafilm, draws attention to its status as an artefact and/or (acoustic) medium. The neglect of this aspect in research is easy to understand, for instrumental music has well-known difficulties not only with (hetero-)reference but also, and a fortiori, with explicit metareference, since it is unable to make overtly metareferential statements. Yet, this does not necessarily entail that instrumental music cannot at least covertly foreground its status as music and thus testify to a potential for implicit metareference.

In the first part of this essay, the concept of 'metareference' as a special case of 'self-reference' is explained, and its principal forms (which are derived from metafiction) are presented. The main part opens with general reflections on the potential, but also the limits, of instrumental music to produce these forms and, where applicable, to mark metareference. This is followed by a discussion of forms and functions of 'metamusic' in some examples, in particular Mozart's sextet, *Ein musikalischer Spaß* (K 522).

The overall aim of this contribution is to highlight yet another aspect under which (instrumental) music can be shown to possess transmedial features which have traditionally been attributed to other media. The transmedial perspective on 'words and music' adopted in this essay reveals that, in spite of appearances and obvious restrictions, music can in fact be aligned with other media, and in particular with verbal media, even in the field of metareference.

1. Introduction: metareference in music – a 'new hat'?

'Metareference' is old hat in the verbal media, at least as far as the substance of the matter is concerned. This becomes clear as soon as one does not use the partly unfamiliar term 'metareference', which will be explained in the following, but rather 'metatextuality' or the even more well-known term 'metafiction'[1]. As the relative clause in the preceding sentence and indeed the very sentence you are just reading illustrates, it is easy to produce verbal metareference, and it is as easy to identify such texts as metatextual. As early as in their first few semesters, students of linguistics learn what metalanguage is, and students of literature, in particular of postmodernist fiction, are also regularly confronted with metafiction. Yet, with regard to music, the situation is quite different. Compared to the old hats 'metalanguage' in linguistics and 'metafiction' in literary studies, 'metamusic' appears to be relatively 'new hat', or at least a rather obscure notion. Who has ever heard of it? Except for isolated occurrences, for example in Mittmann (1999), Burnham (2005: 74), an essay of mine (Wolf 2007a) and some contributions to a project on *Metareference in the Arts and Media* (Wolf, ed. 2009), to which the present investigation also belongs, the term 'metamusic' seems to be virtually non-existent in musicology[2].

As for the concept designated by the term I am using, 'metamusic', which denotes music that self-reflexively refers to itself as a medium

---

[1]   Metafiction (formerly 'literary self-consciousness') has been discussed for more than fifty years with increasing intensity. As it is futile to attempt a list of the publications in the field and as the term and the concept are by now well-known in literary studies, it may suffice here to name just a few studies: Hutcheon 1980/1984, Waugh 1984, Stonehill 1988, Wolf 1993 (ch. 3.2.) and 2001a, Currie, ed. 1995, Scheffel 1997.

[2]   Searching for 'metamusic' on Google leads to several references to music therapy (e. g. as conducted by the jazz band The Diamond Jubilators, who advertise their services with the slogan "Metamusic: Life enhancement through music") as well as to a composition by Valentin Silvestrov called "Metamusik", in which this title is explained as being used "in the sense of 'beyond music'" (Tuttle 2003: online). Such references have nothing to do with metamusic as a form of musical self-reflexivity; this also applies to Xenakis 1967/1971, an essay which, in spite of the misleading title "Towards a Metamusic", simply deals with 'musicology', and moreover to Kelkel 1988, for whom 'metamusic' – as for the organizers of a series of festivals of 'Metamusik' held in Berlin since 1974 – means 'exotic' or 'ethnic' music. Kelkel, strangely enough, also includes "l'alchimie" and "le Yoga musical" (1988: 5) in his investigation of the "au-delà de la musique et de la musicology" (ibid.: 3). Even a search of the online version of the renowned *Grove Dictionary of Music and Musicians 2007–2010* (Grove Music Online as part of Oxford Music Online) yields only two hits for 'metamusic', both referring to the Swedish composer Jan W. Morthenson (born in 1940; for more detailed biographical information see Haglund 2007–2010).

and/or artefact, it has received some attention, in particular in recent research, albeit under different designations such as 'music on music' or 'musical self-reflexivity'. As Tobias Janz, co-organizer of the research project 'Musikalische Selbstreflexivität', currently arguably the most promising project in the field[3], mentions in the project description, the phrase "Musik der Musik" ('music of music') was already used by Jean Paul with reference to Haydn in *Flegeljahre* (1804–1805/1959: first subtitle to no. 25 of vol. 2[4]), and the expression "Musik über Musik" ('music on music') can be traced back to a comment by Nietzsche on Beethoven (in *Menschliches, Allzumenschliches*, 3, § 152 [1954/1997: III, 935])[5]. 'Music on music' was later used as a critical phrase by Adorno (1949/1975: 165–189) in his critique of Stravinsky and by others, most prominently in the title of Klaus Schneider's recent (2004) *Lexikon 'Musik über Musik': Variationen – Transkriptionen – Hommagen – Stilimitationen – B–A–C–H*. As for 'musical self-reflexivity', this notion has, for instance, been used in order to characterize Brahms' music (see Schmidt 2000). In sum, therefore, one can say that the idea of metamusic is not entirely new, even though it is definitely not a central concept in musicology. Yet, as far as it has been used, and as far as I can see, musical metareference has hitherto almost exlusively been discussed in order to highlight individual composers or epochs[6]. Moreover, musicological

---

[3] It is being carried out at the University of Cologne and financed by the Deutsche Forschungsgemeinschaft. For further information see the project website at http:// selbstreflexion.uni-koeln.de. I am grateful to Tobias Janz for having attracted my attention to this project as well as for giving me valuable hints concerning the research history in the field.

[4] The ensuing text, the description of a concert (cf. 1804–1805/1959: 742–746), however, does not bear out expectations of metareference.

[5] See Janz (2006: online).

[6] Even the aforementioned research project at the University of Cologne concentrates on historical parameters (in particular the 'long 19th century' and modernism), rather than on intermedial comparisons. As for individual composers, one could, for instance, mention Finscher's discussion of Beethoven's piano sonata opus 31, 3 as a 'sonata on the sonata' ("eine Sonate über die Sonate", "'Musik über Musik'" [1967: 396]) or Mittmann 1999, who attributes self-reflexivity to a composition by Mauricio Kagel entitled "Metapiece" (which, incidentally, is identical to the title of a piece by the Australian composer Rainer Linz): Mittmann regards Kagel's "Metapiece" as belonging to a class of compositions that constitute a metamusical reflection on the 'performative act of music playing' ("Kompositionen [...], die den performativen Akt

research in the field appears to be largely untheoretical: 'music on music' is mostly regarded as a mere intramusical reference (e. g. by Dibelius 1966/1998), and the question of whether such intramusical self-reference in the sense of 'pointing at' (see below) could also invite metareferential self-reflection and thus be likened to meta-phenomena in other arts and media has hardly ever been asked.

It is therefore no great surprise that transmedial comparisons be-tween the metareferential potentials of the two media in focus in the present volume, namely words (verbal art) and music, have never been attempted in a systematic way. Admittedly, there have been occasion-al hints at literary-musical analogies in the field, notably between Joseph Haydn's 'humour' and the self-reflexive humour in Laurence Sterne's *Tristram Shandy* – this comparison even dates back to Jean Paul's *Vorschule der Ästhetik*[7]. Yet, most preceding discussions do not focus, from a theoretical point of view, on the general potentials as

---

des Musizierens 'metamusikalisch' reflektieren" [1999: 236f.]). Mittmann's point of departure is linguistics; his conclusion concerning his object of analysis (which corresponds to what I will term 'critical intracompositional metareference') is predominantly sceptical, but his whole enterprise – including its failures – shows the extent to which musicological reflection could benefit from applying narratological investigations on metareference. Together with Mittmann, Burnham (cf. 2005: 74) is one of the very few musicologists to have used the term 'metamusic'. (Yet, as his main subject is musical 'humour', he does so only en passant.) Neubauer (cf. 2005: 203–205) deals with "Meta-Reflection in Music", although only with reference to vocal music. Further scholars who have approached the field – mostly concentrating on 'music on music' – include: Burkholder (who sees a historicist tradition at work since the latter part of the 19th century, which produces "music about music" [1983: 130] through "Museum Pieces" [ibid.: 115] that are meant as "commentary on or foil for" the music of the past few centuries [ibid.: 125]); Karbusicky (who acknowledges the possibility of music possessing 'analytical metalanguages' ["'analysierende Metasprachen'"; 1986: 21]); Danuser 1996 (who focuses on one part of the field, namely homage-compositions, albeit without theoretical ambitions); Schmidt 2000 (an illuminating study on Brahms' self-reflexive historicism); and Schneider 2004 (a theoretically unambitious dictionary of examples of 'music on music', which, however, does not include compositions that show a potential for general metamusical reflections on music as a system or medium).

[7]   First part, seventh 'programme', § 33 (cf. 1804/1963: 131f.; Jean Paul does not deal with meta-issues, though), see again Janz (online). For the comparison cf. also Burnham (2005: 74; Burnham uses the comparison in the context of a mention of "meta-music").

well as the limitations of both music and verbal art in expressing metareference[8]. My remarks which follow attempt to fill this lacuna.

In order to highlight these general issues from a media-comparative point of view, I will concentrate on instrumental music. For, if one were to include vocal music, the idea of musical metareference would appear treacherously unproblematic and quite similar to metareference in literature. Many songs thematize singing[9], and there are quite a few metaoperas, frequently in the form of opera on opera, such as Richard Strauss' *Ariadne auf Naxos* and *Capriccio* (which deals with the rivalry of word and music in opera[10]). It is, however, clear that in all of these cases metareference tends to enter music via the verbal medium, which is part of vocal music. But what about music unalloyed with words? What about instrumental music?

If we were talking about 'self-reference' in general, the question could again easily be answered, for music is perhaps the most self-referential medium of all. Yet *meta*reference is not exactly the same thing as *self*-reference, nor self-*reflection* for that matter, although these terms – as well as the related notions – are often confused and used indiscriminately (see, e. g., Fricke 2001 or Danuser 2007). It is not self-evident what metareference actually is, so some theoretical explanations are not amiss before one can address the central questions of the present contribution: is there such a thing as instrumental metamusic? If so, in what forms can it appear? And finally, what is the benefit of identifying metamusic in the first place?[11]

---

[8]   In view of the advanced state of 'meta-research' in literature, it is no coincidence that one of the earliest hints at musical self-reflexivity from a media-comparative point of view (although only casually mentioned) did not come from musicology but from a literary scholar dealing with metafiction, namely from Linda Hutcheon: "[...] the visual arts and music both have also shown signs of self-reflectiveness" (1980/ 1984: 8; cf. also 17). Among the rare exceptions of those who deal with metamusic from a (to a certain extent) media-comparative and more theoretical point of view are the following musicological contributions to the aforementioned project on metareference in the arts and media: Janz 2009, Michaelsen 2009, and Mittmann 2009.

[9]   For an example by Schubert discussed in an earlier volume of Word and Music Studies see Wolf 2001b.

[10]   See also, as further case studies, Frieder v. Ammon's and Walter Bernhart's contributions to this volume, and moreover the seminal article on "Oper in der Oper" by Harald Fricke (2001), as well as Danuser 2005 for metaopera in general.

[11]   For previous discussions of these issues, on which I am partly drawing here, see Wolf 2007a and 2007b.

2. 'Metareference': the concept[12]

2.1. Metareference as a special case of self-reference

For the sake of clarifying the central concept under discussion, the difference between self-reference, self-reflection and metareference shall be illustrated by means of three examples from the field of the verbal media[13]:

Example 1:

> Tyger! Tyger! Burning *bright*
> In the forests of the night,
> [...] (Blake 1794/1982: 33; my emphases)

Example 2:

> [...] I desire you to be in perfect charity [with Mr Irwine], far as he may be from satisfying your demands on the clerical character. Perhaps you think he was not – as he ought to have been – a living demonstration of the benefits attached to a national church? But I am not sure of that; at least I know that the people in Broxton and Hayslope would have been very sorry to part with their clergyman [...]. (Eliot 1859/1985: 225)

Example 3:

> *This sentence* contains five *words*.

All three examples can be subsumed under the term '*self-reference*' in a broad sense. In this sense self-reference can be defined as the quality of signs and sign systems that point to themselves or to similar and contrasting elements within one and the same semiotic system. Self-reference as defined here is theoretically opposed to '*hetero-reference*' (or, as Nöth calls it, "alloreference" [2007: 62]), which denotes the 'normal' or 'default' quality of signs, namely to point to what is conventionally conceived of as 'reality outside' a semiotic system[14]. In

---

[12] For a more detailed discussion of the concept of 'metareference' cf. Wolf 2009: ch. 3.

[13] I am here drawing on, but also modifying, Michael Scheffel's research and a typology which I have published elsewhere. Scheffel was among the first to attempt some systematic ordering in the vast field of terms such as 'self-reference', 'auto-reflexivity', 'metafiction', etc., which had mostly been used as mere synonyms (cf. Scheffel 1997: notably 46–49). In Wolf 2001a I elaborated on Scheffel's distinctions.

[14] In practice, self- and hetero-reference can, of course, be combined and occur simultaneously.

spite of this common self-referentiality there are important differences between the three examples:

Example 1 contains, in the highlighted parts, specimens of *formal* verbal *self-reference*: the alliterations and the rhymes form acoustic recurrences within one and the same system, here William Blake's famous poem "The Tyger", and can be said to point to one another in much the same way as the second occurrence of a theme in a musical composition points back to its exposition[15]. It is this kind of non-semantic self-reference through *similarities, contrasts* or the formation of an *ordered series*[16] which is referred to when we speak about the overwhelming general self-reference of music[17].

Example 2, an excerpt from chapter 17 of George Eliot's realistic novel *Adam Bede* (1859), is a narratorial comment on the failure of a clerical character, Mr Irwine, the rector of a village named Broxton, to admonish the son of the local squire in a moral affair. Clearly, this comment refers to a part of the text from which it is taken, and therefore is also self-referential. However, the self-referentiality here is not merely an effect of formal phenomena (similarity, contrast, ordered series[18]) but emerges due to a specific semantic or *discursive* meaning and invites the recipient to 'reflect' on what he or she has previously learnt about Rector Irwine. It may thus be said to be an instance of '*self-reflection*'.

Example 3 is clearly also self-referential and operates with self-reflexive meaning like Example 2. Yet the kind of meaning is differ-

---

[15]   There are, of course, many more possibilities of self-reference which obey the minimal condition of a link between elements of one and the same system; in the verbal media this includes, notably, all the variants of Jakobson's 'poetic function' (see 1960), in addition, semantic recurrences ('isotopies') and grammatical *accord* as in "Galli*a* est omnis divis*a* in partes tres [...]".

[16]   Fricke (cf. 2000: 36) used these three forms in order to clarify intratextual deviations from standard language.

[17]   It is the same kind of non-semantic (dereferentialized) self-reference which authors and aestheticians of the Romantic and post-Romantic eras had in mind when attempting to create or celebrate similarities between music and poetry, or indeed all the arts.

[18]   Intertextual and intermedial references would also be classifiable as formal self-reference, since intertextuality and intermediality always imply similarity or contrast in the text/text or medium/medium reference. In addition, both intertextuality and intermediality may acquire a metareferential quality under certain conditions (for a more detailed discussion of this see Wolf 2009: ch. 5.4. and below, section 3).

ent: the narrator's statement in Example 2 is formally self-referential because it discusses an element of the novel we are currently reading, but in doing so, Rector Irwine appears as a person existing beyond the text. In fact, in the quoted passage nothing implies that he is actually a fictional figure and nothing points to the medium of fiction. Rather, the comment combines formal self-reference with semantic 'hetero-reference'. In contrast to this, Example 3 implies or triggers an awareness of the fact that we are reading a sentence and hence focusses on signifiers rather than on hetero-referential signifieds. The sentence thus self-reflexively refers to the medium or macro-system 'verbal language' and even to the micro-system 'sentence' of which it is itself a part. This is self-reflection with a meta-dimension, or what I call *metareference*. Metareference thus appears to be a special kind of self-reference (and also of self-reflection), as can be seen in the classification of Examples 1–3 in *Figure 1*. More precisely, it is an umbrella term for all phenomena that fulfil the following three conditions:

1) the existence of self-reference within a given system;
2) the discursive quality of this self-reference: it does not interlink elements of the system only through similarity, difference or in a serial way but rather triggers *reflections* in the recipient;
3) a specific logical location and content of these reflections, namely that they issue from a meta-level existing or implied in the work in question and are *focussed on (aspects of) the medium or the system referred to and related issues.*

It should be noted that metareference always involves a logical difference between an object-level (in Example 3 this is the entire sentence seen as a chain of signifiers) and a meta-level (in Example 3 this comprises the entire sentence with the words in italics as particularly clear metareferential signifieds). Owing to this differentiation, metareference appeals predominantly to reason and presupposes that a recipient is aware of the nature, forms and conventions of the signifying systems and media in question[19]. In addition, it implies that the metareferential phenomenon is not accidental but that it is, or can be

---

[19]   The fact that media-awareness is an effect of enculturation and familiarity with media may explain why ontogenetically (and perhaps also phylogenetically) metareference occurs and/or is perceived as such at a relatively late stage. Thus small children do not seem to be aware of metareference even in highly metareferential works such as Carroll's *Alice* stories.

perceived as, purposeful and thus is part of the meaning of the text or work under discussion[20].

FORMS OF SELF-REFERENCE	CRITERIA FOR THE DISTINCTION BETWEEN DIFFERENT FORMS OF SELF-REFERENCE		
	intra-systemic reference (= self-reference)	*Discursive (not merely formal) quality of the intra-systemic reference (forms or implies a statement with variable contents)*	*reference to (aspects of) the medium or related issues from a meta-level (thereby eliciting 'medium-awareness' in the recipient)*
Example 1 *formal self-reference* through similarity/contrast/ serialization	✓		
Example 2 *general self-reflection* without a meta-dimension	✓	✓	
Example 3 self-reflection with a meta-dimension: *'METAREFERENCE'*	✓	✓	✓

Figure 1: Metareference in the context of other forms of self-reference

Using the three criteria illustrated in *Figure 1*, *metareference* can thus be *defined* as follows for the field of the arts and media: it is a special, transmedial form of non-accidental self-reference produced by signs or sign configurations located on a meta-level within an artefact or performance[21]; this self-reference, which can extend from the artefact to the entire system of the arts and media, forms or implies a statement

---

[20]   This involves the hotly disputed issue of intentionality, yet even though metareference, like all reception phenomena, can be conceived of as ultimately taking place within the recipient's mind (see below, section 3), the artefact or text eliciting meta-awareness in the recipient should at least be said to give non-accidental 'signals' that invite a 'meta-reading'. Their decoding will be felt to contribute to the meaningful decoding of the artefact or text under discussion. Accidentals would hardly have this effect.

[21]   The fact that metareference cannot only proceed from 'works' (texts, artefacts, compositions) but also performances is, of course, particularly relevant in the case of a performative art such as music.

about an object-level, namely on (aspects of) the medium/system referred to. Where metareference is adequately understood, an at least
minimal corresponding 'meta-awareness' is elicited in the recipient,
who thus becomes conscious of both the medial (or 'fictional', in the
sense of artificial, and, sometimes in addition, 'invented') status of the
work under discussion and the fact that media-related phenomena are
at issue, rather than (hetero-)references to the world outside the arts
and media.

2.2. Important forms of metareference

Metareference, as just defined, can occur in many forms. I will here
single out four of the most important typological pairs and illustrate
them again – for the time being – with verbal examples, notably from
metafiction. This will prepare the ground for a brief discussion of the
extent to which these forms are also relevant to (meta)music.

2.2.1. Explicit vs. implicit metareference

The first opposition concerns *explicit* vs. *implicit metareference*,
which will be illustrated using two examples taken from Sterne's emi-
nently metafictional anti-novel *Tristram Shandy* (1759–1767):
Example 4:
> Unhappy Mrs Wadman!
> – For nothing can make *this chapter* go off with spirit but *an apostrophe* to thee –
> but my heart tells me, that in such a crisis *an apostrophe* is but an insult in
> disguise, and ere I would offer one to a woman in distress – let *the chapter* go to
> the devil; provided any damned *critic in keeping* will be but at the trouble to take
> it with him. (1759–1767/1967: 608, end of ch. IX/26 [my emphases])

Example 5:
> CHAPTER TWENTY-SEVEN
> My uncle Toby's Map is carried down into the kitchen.
> CHAPTER TWENTY-EIGHT
> [...]   (ibid.: 608, ch. IX/27–28)

Explicit metareference means that the meta-element is unmistakably
to be perceived on the 'surface' of the work or text in question due to
the conventional, denotational meaning of a sign (configuration). In
the case of verbal media, this implies the quotability of semantically
metareferential words such as the emphasized terms 'chapter', 'apos-
trophe' or 'critic' in Example 4, which are all expressions connected
to literature.

Implicit metareference does not use overt but rather covert means to establish a meta-level in a work (or performance) and trigger meta-thoughts in the recipient. In Example 5, we see a curious chapter 27, which oddly contains only one short sentence. This chapter structure saliently and, we may assume, intentionally deviates from standard forms of text segmentation. By this deviation, the text makes the reader aware of the corresponding literary convention. But why is it correct to classify this departure from the norm as an instance of metareference? It is obvious that implicit metareference is often not easy to identify and therefore frequently requires the support of explicit metareference in order not to be misread, for instance, as a mere oddity. In our example, this explicit meta-context is given in the narrator's meta-reflections on chapters which immediately precede chapter 27.

2.2.2. Intracompositional/direct vs. extracompositional/indirect meta-reference

The second pair of forms will, as in an earlier example, be illustrated with excerpts from chapter 17 of Eliot's *Adam Bede* (1859). There is one meta-variant that directly refers to the text or work in question, as in Example 6, in which the narrator comments on her own story. I have called this variant *intracompositional* or *direct metareference*.

Example 6:
> So I am content to tell *my simple story*, without trying to make things better than they were; dreading nothing, indeed but falsity, which, in spite of one's best efforts, there is reason to dread. Falsehood is so easy, truth so difficult. (Eliot 1859/1985: 222 [my emphasis])

Alternatively, there are *extracompositional* metareferences concerning other works or general medial or artistic issues, as in Example 7[22], in which the narrator comments on another art:

Example 7:
> It is for this rare, precious quality of truthfulness that I delight in my *Dutch paintings*, which lofty-minded people despise. (Ibid.: 223 [my emphasis])

---

[22] As can be seen in these examples, the 'system' within which self- as well as metareference operate can have different extensions. Although these extensions resemble a continuum rather than a binary opposition, it makes sense to identify the work or text in question as the most important unit near the lower end of the continuum, and the entirety of the media and arts (as opposed to 'reality outside them') as the largest unit.

Although the metareference in Example 7 is not directly concerned with *Adam Bede,* it is clear that the narrator's intermedial meta-comment on 'truthful' realistic Dutch paintings indirectly also concerns the realist aesthetic underlying the novel. Therefore, such extracompositional metareferences can also be called '*indirect metareferences*'.

2.2.3. Generally mediality-centred vs. truth-/fiction-centred metaref-erence

Examples 8 and 9, taken from the "Preface" to *Robinson Crusoe* (1719), illustrate two content-related meta-forms: Example 8 only concerns *generally mediality-centred* issues[23], namely the fact that we are going to read a novel and that it will be interesting.

Example 8:
> If ever the story of any private man's adventures in the world were worth making public, and were acceptable when published, the editor of this account thinks this will be so. (Defoe 1719/1965: 25)

In contrast, Example 9 focusses in addition on the opposition of truth vs. fiction by claiming factuality for the story.

Example 9:
> The editor believes the thing to be a just history of fact; neither is there any appearance of fiction in it [...]. (Ibid.)

Such *truth-/fiction-centred metareference* regularly also implies a generally mediality-centred utterance (in representations, fictionality as 'invention' presupposes mediality) and is thus a special case of me-tareference that is particularly noteworthy[24].

2.2.4. Critical vs. non-critical metareference

The last pair of meta-forms concerns one possible set of metareferen-tial functions: there is a prevailing notion that, particularly in post-

---

[23] 'Mediality' here includes all facets of medial or generic transmission, conventions etc.

[24] This special case is of particular relevance to literature since in combination with 'critical' metareference (see below) it can severely undermine aesthetic illusion (cf. Wolf 1993: ch. 3.2.4., where '*fictio*-metafiction' corresponds to what I here call 'generally mediality-centred metareference', and '*fictum*-metafiction' to 'truth-/ fiction-centred metareference').

modernist texts such as John Fowles' *The French Lieutenant's Woman*, from which Example 10 is taken, metafiction normally serves the *critical function* of laying bare the fictionality or 'untruthfulness', in the sense of 'inventedness', of the text in question and thus functions as the vehicle of an 'alienation effect'. However, metareferences can also have a more *neutral* or even a *positive*, supportive purpose, as in Example 11, which is identical with Example 9 and comprises a fictional truth-claim.

Example 10:
> This story I am telling is all imagination: these characters I create never existed outside my own mind. (Fowles 1969/1977: 85)

Example 11 = Example 9

The double use of one example for different forms of metareference here also shows thatthe same instance of metareference can, of course, involve forms from more than one of the aforementioned typological pairs and can thus be classified in multiple ways. The typology of metareferential subforms which I have just outlined must hence be understood to function in a cumulative way[25].

3. Applications to instrumental music (I): preliminary theoretical reflections

Having formulated and explained the concept of metareference as well as its principal distinguishable forms mainly through examples from fiction, one ought to maintain that meta-phenomena are by no means restricted to the verbal media. For it, much to the contrary, constitutes a transmedial phenomenon, metareference can, in fact, be regarded as a hypernym of many medial and generic variants, such as metapoetry, metadrama, metafilm, or metapainting. It should be clear by now what 'metareference' is as well as which principal meta-forms can be distinguished – at least in fiction. In spite of the fact that I have so far illustrated metareference with examples mostly taken from fiction, it is not just restricted to verbal media but is – like, for example, narra-

---

[25] Other subdivisions are possible: for instance, Nünning (2004) differentiates between 'meta-narrative' and 'meta-fictional' forms, which roughly correspond to my generally mediality-centred vs. truth-/fiction-centred metareference. Yet Nünning's terminology is only applicable to narratives and therefore useless for a transmedial application including music (which is normally non-narrative).

tivity or descriptivity – a transmedial phenomenon. The term 'metareference' can thus be regarded as a hypernym of many medial and
generic variants, such as metapoetry, metadrama, metafilm, or metapainting. However, it still remains to be seen to what extent metareference is relevant to instrumental music.

Before discussing specific examples we can, from a theoretical
point of view, already discard as inapplicable to instrumental music
some variants that occur in verbal media. Since music as such cannot
make explicit semantic statements, let alone make truth claims or lie,
the *explicit* as well as the *truth-/fiction-centred variant* of metareference cannot be realized in instrumental music. All instrumental metamusic – if it indeed exists – must therefore not only be *implicit* but
must also refer to *general medial or generic* musical *concerns* only.

There are essentially two devices through which implicit metareference could be realized in the composition and/or performance of
music:

a) deviations from standard practice, either by surpassing the standard
   or by conspicuously falling short of it; or

b) 'intermusical reference', be it in the form of references to individual compositions or in the form of 'system reference' (references to
   historical or composers' styles, to individual musical genres or
   compositional devices, etc.). In analogy to literary intertextuality,
   'intermusical' references occur in different functional variants:
   they can be critical or non-critical (like metareference), and they
   can focus on the 'pre-text' or on the work in which the 'quotation'
   occurs (for the resulting four functional variants see *Figure 2*).

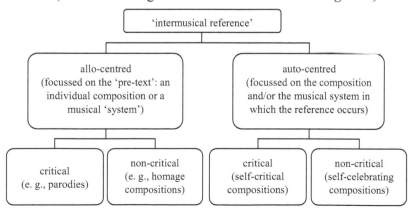

Figure 2: Variants of 'intermusical reference'

However, deviations and intermusicality per se do not in themselves guarantee the occurrence of metamusic. In the definition of metareference given above, eliciting meta-thoughts in a recipient was an important part and must consequently occur if a given case of deviation or intermediality is to be classified as metamusical. As seen, metareference is a phenomenon that not only involves artefacts and specific 'devices' but also recipients and, with this, cultural contexts which may to a considerable extent influence the recipients' cognitive meta-awareness in the first place[26]. While the work in question serves as a trigger of metareference, metareference is actually realized in the recipient's mind. Recipients depend on cultural contexts, and these are in turn influenced by the arts and media – which again influence culture since they are part of it. Thus, from a cognitive and communicative perspective, metareference is a phenomenon produced from a plurality of interdependent factors, among which the author (or performer) and the medium must also be taken into account.

The fact that the occurence of metamusic, like all metareference, depends on such a plurality of factors, together with the restriction of metamusic to implicit meta-forms, creates several problems. It may, for instance, be the case that the trigger in the work is too weak or ambiguous, that it lacks support from a cultural context, or meets with an unresponsive listener, so that no meta-awareness is elicited. In addition, a crucial difference can become an issue: namely that between the suggestion or implication of a meta-level (including the elicitation of a corresponding meta-awareness) and a 'normal' appreciation of a composer's or performer's skills. It would obviously not make much sense to regard compositions or performances that trigger such a normal appreciation as 'metamusic', for, if one did so, almost all well composed or well performed music would imply a meta-dimension. There may even be a continuum between ordinary appreciation and meta-awareness, but when do we know that we have crossed the line into 'meta-land'? This question implies the problem of *marking metareference*, a general problem of all implicit metareference and particularly so with potential metamusic. There are essentially two composition-related forms of marking:

---

[26]   For more details on this issue as well as on some others treated in this chapter cf. Wolf 2009: ch. 3.3.

a) marking through a *salient* and often *combined* use of the two
   aforementioned devices – intermusical references and highly unusual deviations from standard musical practice – so that reflections on music, its composition, performance, etc. are triggered.
   Yet even such 'marking' could be ambiguous or not sufficiently
   efficient so that this form will often occur in conjunction with a
   second one:

b) intermedial marking through *verbal paratexts* (for instance titles of
   compositions) or contextual documents (in a programme or a
   composer's comments).

While marking metareference through paratexts actually involves a
variant of explicit verbal metareference which makes it relatively
transparent[27], marking through deviations and intermusical reference
once more shows the precariousness of metamusic. As for deviations,
not all of them can be regarded as metareferences (they could, for
instance, simply stem from an incompetent composer or rather point
to narrativity [see Wolf 2008]). Moreover, deviations depend on cultural contexts and the listener's awareness of them. In order to function as markers of metamusic, deviations therefore should not only be
salient but ought to prevent listeners from attributing them to regular
non-metareferential causes and should occur in a context in which a
meta-awareness can plausibly be assumed.

As for intermusical reference, it is no less problematic as an indicator of metamusic. It would certainly be an exaggeration to claim that
all musical 'quotations' are automatically a form of metamusic[28], and
even more so that they therefore *mark* metamusic. Thus the occurrence of hymns in Romantic symphonies will trigger connotations, but
not necessarily metareferential ones, since they could also elicit
'hetero-referential' notions. If quotations, however, become so salient
that a composition appears to turn into a pastiche, or if the quotations
do not 'organically' fit into the work in question, this may well be perceived as a trigger of a metareferential awareness.

---

[27] For the role of titles in metamusical compositions see Danuser 2009.

[28] A similar problem occurs in fiction. Thus, if a text such as the Bible or a novel is a
probable part of the fictional world, e. g., of a short story, references to biblical stories
or to novel-reading by a character may not by themselves elicit an awareness of a
textual medium in the readers and therefore remain below the meta-threshold, so to
speak. As instrumental music does not form possible worlds, this argument is, however, not directly transferable to it.

In looking for potential metamusic, it will hence prove advantageous to search for compositions with unusual titles that foreground music or compositional practices as such. These compositions should, in addition, have been created in (historical) contexts in which a certain musical 'self-consciousness' can be assumed, and should moreover be highly idiosyncratic works whose internal make-up is apt to elicit reflections on music through salient deviations and/or intermusicality to a higher degree than is normally the case. Are there examples of such compositions which could be used to test the claim that instrumental music can in principle become metareferential and thus resemble certain forms of metafiction?

4. Applications to instrumental music (II): examples

In both drama and epic narratives, the oldest examples of metareference tend to come from comic genres such as Ancient Greek comedy or the parodic mock epic *Batrachomyomachia* ('The Battle of the Frogs and Mice' by Pseudo-Homer). This link between metareference and the comic arguably stems from the affinity between the cognitive distance implied in all metareference and the emotional distance involved in all matters comic. It consequently does not come as a surprise that many, albeit not all, potential examples of metamusic are also humorous. My first test case, Mozart's 'Musical Joke' (*Ein musikalischer Spaß*, K 522, composed in 1787) may illustrate this, although its completion, on June 14, 1787, was set in a decidedly non-humorous biographical context, as "it was the first composition [Mozart] completed after receiving the news of his father's death (28 May 1787)" (Lister 1994: 101).

This sextet (Schipperges 2005: 597 classifies it as a 'serenade') has an apocryphical title, "Dorfmusikantensextett" ('Country musicians' sextet'), which alludes to salient deviations apparently occurring in the performance of the composition: strident dissonances which seem to constitute a parodic system reference to incompetent musical performance. Apart from the final chord and some blatantly wrong notes at the end of the cadence in movement III, movement II, *Menuetto Maestoso* (!), contains a particularly humorous form of this kind of 'parody', namely jarring notes in the horns.

Example 1: Mozart, Ein musikalischer Spaß, *K 522, second movement (Menuetto Maestoso), mm. 16–22.*

The wrong notes in the horns could, in principle, be accidental and therefore not conform to our definition of metareference. However, we know or can see from the score (*Example 1*) that they are there on purpose, and this shows that in this case the salient falling short of standard expectations not only presupposes but activates our awareness of the musical system (here: tonality) and is therefore an instance of metamusic.

However, as Wolfgang Hildesheimer has pertinently remarked (see 1977/1982: 218; cf. also Schipperges 2005: 597), the principal butt of Mozart's joke is *not* incompetent *performers*[29] but incompetent *composers*[30]. This is indeed convincing and can be seen clearly from the compositional structure, in which a salient banality of the material is coupled with constantly failing attempts at fulfilling musical conventions. The following examples illustrate this.

The first example (*Example 2*) is the beginning of the opening movement, which is composed in sonata form. Here, a remarkably uninspired first theme extends over only three, rather than the regular four, measures and is repeated in an odd way so that the last chord of the theme is at the same time the first chord of its repetition:

---

[29] Contrary to appearances, *Ein musikalischer Spaß* is very difficult to perform, in particular for the horn players, whose part is composed in seeming oblivion of the instrument's limitations. (I am grateful to Michael Halliwell, who as a horn player has an intimate knowledge of the horn part, for his private communication.) Schipperges (cf. 2005: 597) also considers the violin 'cadenza' in the third movement to clearly go beyond the scope of inexpert performers.

[30] Lister (cf. 1994: 104f.) also mentions the further possibility that part of the joke is directed against Mozart's own compositional style as a child.

Example 2: Mozart, Ein musikalischer Spaß, *K 522, first movement (Allegro), mm. 1–7 (!).*

The following examples are all taken from the last (fourth) movement. It is a rondo following a slow movement, which ought to have come as the second rather than the third movement. (The second movement is the aforementioned minuet; this internal sequence constitutes an odd deviation from standard practice and arguably forms a further covert metamusical element.)

Example 3: Mozart, Ein musikalischer Spaß, *K 522, fourth movement (Presto), mm. 29–55.*

The opening section of the final rondo is particularly interesting since the first interlude starts like a fugue in five parts, again with an over-simplistic theme, but does not advance further than a very short exposition (see *Example 3*; this is obviously a critical intermusical system reference to a form which is not normally used in rondos).

The second example (*Example 4*) from the final rondo contains a parody of 'thematic work', which is executed here in both an obtrusive and again over-simplistic manner:

Example 4: Mozart, Ein musikalischer Spaß, *K 522, fourth movement (Presto), mm. 182–206.*

There are many more instances of compositional blunders until the final part of the rondo, which sports some enervating repetitions of banal phrases, a second attempt at the failed fugue from the beginning, a mock-effective general rest, and the well-known final discord, which again seems to be an effect of a failed performance.

The fact that Mozart's composition contains salient and highly idiosyncratic deviations from standard practice is clear enough. Yet is all of this[31] really metamusic, or does it merely indicate a particularly uninspired work (and that the supposed implicit metamusical devices are mere accidents)? Apart from the almost 'blasphemous' implication that the 31-year-old Mozart would have composed so many blunders without any ulterior motive, it would arguably still be discernible as metamusic owing to its revealing (original) title, *Ein musikalischer Spaß* ('A Musical Joke'). And yet, does this title not merely point to a joke, which is not necessarily identical with marking metareference? Research seems to have limited itself to just this dimension: the 'jokes' and their musical details have been recognized and have received detailed discussion (cf. for instance Greither 1962: 126f., Abert 1955/1973: 326–330, Hildesheimer 1977/1982: 217–219, Lister 1994:

---

[31]   There are many more deviations from standard expectations, pertinently discussed in detail by Lister (cf. 1994: 101–179), such as incompetent modulations, wrong trills, rhythmic, melodic and dynamic 'mistakes', including "Accompaniment Without Melody" (ibid.: 111) and an incongruous use of the "subito forte technique" (ibid: 137). However, since I purport to 'read' such 'odd' elements in K 522 not merely as 'musical humour' but as occurrences of metamusic, the details mentioned so far may suffice.

$101-179^{32}$). Yet the fact that this is a good example of metamusic and to that extent comparable to literary parodies, which are metareferential by definition (see Rose 1979), has to my knowledge not been observed by anybody so far.

The 'jokes' or – with generic singular – the joke, whether directed at bad composers or bad performers, is first and foremost a *joke about music* and presupposes at least some knowledge of contemporary music in order to be appreciated (in particular of the sonata, which by 1787 had become an established form). Thus the title does not only indicate music as the *means* by which the *Spaß* is carried out, but also as its *object* – and thus signals a metareferential dimension in K 522. As mentioned before, the principal function of the metareference is a critical, parodic system reference to contemporary practice by colleagues of Mozart, but the little piece may arguably also have been conceived of in order to furnish intelligent amusement to well informed listeners: by inviting them to exercise their musical knowledge and decipher the 'blunders', K 522 not only makes them appreciate Mozart's (negative) skill but also allows them to become aware of their *own* expertise – the 'self-conscious', metareferential nature of the composition thus has its counterpart in a gratifying self-consciousness on the part of the listeners.

* * *

Mozart's *Musikalischer Spaß* is, of course, not the only humorous example of metamusic. In fact there are so many examples, even if one only focuses on Western music of the past two to three centuries, that I can only mention some of them. First and foremost they come from Mozart's famous contemporary, Joseph Haydn, whose capacity for musical humour is well known (see Wheelock 1992, Burnham

---

[32] Lister differentiates between 'referential' and 'absolute' humour in music. To her the latter form, for which the term 'self-referential' would have been more appropriate, "consists of a play with or distortion of the expectations set up by the music" (1994: 79). Curiously, Lister classifies Mozart's making fun of "inadequate composing" as "referential in nature" (ibid.: 178), thereby entirely missing the *meta*reference implied in this generic parody. Lister's discussion, illuminating as it is with respect to musical humour, also shows that the absence of the concept of metamusic can lead to quite misleading comments.

2005[33]; cf. Walter 2007: 19–21[34] and 109–123[35]). As in the case of Mozart's *Spaß*, the fact that this so-called humour also has a serious, metareferential dimension has largely escaped scholarly attention, but it is a noteworthy indicator that musical 'self-consciousness' is part of the cultural context in which Mozart composed.

The same rubric of humorous metamusic could not only be used for the classification of musical parodies but also of pastiches as metamusic. For pastiches often imply a self-critical dimension (by laying themselves bare as pastiches) and also a non-critical reverence towards the composers or styles employed. In pastiches, there is moreover a possibility of employing self-irony not in a destructive but in a *self-protective* way, which I have discussed elsewhere with reference to the 'protective irony' in Friedrich Gulda's "Piano Concerto for Myself" (see Wolf 2007c: 41f., and 2007a: 314).

However, not all metamusic is humorous. Thus homage music, as collected by Schneider 2004, can be regarded as serious (non-critical) metamusic if the style or parts of the work of the honoured person or period are recognizable as a specific kind of music and as forming part of the meaning of the composition in question[36]. Other non-humorous

---

[33]   Burnham, in an excellent article on Haydn's humour, likens Haydn's "foregrounding [of] the articulative junctures of his music" to "the self-reflexive literary art of Laurence Sterne" and even once calls the witty products of this composer "a kind of meta-music", which he rightly sees to have the effect of "distanc[ing]" the listener from the "musical material" (another way of describing the difference between object- and metalevel) and rendering the listeners "aware of [their] expectations" (2005: 73f.).

[34]   Walter (cf. 2007: 19) quotes an eighteenth-century source (*Musikalischer Almanach auf das Jahr 1782*), which testifies to the fact that Haydn's contemporaries were well aware of the witty, humorous quality of much of his music.

[35]   Particularly illuminating in this chapter on "Publikumsgeschmack und Ironie" is Walter's discussion of the slow movement in Haydn's symphony no. 95 ("Surprise"). Walter regards the banality of its main theme as well as the unmotivated fortissimo chord near the beginning of the movement, which gave rise to the symphony's name (in German: "mit dem Paukenschlag"), as an ironic undercutting of the London public's expectation of simplicity without, however, commenting on the meta-dimension of this composition.

[36]   Examples of an homage to a specific composer would be Luciano Berio's *Sinfonia*, whose third part was intended as a celebration of Gustav Mahler (cf. Berio n. d.) and structurally follows the third movement of Mahler's second symphony, as well as Mauricio Kagel's *Ludwig van*, which the composer called a "Metacollage" (Kagel n. d.). An example of an homage to an entire musical period is Grieg's *Fra*

variants of metamusic, which sometimes border on self-celebration, would be compositions that saliently surpass existing standards and self-consciously flaunt their own compositional particularities or perfections. A case in point would be Johann Sebastian Bach's *Kunst der Fuge* or "Kleines harmonisches Labyrinth" (attributed to Bach), which I have discussed elsewhere as metamusic that foregrounds the possibilities of modulation and chromaticism (cf. Wolf 2007a: 310–312, and 2007b: 56–58). One should also enlist in the range of potential metamusic virtuoso performances, whether composed or improvised, whether from classical music or jazz. For in all of these forms the skill of the performer is often conspicuously foregrounded as well as the technical potential and limits of the instruments played, so that in such cases the 'medium becomes the message' and the medium-awareness thereby elicited fulfils an important condition of metareference. (Of course, as mentioned before, in these cases the problem of distinguishing between 'ordinary' expert execution and metamusical performance applies; arguably individual performances will contain relevant 'keys' that facilitate the decision on the frame to be applied.) From a historical point of view one should add to the non-humorous variants of metamusic compositions written in particular from the second half of the 19th century onwards, which Burkolder discusses in his noteworthy essay of 1983 as "museum pieces". Burkholder claims that musical self-consciousness has become increasingly discernible in compositions since the mid-19th century. He explains this by the endeavour of many composers (such as Schumann in his second symphony in C major) to inscribe themselves – through self-conscious emulation, allusion and transparent references to 'old masters' – into the tradition of culturally valuable music that, it is hoped, will survive in the museum of cultural memory (see also Seaton 2008).

*   *   *

There is not enough space in this volume to go into detail on further examples. Suffice it to say that metamusic, in fact, exists, although certain conditions must apply to allow us to speak meaningfully of it. As for the different forms of musical metareference, they are substantially limited in comparison to metafiction since explicit and truth-/

Holbergs Tid ('From Holberg's Time'). Note that in the two latter cases the titles of the compositions contribute to marking metareference.

fiction-centred variants are excluded from instrumental music. Still, the remaining reservoir of forms is rich enough to claim that music, contrary to what one may have expected, can contribute to the meta-referential field in its own right.

		META-FICTION	META-MUSIC	MUSICAL EXAMPLES
A. explicitness of metareference	explicit	✓	–	–
	implicit	✓	✓	Mozart, *Mus. Spaß*
B. extension of metareference	intra-compositional/direct	✓	✓	Bach, "Kleines harmon. Labyrinth"; virtuoso impro-visations in jazz
	extra-compositional/indirect	✓	✓	Mozart, *Mus. Spaß*
C. content of metareference	generally mediality-centred	✓	✓	Mozart, *Mus. Spaß*
	truth-/fiction-centred	✓	–	–
D. evaluative function of metareference	critical	✓	✓	Mozart, *Mus. Spaß*
	non-critical	✓	✓	Bach, "Kleines harmon. Labyrinth"; virtuoso improvisa-tions in jazz

Figure 3: Forms of metareference in fiction as compared to instrumental metamusic with musical examples.

Figure 3 gives an overview of possible forms of metamusic in comparison to metafiction. It also contains a classification of the metareferential forms encountered in Mozart's 'Musical Joke', as well as in two other cases where Mozart's composition cannot be used as an illustration.

5. Conclusion: Why the identification of metamusic matters

I hope I have convincingly shown that some instrumental music can indeed be classified as 'metamusic'. Yet, what is the benefit of such a classification? The question merits attention, not least because metamusic is such a novel notion in musicology. There are in fact a num-

ber of reasons which point to considerable advantages which the introduction and use of this concept in musicology would bring about:

a) it enables us to see connections between phenomena such as homage compositions and musical jokes that hitherto have been studied
under completely different headings;

b) due to a well-known cognitive mechanism, the existence of a term
sharpens our awareness of the corresponding phenomenon and
helps us to identify relevant musical compositions and show them
in a new light. This especially concerns the various cultural functions metareference can fulfil – from providing amusement for an
elite of connoisseurs to criticising traditions and propelling new
developments. This could also be illuminating for musical genre
theory, for instance concerning the question as to whether there are
musical genres, such as themes with variations or compositions
that favour virtuoso performances, which per se tend towards metareference as they draw attention to compositional and/or performative brilliance;

c) in particular, the concept of metamusic may create awareness for
the fact that music is just as capable of metareference as are all other arts and media. Aligning music in this way permits us to carry
out yet another transmedial comparison besides, for instance,
discussing the common narrative or descriptive potential of music
and other media;

d) terminological and conceptual tools related to metareference allow
us to carry out comparative cultural historical enquiries: it would,
for instance, be interesting to see whether Western music shares
the massive increase in metareference, or in other words the 'metareferential turn' which has affected other arts and media over the
past century (cf. Wolf 2007a: 317, and 2007b: 60, as well as Wolf,
ed. 2010, forthcoming)[37], and if it also betrays another tendency
which has been discernible in literature and other media since the
beginning of the twentieth century, namely to considerably increase the proportion of non-humorous metareference; such comparative enquiries would, of course, also apply to possible explana-

---

[37] The interest which a metamusical such as *The Phantom of the Opera* has recently
found may just be one facet of such a development, even if part of the public interest
here, of course, derives from the romantic content. For a critical assessment of the
metereferentiality in *The Phantom of the Opera* see Urrows 2009.

tions of why music follows these developments or does not do so (fully);

e) last but not least, being able to identify metamusic contributes to our understanding of the highly developed human faculty of representing meta-thoughts, which seems to be one of the characteristic features of our species. It would indeed be surprising if music, one of our culture's most elaborate arts, did not show symptoms of this general tendency.

Nevertheless, much remains to be done in the field of metamusic, from collecting more evidence throughout musical history to discussing the multiple functions of musical metareference. These functions considerably exceed the crude distinction between critical and non-critical metamusic which I have introduced above. As for further evidence, the few examples I have discussed or mentioned here mirror my own limited knowledge and 'classical' musical taste rather than the range of periods and compositions that ought to be investigated. So in this respect, too, there is still ample room for further activities. Nevertheless, I hope that my remarks have contributed to filling at least some of the lacunae that exist in the field. I moreover trust that the foregoing reflections have thrown some light on an exciting new field, in which music can be heard to add its voice to the chorus of all the other 'self-conscious' arts and media humanity has produced.

References

Abert, Hermann (1955/1973). *W. A. Mozart: Neubearbeitete und erweiterte Ausgabe von Otto Jahns Mozart*. 3 vols. 8th ed. Leipzig: Breitkopf und Härtel.

Adorno, Theodor (1949/1975). *Philosophie der neuen Musik*. Gesammelte Schriften 12. Frankfurt/M.: Suhrkamp.

Berio, Luciano (n. d.). *Sinfonia*. Liner notes. CBS. LP 34-61079.

Blake, William (1794/1982). "The Tyger". William Blake. *Selected Poems*. Ed. P. H. Butter. London: Dent. 33.

Burkholder, J. Peter (1983). "Museum Pieces: The Historicist Mainstream in Music of the Last Hundred Years". *The Journal of Musicology* 2: 115–134.

Burnham, Scott (2005). "Haydn and Humor". Caryl Clark, ed. *The Cambridge Companion to Joseph Haydn*. Cambridge: Cambridge Univ. Press. 61–76.

Currie, Mark, ed. (1995). *Metafiction*. Longman Critical Readers. London: Longman.

Danuser, Hermann (1996). "Hommage-Komposition als 'Musik über Musik'". Günther Wagner, ed. *Jahrbuch des Staatlichen Instituts für Musikforschung Preußischer Kulturbesitz*. Stuttgart: Metzler. 52–64.

— (2005). "The Textualization of the Context: Comic Strategies in Meta-Operas of the Eighteenth and Twentieth Centuries". Karol Berger, Anthony Newcomb, eds. *Music and the Aesthetics of Modernity: Essays*. Harvard Publications in Music 21. Cambridge, MA: Harvard Univ. Press. 65–97.

— (2007). "Robert Schumann und die romantische Idee einer selbstreflexiven Kunst". Henriette Herwig et al., eds. *Übergänge zwischen Künsten und Kulturen: Internationaler Kongress zum 150. Todesjahr von Heinrich Heine und Robert Schumann*. Stuttgart: Metzler. 471–491.

— (2009). "Generic Titles: On Paratextual Metareference in Music". Wolf, ed. 191–210.

Defoe, Daniel (1719/1965). *Robinson Crusoe*. Ed. Angus Ross. Harmondsworth: Penguin.

Diamondcentre: online. http://www.diamondcenter.net/jubilators/ met amusic.htm. [07/02/2005.]

Dibelius, Ulrich (1966/1998). "Musik über Musik". Ulrich Dibelius. *Moderne Musik nach 1945*. Munich: Piper. 607–628.

Eliot, George (1859/1985). *Adam Bede*. Ed. Stephen Gill. Harmondsworth: Penguin.

Finscher, Ludwig (1967). "Beethovens Klaviersonate opus 31, 3: Versuch einer Interpretation". Ludwig Finscher, Christoph-Hellmut Mahling, eds. *Festschrift für Walter Wiora zum 30. Dezember 1966*. Kassel: Bärenreiter. 385–396.

Fowles, John (1969/1977). *The French Lieutenant's Woman*. London: Triad Panther.

Fricke, Harald (2000). *Gesetz und Freiheit: Eine Philosophie der Kunst*. Munich: Beck.

— (2001). "Oper in der Oper: Potenzierung, Ipsoreflexion, Mise en abyme im Musiktheater". Francois Seydoux, Giuliano Castellani, Axel Leuthold, eds. *Fiori Musicologici: Studi in Onore di Luigi Ferdinando Tagliavini nella Recorrenza del Suo LXX Compleanno*. Bologna: Patron. 219–245.

Greither, Aloys (1962). *Wolfgang Amadé Mozart in Selbstzeugnissen und Bilddokumenten.* Reinbek bei Hamburg: Rowohlt.

Haglund, Rolf (2007–2010). "Morthenson, Jan W(ilhelm)". *Oxford Music Online.* http://www.oxfordmusiconline.com:80/subscriber/article/grove/music/19177. [23/02/2010.]

Hildesheimer, Wolfgang (1977/1982). *Mozart.* Suhrkamp Taschenbuch 598. Frankfurt/M.: Suhrkamp.

Hutcheon, Linda (1980/1984). *Narcissistic Narrative: The Metafictional Paradox.* London: Methuen.

Jakobson, Roman (1960). "Closing Statement: Linguistics and Poetics". Thomas A. Sebeok, ed. *Style in Language.* Cambridge, MA: M.I.T. Press. 350–377.

Janz, Tobias (2006: online). "Projektbeschreibung". Musikalische Selbstreflexion. University of Cologne. http://selbstreflexion.uni-koeln.de. [6/8/2008.]

— (2009). "'Music about Music': Metaization and Intertextuality in Beethoven's *Prometheus Variations op. 35*". Wolf, ed. 211–233.

Jean Paul (1804/1963). *Vorschule der Ästhetik.* Jean Paul. *Werke.* Ed. Norbert Miller. Vol 5. Munich: Hanser. 7–456.

— (1804–1805/1959). *Flegeljahre.* Jean Paul. *Werke.* Ed. Gustav Lohmann. Vol 2. Munich: Hanser. 567–1065.

Kagel, Mauricio (n. d.). *Ludwig van.* Liner Notes. Deutsche Grammophon. LP 14931.

Karbusicky, Vladimir (1986). *Grundriß der musikalischen Semantik.* Grundrisse 7. Darmstadt: Wissenschaftliche Buchgesellschaft.

Kelkel, Manfred (1988). *Musique des mondes: Essai sur la métamusique.* Paris: Vrin.

Lister, Laurie-Jeanne (1994). *Humor as a Concept in Music: A Theoretical Study of Expression in Music, the Concept of Humor and Humor in Music with an Analytical Example – W. A. Mozart, 'Ein musikalischer Spaß, KV 522'.* Publikationen des Instituts für Musikanalytik Wien 2. Frankfurt/M.: Lang.

Michaelsen, René (2009). "Exploring Metareference in Instrumental Music – The Case of Robert Schumann". Wolf, ed. 235–257.

Mittmann, Jörg-Peter (1999). "Meta-Musik: Zum Problem musikalischer Selbstreferenz". Christoph Asmuth, Gunter Scholtz, Franz-Bernhard Stammkötter, eds. *Philosophischer Gedanke und musikalischer Klang: Zum Wechselverhältnis von Musik und Philosophie.* Frankfurt/M.: Campus. 229–238.

— (2009). "'Intramedial Reference' and Metareference in Contemporary Music". Wolf, ed. 279–297.

Neubauer, John (2005). "The Return of the Repressed: Language and Music in the Nineteenth Century". Lilo Moessner, Christa M. Schmidt, eds. *Anglistentag 2004, Aachen: Proceedings*. Proceedings of the Conference of the German Association of University Teachers of English 26. Trier: Wissenschaftlicher Verlag Trier. 199–209.

Nietzsche, Friedrich (1954/1997). *Werke*. Ed. Karl Schlechta. 4 vols. Darmstadt: Wissenschaftliche Buchgesellschaft.

Nöth, Winfried (2007). "Metapictures and Self-Referential Pictures". Winfried Nöth, Nina Bishara, eds. *Self-Reference in the Media*. Approaches to Applied Semiotics 6. Berlin: de Gruyter. 61–78.

Nünning, Ansgar (2004). "On Metanarrative: Towards a Definition, a Typology and an Outline of the Functions of Metanarrative Commentary". John Pier, ed. *The Dynamics of Narrative Form: Studies in Anglo-American Narratology*. Narratologia 4. Berlin: de Gruyter. 11–57.

Rose, Margaret A. (1979). *Parody/Metafiction: An Analysis of Parody as a Critical Mirror to the Writing and Reception of Fiction*. London: Croom Helm.

Scheffel, Michael (1997). *Formen selbstreflexiven Erzählens: Eine Typologie und sechs exemplarische Analysen*. Studien zur deutschen Literatur 145. Tübingen: Niemeyer.

Schipperges, Thomas (2005). "Die Serenaden und Divertimenti". Silke Leopold, ed. *Mozart Handbuch*. Kassel/Stuttgart: Bärenreiter/ Metzler. 562–602.

Schmidt, Matthias (2000). *Johannes Brahms: Ein Versuch über die musikalische Selbstreflexion*. Taschenbücher Musikwissenschaft 137. Wilhelmshaven: Noetzel.

Schneider, Klaus (2004). *Lexikon 'Musik über Musik': Variationen – Transkriptionen – Hommagen – Stilimitationen – B-A-C-H*. Kassel: Bärenreiter.

Seaton, Douglass (2008). "Back from B-A-C-H: Schumann's Symphony no. 2 in C Major". Gregory Butler, George B. Stauffer, Mary Dalton Greer, eds. *About Bach: Festschrift for Christoph Wolff*. Urbana, IL: University of Illinois Press. 191–206.

Sterne, Laurence (1759–1767/1967). *Tristram Shandy*. Ed. Graham Petrie. Harmondsworth: Penguin.

Stonehill, Brian (1988). *The Self-Conscious Novel: Artifice in Fiction from Joyce to Pynchon*. Philadelphia, PA: Univ. of Pennsylvania Press.

Tuttle, Raymond (2003: online). "[CD Review: Valentin Silvestrov – Metamusik, Postludium]". Classical Net. 2003. http://www.classica l.net/music/recs/reviews/e/ecm01790a.php. [07/02/2005.]

Urrows, David Francis (2009) "Phantasmic Metareference: The Pastiche 'Operas' in Lloyd Webber's *Phantom of the Opera*". Wolf, ed. 259–277.

Walter, Michael (2007). *Haydns Sinfonien: Ein musikalischer Werkführer*. Beck Reihe Wissen. Munich: Beck.

Waugh, Patricia (1984). *Metafiction: The Theory and Practice of Self-Conscious Fiction*. New Accents. London: Methuen.

Wheelock, Gretchen A. (1992). *Haydn's Ingenious Jesting with Art: Contexts of Musical Wit and Humor*. New York, NY: Schirmer.

Wolf, Werner (1993). *Ästhetische Illusion und Illusionsdurchbrechung in der Erzählkunst: Theorie und Geschichte mit Schwerpunkt auf englischem illusionsstörenden Erzählen*. Buchreihe der Anglia 32. Tübingen: Niemeyer.

— (2001a). "Formen literarischer Selbstreferenz in der Erzählkunst: Versuch einer Typologie und ein Exkurs zur '*mise en cadre*' und '*mise en reflet/série*'". Jörg Helbig, ed. *Erzählen und Erzähltheorie im zwanzigsten Jahrhundert: Festschrift für Wilhelm Füger*. Heidelberg: Winter. 49–84.

— (2001b). "'Willst zu meinen Liedern deine Leier drehn?': Intermedial Metatextuality in Schubert's 'Der Leiermann' as a Motivation for Song and Accompaniment and a Contribution to the Unity of *Die Winterreise*". Walter Bernhart, Werner Wolf, eds. *Word and Music Studies: Essays on the Song Cycle and on Defining the Field. Proceedings of the Second International Conference on Word and Music Studies at Ann Arbor, 1999*. Word and Music Studies 3. Amsterdam: Rodopi. 121–140.

— (2007a). "Metafiction and Metamusic: Exploring the Limits of Metareference". Winfried Nöth, Nina Bishara, eds. *Self-Reference in the Media*. Approaches to Applied Semiotics 6. Berlin: de Gruyter. 303–324.

— (2007b). "Metaisierung als transgenerisches und transmediales Phänomen: Ein Systematisierungsversuch metareferentieller Formen und Begriffe in Literatur und anderen Medien". Janine Hauthal et al., eds. *Metaisierung in Literatur und anderen Medien: Theoret-*

ische Grundlagen – historische Perspektiven – Metagattungen – Funktionen. Spectrum Literaturwissenschaft. Berlin: de Gruyter. 25–64.

— (2007c). "'Schutzironie' als Akzeptanzstrategie für problematische Diskurse: Zu einer vernachlässigten Nähe erzeugenden Funktion von Ironie". Thomas Honegger, Eva-Maria Orth, Sandra Schwabe, eds. *Irony Revisited: Spurensuche in der englischsprachigen Literatur. Festschrift für Wolfgang G. Müller.* Würzburg: Königshausen & Neumann. 27–50.

— (2008). "Erzählende Musik?: Zum erzähltheoretischen Konzept der Narrativität und dessen Anwendbarkeit auf Instrumentalmusik". Melanie Unseld, Stefan Weiss, eds. *Der Komponist als Erzähler: Narrativität in Dmitri Schostakowitschs Instrumentalmusik.* Ligaturen 2. Hildesheim: Olms. 17–44.

— (2009). "Metareference across Media: The Concept, its Transmedial Potentials and Problems, Main Forms and Functions". Wolf, ed. 1–85.

— ed., in collaboration with Katharina Bantleon and Jeff Thoss (2009). *Metareference Across Media: Theory and Case Studies. Dedicated to Walter Bernhart on the Occasion of his Retirement.* Studies in Intermediality 4. Amsterdam/New York, NY: Rodopi.

— ed., in collaboration with Katharina Bantleon and Jeff Thoss (2010, forthcoming). *The Metareferential Turn: Forms, Functions, Attempts at Explanation.* Studies in Intermediality 5. Amsterdam/ New York, NY: Rodopi.

Xenakis, Iannis (1967/1971). "Towards a Metamusic". Jasia Reichardt, ed. *Cybernetics, Art and Ideas.* London: Studio Vista. 111–123.

Mahler within Mahler
Allusion as Quotation, Self-Reference, and Metareference

Robert Samuels, The Open University

The music of Gustav Mahler (1860–1911) is ideal as a focus for discussion of the role of self-quotation within musical works. Although self-quotation is not in a technical sense the same thing as a narrow usage of self-reference, these two terms converge in the case of Mahler, through his creation of a semiotic 'idiolect' or vocabulary of musical signs which define his works as a single system. This contribution traces a progress from self-quotation, through a more semiotically potent kind of self-reference, to a situation in Mahler's last completed symphony in which one can speak of metareference within the musical text.

Mahler quotes constantly and copiously from other composers and his own works throughout his oeuvre. The most thoroughgoing examination of this habit to date is a 1997 article by Henry Louis de La Grange, whose observations are summarised and discussed here. The concern of this contribution is to focus on Mahler's self-quotations, and to investigate whether these are a special case, in semiotic terms, and whether their use develops over time.

The most straightforward case, in terms of sign functioning, is provided by Mahler's First Symphony and its quotation of his own song, "Gieng heut' Morgens über's Feld". This is a use of quotation to incorporate the suppressed text of the poem within the semiotic economy of the symphonic narrative.

A more tangential and allusive technique is seen in the Fifth Symphony, where the relationship to pre-existing songs and their texts is more distant, and their function within the symphony is indirect and subtle, whilst remaining undeniable.

Finally, the present contribution discusses the closing bars of the Ninth Symphony, hearing in them a Proustian representation of the operation of memory through Mahler's use of fragmented units, which are self-referential within the Mahlerian idiolect. This way of composing attains a modernist, metareferential form of signification.

Introduction: quotation, self-reference and metareference

On discovering that the 2007 conference, the proceedings of which form the present volume, was to be themed around the idea of 'self-reference', it was immediately clear to me that I could not avoid offering this essay as a contribution. In engaging with the debate opened up by Werner Wolf's essays on 'metareference' (see Wolf 2007 and in this vol.), I am returning to the two intellectual fields of my book of 1995: the music of the Austrian symphonist Gustav Mahler (1860–1911), and what I termed in the title of that book 'musical semiotics'. What I want to do in the present article is to pursue some examples of self-quotation within Mahler's works, and to try to suggest some ways of analysing the semiotics of these particular musical elements; but in doing this, I regard myself as in dialogue with Wolf's more theoretical and taxonomic concerns.

First of all, some terms need to be defined. Wolf is particularly concerned to define 'self-reference' as essentially synonymous with what many British or American semioticians would term 'introversive semiosis', where signifieds are located within the same text as their signifiers[1]. As Wolf comments, "each repetition or variation of a theme within a fugue or a sonata can be regarded as an instance of self-reference" (Wolf 2007: 302). This indicates one of the most distinctive features of music as a semiotic system since, as Wolf also comments, signs are often assumed to function by pointing to referents outside the text, in 'extroversive semiosis'[2]. Whether musical signification is limited only to introversive semiosis – in other words, whether reference outside of the 'text' is even possible in the case of music – is an issue which has been much debated, but is not a question which need concern us here. Mahler's musical procedure presents a different question, which is how the recurrence of music between works functions within the semiotic economy of those works. In other words, his practice foregrounds the question of musical quotation and its relationship with musical meaning.

Self-reference arguably goes beyond quotation. In order to function as part of a sign, a repetition of a musical unit (for instance, the return of the opening gesture of a sonata movement at the recapitulation) has to function as the *referent* or *signified* of the first occurrence, rather than simply as a recurrence or quotation of it. The second occurrence must be interpreted as signifying a function ('recapitulation', perhaps) something that requires the interpreter to create an 'interpretant' (to use a term from Charles Sanders Peirce). In what follows, I shall be

---

[1]   For example, "introversive semiosis" is the title of the third chapter of Kofi Agawu's influential study *Playing with Signs: A Semiotic Interpretation of Classic Music* (1991).

[2]   "Extroversive semiosis" is the title of the fourth chapter of Agawu 1991.

discussing quotation within Mahler's works, but one of the questions I wish to ask is whether his practice of quotation should be regarded as self-reference. The most obvious terminological problem with this is that quotation, by its nature, involves reference *between* rather than *within* works. However, herein lies one of the most interesting features of Mahler's compositional procedure. One of the semiotic effects of his practice of self-quotation, in my view at least, is the positing of his own works – all of them – as a *single system*. Quotation between his works builds up a vocabulary unique to those works and distinctive of them: a Mahlerian 'idiolect'. Seen in this light, self-quotation does indeed become a clear instance of self-reference.

This is to run ahead of myself slightly, though. The interplay between quotation and reference will be discussed below. The remaining question in terms of terminology is whether self-quotation, and indeed self-reference, ever assumes the status of 'metareference'. In other words, the question is in this case whether Mahler's quotations of his own works have the effect of commentary on the practice of quotation, on the mechanisms of referentiality itself, or on other aspects of the musical medium. My answer to this question is not going to be a simple 'yes' or 'no'. But it is indeed my conclusion that Mahler's music does, at least occasionally, and at least to some extent, attain the status of 'music about music'. If this is so, it poses interesting questions in turn about the relationship between music and literature, which account for my own fascination with Mahler's works within the nineteenth-century history of word-music relations. Whilst musical narrativity, which is often perceived by commentators on Mahler's symphonies, does not necessarily imply metareferentiality, if this music is 'telling a story' *about itself*, then how does it create this effect? Answering this question is my task in the remainder of this article.

Mahler and the inevitability of quotation

Mahler's music is inseparable from the idea of quotation, something that has been noted and discussed since his own day. That Mahler quotes copiously from previous music is beyond doubt. The significance of this habit, however – why he does what he does – is much more open to analysis and discussion. In a recent authoritative survey of contemporary Mahler research, John Williamson comments:

The question of categorizing seeming quotations from other composers is central to discussion of Mahler. Because the charge of banality was countered amongst the composer's earlier admirers with concepts such as irony and parody, analysts have tended to point to supposed allusions with a degree of pride, though in many ways they demonstrate the continuing belief in Mahler's lack of thematic originality. (2007: 267)

This practice, Williamson points out, may not be in itself as distinctive of Mahler as it has sometimes appeared: "the greater prevalence of the phenomenon [quotation in symphonies] in Bruckner, Mahler and Strauss in comparison with the generation of Mendelssohn and Berlioz is striking" (ibid.). Self-quotation, however, is a slightly different matter. It has been taken both as a measure of the depth and complexity of the subjectivity to which Mahler's music gives access, and as a stick to beat him with. Viewed positively, the many invitations to hear references between works, and therefore to interpret moments or entire works according to their relationship with a pre-existent work within Mahler's oeuvre, are an attestation of interpretive richness; viewed negatively, the frequent resort to material which has been heard (or, more often, half-heard) elsewhere indicates a lack of originality, or an unacceptable degree of self-indulgence.

The most extended discussion of this topic to date is a 1997 article by the great Mahler biographer, Henry-Louis de La Grange, entitled "Music about Music in Mahler: Reminiscences, Allusions, or Quotations?". De La Grange knows Mahler's music more intimately, and has listened to it more intently, than I ever shall; and he provides as an appendix to the article a modest list of some sixty-one examples of passages where he hears Mahler's works quoting other musical works. He describes these examples as "reminiscences", and their identification as "an ongoing game" (1997: 129). They range, too, from direct, unmistakable quotation to quite distant, questionable association. There are several things which strike me in de La Grange's lengthy and careful discussion. One is that he tends to include Mahler's adoption of 'folk-like' style, which can be described as musical allusion to popular forms – such as military march, peasant dance, popular or folk song, and so forth – along with references to individual, identifiable musical works. He wants to discuss the heterogeneity of Mahler's style, and emphasise its difference in this from earlier symphonic music; direct musical quotation, as he remarks, has a much longer history and is not, in itself, revolutionary. But in taking this perspective, de La Grange does not wish or need to ask questions about the specific semiotic economy of direct (or indeed indirect) quotation of identifiable music. Another curious feature of this article is its typology of the moments it inventories. De La Grange says:

> In my view, the main categories to be distinguished are (1) reminiscences, which are in principle unintentional, and (2) allusions or quotations, which are intentional. (Ibid.: 127)

In making intentionality the criterion for distinguishing between examples of intertextual reference, de La Grange appears to be adopting the unprovable as a principle. However, he is quite in line with earlier Mahlerians in doing this. He summarizes the typologies of Monika Tibbe and Marius Flothuis thus:

> *Zitat* (quotation), *Gedächtniszitat* (quotation from memory), *Selbstzitat* (self-quotation), *Paraphrase, Anspielung* (allusion), *Anlehnung* (taking something as a model), *Entlehnung* (borrowing), *Anklang* (echo or reminiscence), *Ähnlichkeit* (similarity), and *Huldigung* (homage). (Ibid.)

The looseness of criteria for compiling this list means that, whilst all these authors identify and delineate an immense quantity of material, they do not wish to ask how these moments of external reference participate in the semiotic richness of the music. The third aspect of de La Grange's article which strikes me is his apparent coyness in discussing Mahler's self-quotation, either as an example of quotation or allusion generally, or as a topic in its own right. He writes:

> But although these borrowings constitute an important feature of Mahler's compositional practice, they fall outside the framework of this paper, which focuses upon the various procedures Mahler employed for "music about music". (Ibid.: 142)

It is not clear to me why self-quotation cannot constitute 'music about music'. In making this statement, de La Grange is accepting self-quotation as "an important feature", but in terms of assessing its functioning, he seems not to want to enter into discussion concerning the nature of its workings. This is an avoidance which suggests that the topic of the present paper is worth pursuing, at the least.

Unsurprisingly, given the comments just quoted, de La Grange concludes that "in my opinion, they [musical allusions] really do not matter that much" (ibid.: 144). Despite the title of his article, it is contestable whether de La Grange is actually trying to identify or describe 'music about music'. The phrase suggests the sort of 'meta-reference' that Wolf is trying to pursue, but de La Grange is not interested in distinguishing between situations according to their possible signification. For instance: (1) where the presence of earlier music within the text is part of a contextualisation of the composition in question, situating it within a discourse, general ('Western art music') or specific ('nineteenth-century Austrian symphonies'); (2) where a direct reference to another work is part of a specific semiotic economy (tying in one work to Mahler's oeuvre as a single system – an instance of the 'Mahlerian idiolect' at work); and (3) those where there is a critical 'metareferential' interpretation to the quotation.

This trio of possibilities is only one of several semiotic spectra which could be suggested. My thumbnail descriptions of them here perhaps suggest C. S. Peirce's distinction of 'Firstness', 'Secondness' and 'Thirdness' in semiotic function (possibility, fact, and argument as three sign-types). I am taking this sideways glance at the complexity of the semiotic theory involved in analysing the functioning of musical signs from Naomi Cumming's book *The Sonic Self* (2000). I would affirm, along with Cumming, that a single musical moment may be functioning in more than one way at a time, semiotically speaking; the question is how this multivalency of the text presents possible interpretations to the listener.

Direct quotation

It is time to consider some specific musical examples. I want to begin at the beginning, with the opening of Mahler's First Symphony of 1888. Theodor Adorno likens the sound of this opening to the whistling made by old-fashioned steam engines (cf. 1992: 4). But it is also already a musical reference, since it recalls the opening of Beethoven's Ninth Symphony – the pedal A naturals, the slow descent using the interval of a fourth, the key (D major in Mahler and D minor in Beethoven). However, this allusiveness, whilst convincing to my ear, is vague enough to have escaped de La Grange's inventory. If the similarity is accepted as a genuinely significant resemblance, then it is no more than a potential sign, a feature which gives a possibility of interpretation: an instance of Peirce's Firstness. Its interpretation is of course debatable. Perhaps the twenty-eight-year-old composer wished to affirm, even if subconsciously, the noble musical tradition, and the titanic figure of Beethoven within it, that his first contribution to the genre wished to join. Perhaps he arrogantly wished to be heard as Beethoven's successor, his own first symphony taking over from – or even outclassing – Beethoven's last. The multiplicity of the possible interpretations reflects the looseness of the connection.

However, this is not the case five minutes later, once the very lengthy introduction finally produces the symphonic first subject. This is another allusion, and indeed this time a self-quotation. The source in question is a song composed by Mahler to a text of his own, in 1883–1885, "Gieng heut' Morgens über's Feld". There isn't any room for doubt here: the symphony quotes the song; Mahler is quoting himself. However, care has to be exercised even in stating this obvious fact as obvious. There are differences between the song and the symphonic melody, and all the differences are significant. Mahler does not simply set the melody as a 'song without words'. He allows it to emerge gradually and, initially, quietly, out of the introduction's pedal A naturals (so cruel in their demands on the orchestral players who have to sustain them, especially the double-bass players); he repeats small phrases, fragments the melody through its instrumentation, re-combines its elements. These are all techniques typical of his procedure in developing and recapitulating themes in his early symphonies. They also provide a distance, a kind of semiotic space, in which an interpretation of the symphony as different from the song can be created. In this case, however, I for one would not wish to argue for a metareferential aspect to the music. I remain guided by the text of the song in this: "Gieng heut' Morgens über's Feld" ('This morning I went out across the field') seems to me pretty much consonant with the emergence of the symphonic protagonist from the inchoate *Naturlaut* of the opening. The optimism of Mahler's poem is sustained right up to the final couplet, where the poet's unhappiness in love undercuts the beauty of the natural world in a Heine-like 're-versal'; but the symphony is to replicate this poetic structure, by undercutting the optimism of the first subject, only much later in the musical argument. The melody itself, for simple and for not-so-simple reasons, invokes a musical representation not distant from another Beethoven symphony, the 'Pastoral' Sixth. One of the results of this is that it really does not matter to the interpretation of the passage whether the melody is invented by Mahler or an 'authentic' folk tune, whether one knows the text set to it, or whether the song precedes the symphony. All these questions are interesting, and the answers readily ascertainable; but they do not affect my interpretation of the music. Just for once, as far as Mahler's music goes, I prefer to hear it without irony, as an arresting and intriguing combination of naivety (as a sign of youth and innocence) and sophistication (as a reinterpretation of the symphony as a genre).

Before moving on, however, I want to note a couple of features here. The facts that this direct quotation is a self-quotation, and that it is of a song, remain generally true throughout Mahler's work. His references to other composers are oblique and contestable; direct quotation is of his own works. This is part of what I called earlier the 'Mahlerian idiolect' – the construction of a musical vocabulary unique to Mahler, a literal 'sound world'. I shall return to this technique later. But the other thing I want to observe now is that the link between song and symphony reflects the narrative nature of the symphonic argument. The parallelism of the first subject's musical journey and the text of the poem is not accidental, but neither is the one generated by the other. Both are made possible by the interpretation of the music according to a narrative scheme. Mahler himself was quite happy to talk or write about 'the hero of the symphony', and indeed he applied the title *Titan* to this symphony, allying it with the novel by Jean Paul. There is no discernible connection between the poem and Jean Paul or his novel; but the possibility of interpreting the symphony as a narrative enables the quotation to acquire semiotic significance. The symphonic setting both invokes and suppresses the text of the song. It becomes an element in the musical narrative.

Submerged quotation

It is time to move on, both in terms of Mahler's output, and in terms of the semiotic complexity of self-quotation. My next example is taken from what is possibly Mahler's most famous single movement; certainly it is the one of his works to feature most regularly on the UK radio station Classic FM. This is the Adagietto, the fourth movement out of five, from the Fifth Symphony. Within the structure of the symphony, this movement serves as an extended introduction to the Finale, with which it makes up the third large block of the work, after the opening pair of movements and the immense central scherzo. It is also the nearest thing to a slow movement in the whole of the Fifth Symphony. If one accepts, as I contend, that a symphony for Mahler constitutes a coherent, complex, narrative structure, then the function of the slow movement is often to invoke a more intimate, personal, often erotic counter-narrative to the more public world of the argumentative sonata-allegro opening movement and the social associations of the dance-derived scherzo. Here, the Adagietto is scored virtually for a chamber ensemble: just strings and harp. In form it is indeed a 'song without words' – a lyrical, sustained melody for the first violins is accompanied by the rest of the chamber forces. The melody is well-known, and it resembles those of the songs Mahler composed immediately beforehand and contemporaneously with the symphony. These are settings of poetry by Rückert, which Mahler first composed with piano accompaniment and then later orchestrated, also for chamber-sized forces. *Example 1* shows the opening of the Adagietto's melody.

Example 1: Mahler, Fifth Symphony, Adagietto, first theme, mm. 3–6.

There are two songs which have been most often cited as references for this melody. First of all, *Example 2* shows the third of the *Kindertotenlieder* ('Songs on the Death of Children'), "Nun seh' ich wohl, warum so dunkle Flammen".

Example 2: Mahler, "Nun seh' ich wohl", opening.

The opening gestures are very similar to the opening melodic phrase of the Adagietto. It is worth noting, however, that the actual melodic line of the song varies the motivic vocabulary in ways that prevent the Adagietto from being heard as a re-presentation of the word-setting melody – the Adagietto really is 'without words'.

The other song which approaches the Adagietto, this time in its vocal line, is "Ich bin der Welt abhanden gekommen", often taken as a manifesto of Mahler's attitude to art.

Example 3: Mahler, "Ich bin der Welt abhanden gekommen", mm. 49–53.

The extract of the melody in *Example 3* (from near the end of the song) does resemble, motivically speaking, parts of the Adagietto's opening melody. In more general terms, the Adagietto re-creates and shares in the sound-world of the Rückert settings, and indeed these songs (ten in total, composed between 1900 and 1904) have a motivic reservoir of gestures which are shared between them – another version of self-quotation, and a more specific, restricted form of 'Mahlerian idiolect'.

Before hastening to conclude that Mahler is in the Fifth Symphony simply operating in much the same way as in the First, it is worth pausing. It is too simple, here, to read a straightforward reference from the songs into the symphony. Apart from anything else, these songs are very different from each other. One is mourning the death of a child who in retrospect seems always to have had too much of the heavenly in their eyes to have been detained long on earth; the other is declaring that the poet can live detached from all earthly cares. And the pitfalls of a simple referential reading are further complicated by two other factors. Firstly, the 'narrative curve' of the symphony does not easily accommodate either poem as a possible subtext – quite unlike "Gieng heut' Morgens". Secondly, there is strong evidence that Mahler had a specific aesthetic charge in mind in composing the Adagietto; one that does indeed 'fit' within the symphony, and one which was of entirely personal significance, and so remained un-known for many years, before its discovery and publication by the Mahler scholar and conductor Gilbert Kaplan. The manuscript of the Adagietto exists in two copies, both dating from 1901. The earlier is in Mahler's hand, and the later (prepared very shortly afterwards) is in Alma's hand, and is probably that used by the publisher for engraving. The significance of the existence of two copies is suggested by an anecdote preserved in an annotation to the conducting score of the symphony that belonged to Wilhelm Mengelberg, conductor of the Amsterdam Concertgebouw orchestra, Mahler's close friend, and cham-pion of his music. On the first page of the Adagietto, Mengelberg's handwritten comment describes it as a 'love song' sent by Gustav to Alma (to whom he had just become secretly engaged, only a matter of

weeks after their first meeting), and claims that both partners independently testified to this[3].

Where, then, does this leave my consideration of quotation and self-
quotation? I do not want to claim that publication of Mengelberg's
anecdote transforms our interpretation of the Adagietto or of the Fifth
Symphony. No more did I wish to claim that it was essential to know
the words of the song whose melody is set in the First Symphony. But
neither do I want to discard it as irrelevant, nor to deny that there is
significance in the relationship with the Rückert settings. As I said, the
character of this movement, as an instrumental, 'wordless' version of
a song-setting, is fully consonant with its positioning in the symphony,
where it literally mediates between the social imagery of the scherzo
and the brisk, culminatory optimism of the Rondo-Finale. In other
words, it sounds as if it ought to have words, and we can have a fairly
shrewd guess at what the import of those words ought to be; and,
fortuitously and gratifyingly, we have some evidence of just such a
reading from personal, biographical sources. The importance of the
'narrative drive' to the symphony is confirmed by yet another instance
of self-quotation when the theme of the Adagietto turns up in the
Rondo-Finale, now transformed in character, but again, not to my ear
with irony (see *Example 4*).

*Example 4: Mahler, Fifth Symphony, Rondo, allusion to theme of Adagietto (mm.
190–197).*

As for the connection with the other songs, the moral seems to be not
to look for the meaning of the words set in the songs within the instrumental work that refers to them. At this level, the reference is musical
and not literary – that is the whole point. The musical connections are
almost undeniable, and, of course, there are oblique connections
between the words too – in all three cases (one of which has no actual
words), there is a strong idea of transcendence: the child belongs to a
transcendent realm; the poet wishes to escape into the 'heaven of my
love and my song', and the Adagietto itself gestures equally towards

---

[3]   The relevant page from Mengelberg's copy of the score, as well as both
autographs, are reproduced in Kaplan, ed. 1992.

the transcendent power of love. But in all these cases, the words appear as the outcome of the musical work of signification, rather than as the key to that work. The music is aesthetically prior to the text.

Self-quotation as obsession

My final examples trace a further complexification of musical sign creation through self-quotation, by looking at Mahler's last completed symphony, the Ninth. In this work, self-reference becomes something close to an obsessive compulsion. Mahler is, in many respects, doing in this work what he does in every work: that is, re-thinking and re-casting the institution of symphonic composition itself, which is both the enabling ground of his art and something akin to a patriarchal adversary for him.

A brief example will serve to reinforce this last point. The third movement of the Ninth Symphony, entitled "Rondo. Burleske." by Mahler, is a movement of aggressive savagery, the violence of which is set against the conflicting expectations created by its title(s) and its positioning (Mahler reverses the order of movements, putting the 'rondo' third and concluding with an adagio). Its main material, though, has clear precedents. *Example 5* gives the opening of the Scherzo of the Fifth Symphony, which I mentioned above.

Example 5: Mahler, Fifth Symphony, Scherzo, opening.

And *Example 6* gives the opening of the same symphony's second movement, marked "Mit größter Vehemenz".

Example 6: Mahler, Fifth Symphony, second movement, opening.

And now, *Example 7* gives the opening of the Ninth Symphony's "Rondo. Burleske.".

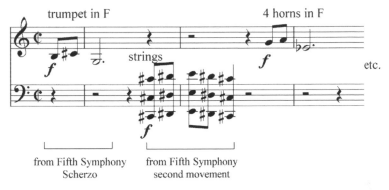

Example 7: Mahler, Ninth Symphony, "Rondo. Burleske.", opening.

This is certainly self-quoting, and this time there is no text, unless it is so far latent in the material as to be irrelevant. But the compulsion to quote, to create music which sounds richly allusive, as if every phrase is a quotation of some sort, is here confirmed and extended by the fact that the elements which are most readily identifiable as quotations are self-quotations. Here, self-quotation is coming much closer to Wolf's 'metareferentiality'. Once again, it seems to me that the semiotic potential of this self-quotation rests upon a kind of narrative, but now a narrative about musical narrativity itself, or, to use the term, a meta-narrative: Mahler's music is here making (or so it seems to me) some sort of statement about the possibility of making sense through symphonic discourse; and it does this through invoking Mahler's own symphonies as the past. It is not simply that Mahler's earlier works are invoked, and the passage of time thereby marked – that is certainly happening, but the effect here is of a different order. In the sound-world of the Ninth Symphony, the earlier works *are* the past; they emblematise it. The music does more than accept its place within the phenomenological world; it posits itself *as* the world. Mahler's often-quoted remark to Sibelius, that the symphony should be 'like the world' is reflected in this practice.

If music does have the potential for (at least implicit) metareference (to use Wolf's term), for the discursive, propositional meaning that Peirce called 'Thirdness', then it has it in virtue of exploiting the temporality of its nature, which enables it to represent temporal processes – the pastness of the past, the operation of memory. In this

semiotic space, self-reference through quotation is a powerful operation, and the locus of metareference.

There is no space here to give any detailed analysis of the complex
semiosis at work in this "Rondo. Burleske.". Instead, I want to consider the very end of the symphony, the point at which, to my mind,
the musical narrative created and developed through the earlier
movements takes on a metanarrative character.

The last movement of the Ninth Symphony is, as I remarked
above, a slow movement. Its entire substance is allusive, and as it
progresses, allusion within the Mahlerian idiolect becomes more no-
ticeable, more obsessive. Its final page is, I would argue, the most
striking and the most 'modernist' of Mahler's repeated attempts to
find an appropriate ending for a symphony – a means by which the
music, and with it the musical argument, is concluded, rather than just
happening to stop as if arbitrarily or through a mindless adherence to
rule. The final page of the work presents fragmentary melodic scraps,
all of which have some sort of self-quoting, idiolectical and potentially metareferential nature. One of the principle points of reference is
the *Rückert-Lieder* or *Kindertotenlieder* style, from which many of the
short (four- or five-note) motivic fragments stem. Semiotically, the
Mahlerian idiolect itself disintegrates before our ears. The harmony
itself becomes atomised, partial, allusive, as *Example 8* exemplifies.

Example 8: Mahler, Nineth Symphony, fourth movement, mm. 155–163.

It is possible to hear, in the violin melody of *Example 8*, a latent or
partial quotation of the melody that sets the final words of the fourth
of the *Kindertotenlieder*, "Oft denk' ich, sie sind nur ausgegangen".
The text of the fragment quoted is "im Sonnenschein! Der Tag ist
schon auf jenen Höh'n!" ('in the sunshine! The day is fine on yonder
height!'). The similarity is shown by *Example 9*, which also demon-

strates how etiolated the rhythm of the symphonic allusion is by comparison.

im Son - nen schein! Der Tag___ ist schön_auf je - nen Höh'n!

Example 9: Mahler, Kindertotenlieder No. 4, "Oft denk' ich, sie sind nur ausgegangen", mm. 63–69.

Another colossus of Mahlerian scholarship, Constantin Floros, interprets the similarity between the earlier song and the symphony's ending unproblematically as Mahler's affirmation of faith in life beyond death (see 1993). Hearing this movement as valedictory is, admittedly, a traditional interpretation; but it is not self-evident, as is demonstrated by Anthony Newcomb's contrary narrative interpretation of the symphony as a version of a 'Bildungsroman' plot in which the end contains the potential for further adventure, as if beyond the bounds of the current story: "[the symphony's] formative energy, always ready to be stirred again into life, passes out of hearing" (1992: 136). Whilst I would not want to accept wholeheartedly Newcomb's choice of the 'Bildungsroman' as a narrative archetype (although Newcomb deliberately chooses Dickens' *Great Expectations* as a point of comparison, hardly the most typical 'Bildungsroman' one could name, as he discusses), the signification of Mahler's closing page is extremely complex. This complexity is intimately bound up with the practice of self-reference; every musical motive has a weight, a history, which has been created not just within this work, but within Mahler's whole corpus and, in the infinitely malleable world of musical resemblances, extending beyond his works to others both identifiable and lost. At this point, Mahler's music becomes literary. The effect, I would suggest, is not dissimilar to that created by Marcel Proust in the final pages of *Le Temps retrouvé*, the volume that closes *A la recherche du temps perdu*. As the immense novel draws towards its close, Proust's narrator experiences a sequence of 'involuntary memories', through which he realises the significance imbued in every experience, every moment of the present through the weight of the past. At the close of the novel, he realises that it is through writing that he is able to reclaim this past, and the final pages turn back to the opening of the first volume, *Du côté de chez Swann*, as the narrator is able to begin writing the novel he wishes he had just read. It is through the narration of how the narrator has become able to begin to narrate that the novel becomes metareferential; and something similar is true of the ending of Mahler's Ninth Symphony. The sparse, fragmented motives are like involuntary memories; they bring back, unbidden, the experience of the past. This is what furnishes Newcomb with the sense that the music's "formative energy, always ready to be stirred again into life, passes out of hearing" (1992: 136). It is also the reason why unproblematic readings such as Floros' are unsatisfying for many Mahlerians. But rather than following a process analogous to the narrative curve of a 'Bildungsroman', I hear the music striving towards a metareferential state in which its potential for narrative reading becomes its own topic.

Conclusion

This study has traced a history in Mahler's use of self-quotation, in which his practice has been seen to vary, and in fact to follow a path of increasing subtlety and complexity in the deployment of this particular technique. The impulse to narrativise this history should be embraced with caution; regarding it as a story of increasing maturity, leaving the naivety of the First Symphony far behind in the sophistication of the Ninth, would be doing the composer something of a disservice. It would be truer to the development of Mahler's aesthetics to see here a progress from the Romanticism of the First Symphony, through a more post-romantic or neo-romantic ideology in the Fifth, to something in the Ninth Symphony closer to the modernism that was about to emerge in the works of Schoenberg and Berg. The relationship between metareference as a strategy and modernism as an aesthetic is an interesting one. For Mahler as for Proust, its importance arises from the realisation that storytelling is not a transparent process. Proust's narration of self-discovery is also a story of how that narration can be achieved; Mahler's symphonic narrative becomes an interrogation of how meaning can be constructed in the passage of music through time. The case of Mahler demonstrates how the overall concern of this volume with self-reference as a phenomenon of musical signification is connected with the relationship between music and literature. Self-reference, in the strict sense of signs which unite signifiers and signifieds (representamens and objects, to use Peirce's terms) within a single semiotic system, is a key to the operation of narrativity in absolute music. It is through this narrative potential that, in Mahler's late style, a metareferential mode can be constructed. Mahlerian self-reference, then, is bound up with word-music relations beyond the plain fact of his habit of quoting melodies previously set to words.

One of the most important recent works in the field of word and music studies is Peter Dayan's book, *Music Writing Literature* (2006). And in Mahler's earlier practice, one can indeed speak of his music as writing a form of literature. This is a literature which narrates in specifically musical terms, in which the poetry of the songs which furnish the material for self-quotation is a component of the narrative, but do not determine or decode it. But as Mahler develops towards a metareferential, modernist style, increasingly the phenomenon in question is a sort of literature writing music: the story being told is less the kind of story which is best told in musical terms, and more a story about musical storytelling itself.

References

Adorno, Theodor (1992). *Mahler: A Musical Physiognomy.* Trans. Edmund Jephcott. Chicago, IL: University of Chicago Press.

Agawu, Kofi (1991). *Playing with Signs: A Semiotic Interpretation of Classic Music.* Princeton, MA: Princeton University Press.

Cumming, Naomi (2000). *The Sonic Self: Musical Subjectivity and Signification.* Advances in Semiotics. Bloomington, IN: Indiana University Press.

Dayan, Peter (2006). *Music Writing Literature: From Sand to Derrida via Debussy.* Aldershot: Ashgate.

Floros, Constantin (1993). *Gustav Mahler: The Symphonies.* Trans. Vernon Wicker. Aldershot: Scolar Press.

Kaplan, Gilbert, ed. (1992). *Gustav Mahler, Adagietto. Facsimile, Documentation, Recording.* New York, NY: The Kaplan Foundation.

La Grange, Henry-Louis de (1997). "Music About Music in Mahler: Reminiscences, Allusion, or Quotations?" Stephen Hefling, ed. *Mahler Studies.* Cambridge: Cambridge University Press. 122–168.

Newcomb, Anthony (1992). "Narrative Archetypes and Mahler's Ninth Symphony". Steven Paul Scher, ed. *Music and Text: Critical Inquiries*. Cambridge: Cambridge University Press. 118–136.

Samuels, Robert (1995) *Mahler's Sixth Symphony: A Study in Musical Semiotics*. Cambridge: Cambridge University Press.

Williamson, John (2007). "New Research Paths in Criticism, Analysis and Interpretation". Jeremy Barham, ed. *The Cambridge Companion to Mahler*. Cambridge: Cambridge University Press. 262–274.

Wolf, Werner (2007). "Metafiction and Metamusic: Exploring the Limits of Metareference." Winfried Nöth, Nina Bishara, eds. *Self-Reference in the Media*. Berlin: de Gruyter. 303–324.

Medial Self-Reference between Words and Music in Erik Satie's Piano Pieces

Peter Dayan, Edinburgh

Erik Satie (1866–1925) was the inventor of a peculiar hybrid kind of work: piano pieces with words on the score, strange little tales or poems, that are meant neither to be sung, nor to be read out, nor to be on concert programmes, and which therefore remain unknown to audiences, though not to pianists. When these words refer to the music, is this to be construed as self-reference within the work? Yes, doubtless, if they are seen as part of the same work as the music they accompany; but this depends on one's point of view. This difficulty of defining what, exactly, constitutes the work's self, the 'self' to which self-reference might refer, is endemic in Satie. He provokes it also by playing games with repetitions (of which, in the case of *Vexations*, he suggests 840) and with inaccurate or false self-reference between words and music, in order to destabilise our sense of the identity of the work of art. The result is a strange displacement of what might be called the 'truth' in art. Art, for Satie, never tells the truth about anything, and he feels no need to tell the truth in self-reference within the work. But that absence of the truth in art is not an indifference to truth; rather, it is the creation of a dynamic that lures us onto an endless search for a truth that, like the 'self' of the work's self-reference, can never be precisely located. That combination of attractiveness and elusiveness, of uniqueness and dispersion, is the true character of art, in Satie's world.

> J'ai toujours dit – & je le répéterai encore très longtemps après ma mort – qu'il n'y a pas de Vérité en Art (de Vérité unique, s'entend). (Satie 1981: 61)[1]

Nearly a century after Satie wrote these words, they may seem to have become a banal truth. It is now universally accepted, at least in academia, that there is no unique Truth in Art. Indeed, that has become a fundamental tenet, it seems to me, of cultural studies and of the human sciences generally. Art, we now think, is not a word that designates a stable category; its meaning shifts with the times; so there can be no stable truth within it. Was that Erik Satie's opinion? It might at first appear so. But anyone who is used to reading Satie soon learns to be

---

[1] 'I have always said – & I will continue to repeat it long, long after my death – that there is no Truth in Art (no unique Truth, that is).' [Unless otherwise indicated, all translations are mine.]

suspicious of such appearances. Every apparently clear statement by Satie is always cunningly hedged about with reasons to doubt its validity. Parentheses of all kinds are often used by Satie as seed-beds for sowing such doubts; they are always worth examining carefully. There are two such parentheses in the above quote: one between two dashes; the other at the end, in brackets. I shall begin with the former.

Satie will, he says, continue to repeat long after his death that there is no Truth in Art. Of course, in one sense this is true. He is still saying so now; it is repeated every time this article is re-printed, or perhaps every time it is read. But in another sense, it is ridiculous to say that he is repeating it after his death, because it is not Erik Satie who is repeating it. It is whoever prints or reads the sentence. It cannot be Erik Satie himself, speaking with his own voice, or writing with his own pen, because Erik Satie is now forever absent. The repetition, in other words, is not exactly a repetition, because the self that repeats is not the same self. This is a fundamental principle of Satie's aesthetics: the truth about the truth in art requires endless repetition, endless re-affirmation; yet no repetition that depends on a voice, on a self, is ever simply repetition. We will return to this subject.

The second parenthesis suggests that what we hear or understand, when Satie repeats his principle, is not that there is no Truth in Art; it is that there is no *unique* Truth in Art. So perhaps there remains in art, we would like to believe, a kind of truth that is not unique. But what has Satie just said? What if the absence of Truth in Art were, in fact, the unique truth? What if the unique Truth in Art were the fact that Art is precisely that space where there is no Truth, whether unique or not? And what if the absence of Truth were precisely created by the peculiar status of repetition in Art, which may or may not be the repetition of the artist, of the speaker, of the self?

I should like to suggest that self-reference in the art of Erik Satie is in fact a dramatisation of the peculiar dynamics of repetition in art. These dynamics explain why the Truth in Art can never be located precisely – except, perhaps, in its own absence.

Erik Satie himself, and his art, are certainly truly unique. Among his many inventions, one may include an entirely new artistic genre, which he developed in the years just before and during the First World War, and which remains peculiarly his, since, unlike some of his other inventions, it never really caught on. It is piano music with words by the composer; words not to be sung or read out, or even to be read by the audience, but simply there on the piano score. Some examples of this, taken from his *Sonatine bureaucratique* and *Embryons desséchés*, are given below.

The relationship between the words and the music in these pieces has been the subject, not of controversy since the subject seems not to be much debated, but, more simply, of utterly opposing views. Vladimir Jankélévitch, for example, maintained that the words and music do not refer to each other at all. According to him, there is no meaningful connection between them.

> Souvent Satie plaque sur sa musique un scénario saugrenu qui lui sert non point du tout à en préciser le sens, mais au contraire à en dissimuler les véritables intentions [...] Ces soliloques sans aucun rapport avec la musique semblent nous dire: parlons, si vous le voulez bien, d'autre chose [...]. (1957: 142)[2]

Whereas Jean-Pierre Armengaud, on the contrary, sees Satie's music as a perfect illustration of his words[3]; and Vincent Lajoinie goes so far as to produce a typology of text-music relations in Satie with three categories, all of which suppose that the relationship is one of "illustration musicale" (cf. 1985: 265–267): the music illustrates the text (cf. ibid.). Neither Armengaud nor Lajoinie engages with or even mentions Jankélévitch's opinion, although Jankélévitch is certainly the most famous (and best) early academic 'satiste', and his book was published some thirty years before those of the other two authors. I do not propose to take sides in this non-debate, but I will say that there is one kind of text-music relation in several of these works by Satie which is neither musical illustration, nor, on the face of it, a refusal to talk about what is in the music: it is what I think one might be permitted to call self-reference, where the words explicitly refer to the music.

This is certainly somewhat different from talking about self-reference in a monomedial art form; and the differences are compounded by Satie's staging of it. Let me take, as the archetype of self-

---

[2]   'Often Satie tacks onto his music a whacky scenario which serves, not at all to make the sense of the music clear, but on the contrary to hide its true intentions [...] These monologues, which have no connection at all with the music, seem to say to us: let's just talk about something else, shall we?'

[3]   For example, Armengaud describes the music of "Le porteur de grosses pierres" (from *Chapitres tournés en tous sens*) as "un des exemples les plus étonnants de figuratisme musical" (1988: 83; 'one of the most astonishing examples of figuratism in music'), analysing it as a transposition into music of the scene described by the words.

reference within a monomedial work, the beginning of Francis Ponge's poem "Fable". It starts: "Par le mot *par* commence donc ce texte" ('with the word *with* this texts begins')[4]. Ponge's words here refer to Ponge's words within the work, and the object of the reference is clearly visible, physically present. The position is less clear-cut when Satie's words refer to Satie's music. Certainly, as Werner Wolf points out in his essay in this volume, there are many kinds of self-reference; but every kind must depend on the perception of a 'self' to which reference is being made. Ponge's words refer to something within the work in which they appear; therefore, one could say, the work contains reference to itself. Is the same thing happening in these pieces by Satie? Do they contain reference to themselves? In one sense, they certainly seem to do so: as we shall see, the words on the piano score indubitably refer to the music printed on the same page. However, Satie, as always, provides many reasons for doubting the possibility of any such simple resolution of the question of the identity of the work of art.

The first of these reasons concerns the work's reception. The pianist sees the words on the page; for him or her, as for the musicologist, the work may indeed include the words. However, the concert audience (and in our day, the CD audience) normally does not even know that the words exist. For this audience, there is no self-reference, simply because the work does not include the words. And this is certainly a situation which was not only foreseen, but deliberately preserved by Satie, who never wanted the words read out or distributed in concerts; he wanted the listener to remain ignorant of what the pianist could read. In short, in calling the reference to Satie's music in his words 'self-reference', I am making a certain assumption about the unity of the work; an assumption which is unjustified in the case of the person who hears the piano pieces played without access to the text, as is normally the case. Self-reference, here, then, depends on the position of the person who receives the work, and no single position seems implied by the work itself. This complication may seem to be artificial and easily dismissed. But in fact, like all such obstacles to the apprehension of a unity of sense in Satie's work, it is designed as a reflection, a materialisation, of a more essential obstacle to under-

---

[4]   Derrida discusses this example in a study which has become a classic of self-reference; see, for example, "Psyché. Invention de l'autre" (1987/1998) or "From *Psyche*" (1992).

standing which Satie wishes, not only to preserve (since in his opinion there is no art without it), but also to render sensible. To put it at its simplest: we must never be quite sure what the work of art is about.

I will now comment on the most extended example in Satie's œuvre of self-reference between words and music. It occurs in his "Sonatine bureaucratique". This bureaucratic sonatina certainly has what Jankélévitch might have called a 'whacky scenario'. It describes a working day in the life of a reasonably contented bureaucrat. At one point, we are told that the bureaucrat hears a nearby piano playing a sonatina by Clementi. And indeed, at that point, we hear something that sounds very much like Clementi.

Example 1: "Sonatine bureaucratique" (Satie 1976: 65).

However, as soon as one becomes aware of it, the reference to Clementi expands well beyond that part of the music where it is made explicit.

The title "Sonatine" is already Clementi-esque. So, indeed, is the opening of the work. In fact, as Robert Orledge (cf. 1990: 26–32) and Stephen Moore Whiting (cf. 1999: 484–488) have demonstrated; , most of Satie's "Sonatine" can be analysed as a re-writing of Clementi's Sonatina in C op. 36 no. 1, in rather the same way as Stravinsky, who knew Satie's work well, would later re-write Pergolesi for *Pulcinella*. Nearly all the main musical motifs in Satie's Sonatina can be shown to be derived from Clementi's. This includes a section just before the explicit reference to Clementi, where we are told that the bureaucrat hums an old Peruvian tune which he had collected from a deaf-mute in lower Brittany.

Example 2: "Sonatine bureaucratique" (Satie 1976: 65).

Are the words, at this point, referring to the tune being played by the piano, which we would then have to take as Peruvian? Do we believe in self-reference at least to this extent? If we do, this self-reference is considerably more puzzling than the invocation of Clementi. The Peruvian tune is as much like Clementi as the nearby piano's theme; which is to say, very reminiscent of Clementi, but not exactly the same. And it really does not sound Peruvian at all. One can certainly see why Jankélévitch thinks Satie's text is absurd, and its relations with the music are not to be taken seriously. However, in its very absurdity (and Jankélévitch does do justice to this in his book), the text draws attention to something that can only happen in words, and not in music. That difference between words and music concerns the status of truth and of repetition in the two media. And the end result of this dramatisation of the difference between words and music is a re-situation of the truth in art, beyond the reach of reference.

It is a commonplace that music tends to contain more repeated passages than literary texts. That is certainly the case here. The Peruvian tune comes back unchanged, not many seconds later (which seems entirely in keeping with the conventions of the sonatina). The words that accompany that tune, however, change. The first time we hear the tune, the accompanying words are: "Il chantonne un vieil air péruvien qu'il a recueilli en Basse-Bretagne chez un sourd-muet" (Satie 1976: 65)[5]. The second time, the words are: "L'air froid

---

[5]   'He hums an old Peruvian tune which he collected in Lower Brittany from a deaf-mute'.

péruvien lui remonte à la tête" (ibid.: 66)[6]. The music is repeated; the words change; and the changed words refer, not only to the music, but to the repetition in the music; they signal the fact that the music returns.

Now, one of the differences between music and words is determined by the way in which music refers to itself through the dynamics of repetition. Where we feel we have found self-reference within music (leaving words aside), this can generally be traced back to a perception of repetition, or at the very least of similarity, whose presence can be located within the sound or notes of the music itself[7]. Satie refers to Clementi in music by imitating him, and he refers to his own sonatina, within the music, by repeating or imitating what he has already written. Yet words have other means at their disposal. Their conventional mode of functioning is to refer without repeating or imitating. One can repeat a reference in words without repeating anything concrete or material; the meaning can be separated from the material form of the expression; hence the possibility of translation and also the possibility of lying. Therefore, when self-reference within the work is mediated by words, it need not be true. When we read that the bureaucrat collected that Peruvian tune from a deaf-mute in Lower Brittany, we do not believe what we read. We do not believe it on several levels. We know that the whole text is a fiction, and untrue in the way that, for example, all novels are untrue. But nor do we see in it the truth of 'vraisemblance', of plausibility, because according to our common wisdom, deaf-mutes in Lower Brittany do not sing old Peruvian airs, bureaucrats do not collect tunes, and anyway the tune does not sound Peruvian, it sounds like Clementi. Words can tell lies because they can refer without imitating each other. And it is precisely that capacity of words to tell lies that explains their function in Satie's music.

When Satie says that there is no Truth in Art, he implies that there is Truth outside Art. And in practice, he did indeed believe this; as do we all, I think, if we take 'truth' to mean an adequate relationship between a signifying system and an object of signification outside that system. We believe in the capacity of words to tell the truth because

---

[6]   'The cold Peruvian tune comes back up into his head'.

[7]   Formal contrast, such as inversion, might appear to contradict this generalisation; but one could also say that since it functions by repeating certain elements while modifying others, it, too, relies on a logic of similarity.

we believe in an object of their signification that exists outside language. To take again my archetypical example: when Ponge writes "Par le mot *par* commence donc ce texte", we can say he is telling the truth up to that point, because he is referring to an object which is there on the page: the physical presence of the word 'par'. But every time Satie provides words to go with music, they do not tell the truth, and they always fail to tell the truth on both the levels I mentioned above. Satie's words are obviously fiction; and even as fiction they fail the test of 'vraisemblance', of plausibility. More specifically, when they refer to the music, they always fail to tell the truth about the music. The most famous and straightforward example of this is in the *Embryons desséchés*, where Satie quotes, or rather imitates, Chopin, and writes in the score: *"(Citation de la célèbre mazurka de Schubert)"*[8].

Example 3:"Embryons desséchés, No. 2 d'Edriophthalma" (Satie 1976: 53).

The music that Satie here imitates (rather than quoting – even the word "Citation" is untrue) is not a mazurka, and it is not by Schubert. It is the slow movement of Chopin's Sonata in B flat minor. As with his re-writing of Clementi, using again the strategies so well analysed by Whiting (cf. 1999: 373f.) and Orledge (cf. 1990: 33), Satie carefully preserves the features that are necessary to make the original unmistakably indentifiable, while changing other features to take the music towards an equally unmistakable Satie-esque style. And just as in the case of the Peruvian tune, Satie's words invite us to look for an original that is being repeated, but are utterly untrue as to the location of that original, and its relationship with what we are hearing. What is the point of this misleading reference? My provisional answer would be: in order to rub our noses in the fact that it is always a comical mistake to assume that in any work of art, anything is genuinely and simply a repetition of any original. There is no Truth in Art precisely

---

8   '*(Quotation from the famous mazurka by Schubert)*'.

in the sense that there is never an adequate or stable relationship between the text of the artwork, and anything outside that text. The work
of art tells the truth about nothing; and for that reason, whenever it
appears to repeat anything, that appearance is always an illusion, ripe
for mockery.

This applies even when Satie appears to repeat Satie. We have seen
the difficulties of taking him seriously when he claims he will continue to repeat long after his death his dictum concerning Truth in Art.
Similar difficultes apply to the interpretation of repetition in his music. It has often been observed by musicologists that Satie refuses to
develop his material; he prefers to repeat it, and we have seen how in
the "Sonatine bureaucratique" he repeats his Peruvian passage, note
for note. But the curious thing, to which Satie more than anyone else
systematically and creatively draws attention, is that his repetition is
never exactly repetition. Repeated figures or bars are actually perceived as different because the context of the repeat is different.
Hearing something for the second time is not the same as hearing it
for the first time, and the text in the "Sonatine bureaucratique"
reminds us of this, as do the texts that go with Satie's more extreme
exercises in repetition, which often serve to highlight a general Satie
principle that repetition tends to lead either to a steadily increasing an-
noyance and exasperation, or to a steadily increasing sense of immo-
bility, which he equates with coolness. (Perhaps, indeed, this explains
why on its return, the Peruvian tune is described as 'cold', "froid"
[Satie 1976: 66].) The "Tango (Perpétuel)" from his *Sports et divertis-
sements*[9] is written with a curious pair of repeat signs that, together
with the word in brackets in the title, imply repetition ad infinitum. No
pianist has ever known what to do with or about this implication;
most, I think, lamely repeat it once. By thus drawing attention to the
repetition itself, rather than simply to the music repeated, Satie here
crosses, I think, the line that Werner Wolf draws between self- and
metareference: if one reads the words, not only with the music as it
might be heard, but with the strange way that it is notated, one is

---

[9]   The publication history of this work is complex. The current modern edition (cf.
Satie 1989: 237) omits "(Perpétuel)" from the title of the "Tango". However, the word
is certainly present in Satie's manuscript, and in the edition which appeared in Satie's
lifetime. Cf. Whiting (1999: 399–408), who provides full references both to the original projected and realised editions, and to the publications by Ornella Volta in which
their history is revealed.

pushed to reflect on the dynamics of self-reference within the medium in general[10], rather than simply confronted with an example of it. A more famous example of such border-crossing is provided by Satie's tiny piece *Vexations*, which lasts less than one minute, but is accompanied by the notorious words:

> Pour se jouer 840 fois de suite ce motif, il sera bon de se préparer au préalable, et dans le plus grand silence, par des immobilités sérieuses. (Whiting 1999: 180)[11]

The history of the performance of the piece (described by Stephen Whittington in his article "Serious Immobilities: On the Centenary of Satie's Vexations") is most entertaining. One thing is consistently clear from the reactions of all those who have played or heard it: the effect of playing the piece 840 times is not merely 840 times the effect of playing it once. It drives people crazy, or it drives them away, or it puts them in a trance, but it certainly proves conclusively that repetition is not just repetition.

What, then, of the relationship between repetition and self-reference in music? If self-reference within a musical work can normally be traced back to a perception of repetition or similarity, then *Vexations* must surely be the ultimate example of self-reference in music. But if we allow ourselves to believe this, it brings to centre stage a question that often hovers in the background when self-reference is discussed. Is self-reference uniquely interesting and thought-provoking? Or is it really self-indulgent and boring?

From the 27th–28th May 2007, the Tate Modern in London put on a complete 840-repetition performance of *Vexations*. It lasted more than eighteen hours, and was accompanied throughout by repeated screenings of Andy Warhol's film *Sleep* (1963). Plenty of audience reactions subsequently appeared on web sites[12]. They seem to me to justify fully the gallery's juxtaposition of the two artists. In appreciating Satie as in appreciating Warhol, one of the essential questions is indeed: is self-reference in art uniquely interesting, or really boring? The answer is yes; it is indeed uniquely interesting or uniquely boring. It is never neutral, and it never ceases to be interesting or boring. The reason is precisely that evasiveness of the object of reference which, so I have

---

[10] "Eliciting", as Wolf puts it, "'media-awareness' in the recipient" (in this vol.: 16).

[11] 'To play this motif to oneself 840 times in a row, it will be appropriate to prepare oneself beforehand, in the most profound silence, by serious immobilities.'

[12] Most notably: http://www.youtube.com/watch?v=ov0fOVqqcyo.

been suggesting, characterises art, and art's peculiar relationship to truth in general, and to unique truths in particular.

Let us return to the passage I started from, and pursue the quotation a little further.

> J'ai toujours dit – & je le répéterai encore très longtemps après ma mort – qu'il n'y a pas de Vérité en Art (de Vérité unique, s'entend).
>
> La Vérité de Chopin – ce prodigieux créateur – n'est pas celle de Mozart, ce si luxueux musicien dont l'écriture est un éblouissement impérissable; de même que la Vérité de Gluck n'est pas celle de Pergolèse [...]. (Satie 1981: 61)[13]

This seems to align the absence of Truth in Art with the multiplicity of artistic creators. But there is something apparently illogical in what Satie says. Art, we may understand, does not contain just one single truth; Chopin has a truth, and Mozart has a truth, and Mozart's truth is not Chopin's. And yet all these truths exist within the unique overall category of Art. It would seem wrong, therefore, to maintain that there is no Truth in Art; in fact, there are many. The parenthesis ("de Vérité unique, s'entend") does not entirely save us from this contradiction. For it would be commonplace enough to say that Mozart is unique, and Chopin is unique. Each of them, doubtless, then, has a unique truth. It would seem logical to say that Art contains all these unique truths. Yet Satie has already affirmed that Art contains no Truth; as if Truth could be present when we consider the particular, and then suddenly vanish when we consider the multiple.

And that is indeed exactly what is played out in the dynamics of repetition in art. There is truth in the particular. But as soon as several particulars are considered as equivalent to each other, as they inevitably are when subsumed as examples of the same phenomenon within the overarching category of Art, their truth disappears. The particular cannot repeat itself in the general, because in art, there can be no repetition. The reason for which there can be no repetition in art is that repetition of signs (patterns of notes, letters, or images) within a work of art is always taken, to a greater or lesser extent, as self-reference; and the self that is being referred to has always already changed by the

---

[13] 'I have always said – & I will continue to repeat it long, long after my death – that there is no Truth in Art (no unique Truth, that is).

The Truth of Chopin – that prodigious creator – is not that of Mozart, that luxurious musician whose writing dazzles unendingly; just as the Truth of Gluck is not that of Pergolesi [...].'

time the repetition is registered, which means that the repetition is never received as such.

What I have just said contains an implicit definition of Art without which it is impossible to make sense of Satie's pronouncement. Art always evokes a self that can never be stably situated. Art, in other words, is self-reference to a self that cannot be an object of reference. Of course, there is a sense in which the truth of Mozart, or Chopin, or even doubtless Satie, is permanently contained within something that can be an object of reference, and can be endlessly repeated: the notes of their music, or the words that they wrote. But in fact, it is only perceived as an artistic truth because it appears to be permanently beyond those repeatable signs. When what we actually hear is repetition, that is boring; I would contend that according to Satie's understanding, it is not Art. However, when what we hear in repeated notes is not repetition, but reference to something unique beyond what can be repeated, beyond the words and beyond the notes, then the music becomes uniquely interesting, and at the same time the bearer of a unique artistic truth. In music, as *Vexations* demonstrates, given the right circumstances, this sense of something unlocalised and unrepeatable can indeed be created by repeating the same notes. However, this effect depends on the perception of repetition, not simply as repetition, but as the return of something that is felt, on return, to be different. The notes of the Peruvian tune remain the same; Satie's words remind us that we hear them differently.

It is certainly the case that there is something extraordinary about *Vexations* which renders it singularly apt to produce this effect. Robert Orledge, in "Understanding Satie's *Vexations*" (1990), has explained through analysis what many pianists have felt and commented on: although it is so short, the piece is peculiarly difficult to remember; every time it is played, it has to be thought through anew. Nonetheless, the contribution of words to the experience should not be underestimated. After all, it is only in the words I quoted above that the idea of repeating the work 840 times is expressed; that is not contained in the music. This, then, is another example of the way that Satie presses words into service, in order to draw attention to the instability of the object of reference in music. I pointed out towards the beginning of this essay that for some people, Satie's piano music includes his words, whereas for others, it does not, and this means it is impossible actually to say what the work is. It will now be apparent that this should be seen, not as an accident, still less as a mistake, but rather in the context of Satie's inummerable strategies for situating the object of self-reference in the work of art permanently beyond our ability to determine it. In the same way, the words on his music tell lies precisely in order to make us doubt whether what they refer to can function as the object of truth-telling. Satie's misleading self-references between words and music have an effect comparable to his deformation of the music he quotes: as their falsehood, foolishness, or inaccuracy irritates or amuses us, it also challenges us to say what the truth might have been; the truth that they do not say. And we find ourselves unable to give any clear answer to that question which is not, simply, boring.

I should like to conclude in the most heavy-handed way imaginable, by returning to the Peruvian air. What is the point of describing a Clementi-esque tune as a Peruvian air collected by a bureaucrat from a deaf-mute in Lower Brittany? Why say something that is so palpably untrue? Why this false self-reference, if such it be? I think the answer becomes reasonably clear when one asks oneself what difference it would have made if Satie had written at this point: 'The tune you are now hearing is derived from a Clementi sonatina.' That would have been a truth in a referential sense. But it would, in fact, have been less self-referentially true within the work of art as such; because art is precisely not concerned with such truths *about* things. Art is concerned with the truth *of* itself, and to read that truth, we have to look endlessly, and be endlessly frustrated in our search, for the origin of what is being repeated. The dynamic works differently in music and in words, but it works in both, and each can help to bring it out in the other. The patently un-Peruvian music tells us that Satie's words are not telling an objective truth. And the words remind us that Satie's music is not telling an objective truth. But when the music repeats, and the words refer to repetition, we are reminded that repetition in music is actually not only repetition, but also self-reference which invites us to look for what the self in question might be; and the dynamics of that search are perhaps, if not the truth of art, at least the characteristic that allows us to believe that there is some kind of truth in Satie's art, just as there is a kind of truth, according to Satie himself, in Mozart, Chopin, Gluck, or Pergolesi; even though Satie takes such obvious pleasure in telling us lies.

References

Armengaud, Jean-Pierre (1988). *Les plus que brèves d'Erik Satie.* Paris: Séguier.

Derrida, Jacques (1992). "From *Psyche*". *Acts of Literature.* Ed. Derek Attridge. London: Routledge. 318–336.

— (1987/1998). "Psyché. Invention de l'autre". *Psyché: Inventions de l'autre.* Paris: Galilée. 11–62.

Jankélévitch, Vladimir (1957). *Le Nocturne.* Paris: Albin Michel.

Lajoinie, Vincent (1985). *Erik Satie.* Lausanne: Age d'homme.

Orledge, Robert (1990). *Satie the Composer.* Cambridge: Cambridge University Press.

— (1998). "Understanding Satie's *Vexations*". *Music and Letters* 79: 386–395.

Satie, Erik (1976). *Piano Album.* London: Cramer.

— (1981). Ecrits *réunis et présentés par Ornella Volta.* Paris: Champ libre.

— (1989). *Intégrale des œuvres pour piano publiées aux éditions Salabert.* Paris: Salabert.

Warhol, Andy, dir. (1963). *Sleep.* Film. USA.

Whiting, Steven Moore (1999). *Satie the Bohemian: From Cabaret to Concert Hall.* Oxford: Oxford University Press.

Whittington, Stephen Moore (1999: online). "Serious Immobilities: On the Centenary of Satie's Vexations". http://www.af.lu.se/~fog wall/article3.html. [10/03/2007.]

Opera on Opera (on Opera)
Self-Referential Negotiations of a Difficult Genre

Frieder von Ammon, Munich

This paper focuses on metaopera as a distinctive dramatic genre and examines it from both a systematic and a historical perspective. It is demonstrated that, due to its specific structural complexity, metaopera is located at the very centre of the wide field of 'Self-Reference in Literature and Music'. It is through music that in metaopera the potential for dramatic meta-communication is considerably higher than in purely verbal drama. Furthermore, metaopera is a subject worthy of close study also for the cultural historian as, from its very beginnings, opera has continuously been a self-reflexive genre. Thus operas, as metaoperas, frequently tell the story of the cultural development of opera itself. Such metareferential conditions are demonstrated in this paper by a close analysis of Hofmannsthal and Strauss' *Ariadne auf Naxos*, which, in the light of earlier metaoperas, is interpreted as an example of meta-metaopera representing operatic metareferentiality to the highest degree.

The 7th of February, 1786, is an important date in the history of self-reference in literature and music. In honour of the Low Countries' general governor, Duke August of Sachsen-Teschen, and his wife, the German emperor, Joseph II, had arranged a special event for this day. It took place in the orangery of Castle Schönbrunn in Vienna, for that was the only room with an appropriate heating system, and it bore the beautiful title 'Frühlingsfest an einem Wintertag' ('Spring Festival on a Winter's Day'). One is, however, tempted to speak of a 'Festival of Self-Reference' instead. The Viennese court chronicle describes the event as follows:

> Nach geendigter Tafel, und Mittlerweile, als Seine Majestät mit den sämmtlichen Gästen Sich zu einem der Seitwärts am Ende des Orangerie Hauses errichteten Theater begaben, wurde die ganze Tafel aufgehoben, und aus dem Hause hinweggebracht, und sogleich die ganze Länge des Parterre beederseits herrlich beleuchtet, worauf Seine Majestät mit den Gästen zu dem an dem Anderen Ende dieses Orangerie Hauses errichteten Theater sich erhuben, alwo ein teutsches Schauspiel mit untermengten Arien aufgeführt wurde.

Nach dessen Ende begab sich die ganze Gesellschaft hinab zu dem an dem anderen Ende angebrachten Theater, alwo sofort ein Italienisches Singspiel aufgeführet wurde. (Qtd. Braunbehrens 1989: 151)[1]

The 'German play with added arias' and the 'Italian Singspiel' were *Der Schauspieldirektor* (*The Impresario*), a comedy by the then well-known Viennese playwright and librettist Johann Gottlieb Stephanie the Younger, for which Mozart had composed an ouverture, two arias, a trio, and a vaudeville; and *Prima la musica, poi le parole* (*First the Music, Then the Words*), an opera buffa, the libretto of which had been written by the then also famous poet and librettist Giambattista Casti, with the music composed by Salieri. Both works address the same issue: the contemporary dramatical and theatrical practice and its deplorable state of affairs, and in both cases the subject is treated satirically. Whereas *Der Schauspieldirektor* focuses mainly on players, plays, and related problems, *Prima la musica* is concerned with opera and its specific issues, especially the rivalry between librettist and composer, seria- and buffa-singers, and the disastrous influence of noble patronage on opera: the cause of the conflict is a duke, who demands a new opera to be written in only four days, and his mistress, a seria-singer, to partake in its performance; another aristocrat wants his mistress, a buffa-singer, to take part in the performance, too. Therefore, both works are self-referential, or more specifically, meta-dramatical and metatheatrical works, and thus the 'Festival of Self-Reference' should better be called a 'Festival of Metadrama and Meta-theatre'. Joseph II, who is known for his great interest in dramatic and theatrical affairs, had himself chosen this subject. Obviously he wanted to present in a sophisticated way not only 'his' two renowned composers, Mozart and Salieri – as well as the librettists with whom they had had their greatest successes so far (in Mozart and Stephanie's case, *Die Entführung aus dem Serail*, and in Casti and Salieri's case, *La Grotta di Trifonio*) – but also the two ensembles of his court: 'die National-Hof-Schauspieler' (the national court players) and 'die

---

[1] 'After the end of the banquet, and while His Majesty and all his guests betook themselves to one of the two theatres erected on either end of the orangery, the meal was officially ended, and the dishes were removed, and immediately the entire length of the parterre was marvellously illuminated on both sides, whereupon His Majesty rose with the guests, and went to the theatre which had been built at the other side of the orangery, where a German play with added arias was performed. After this play was over, the entire party betook themselves down to the theatre at the other end of the orangery, where forthwith an Italian Singspiel was performed.' [My translation]

Italiänischen Hof-Operisten' (the Italian court 'operatics'). Each ensemble was supposed to have its own metadrama: the court players a metaplay, and the court operatics a metaopera. It has often been overlooked that *Der Schauspieldirektor* is, in fact, a play with 'only' a few added musical numbers and not an opera or Singspiel. Joseph II, however, made a clear distinction between the German metaplay and the Italian metaopera: Salieri was paid a hundred ducats, Mozart only fifty.

Through this event, metaopera as a distinctive dramatical genre appears in such a salient and prominent context that it cannot be neglected by the cultural historian. In particular, this genre is located at the centre of the wide field of 'Self-Reference in Literature and Music', and therefore allows one to address historical as well as systematic questions of importance to the present volume. The fact that in 2007, when the conference on which this volume is based was held in Edinburgh during the period of the Edinburgh Festival, the Festival programme included not only *Prima la musica* but also Krauss and Strauss' *Capriccio* moreover proves that the genre is likewise of interest to current operatic production. Nevertheless, the subject has for a long time been largely neglected in criticism[2]. In older studies on metadrama or the play within the play, it has been treated only superficially, or not at all[3]; and in a new anthology on metaization viewed as a transmedial phenomenon, metaopera regrettably has still been disregarded[4]. With articles by Harald Fricke (2001)[5], Hermann Danuser (2005), and Michael Halliwell (2005), whose interest is for the first time directed towards metaopera as a genre in its own right, as well as a new anthology on the play within the play, which contains at least a small section on 'the play within the play and opera' (Fischer/Greiner, eds. 2007: 319–357)[6], the situation has begun to change only recently.

---

[2] There are a few articles on aspects closely related to metaopera, such as the operatic subgenre 'Künstleroper' (see Weisstein 2006), composers as operatic characters (see Bretzwieser 1995), and opera rehearsals as subject (see Hager 1986), but they do not address metaopera as such.

[3] See Pfister 1997, Schöpflin 1993, Schmeling 1977, Kokott 1968, and Voigt 1955.

[4] See Hauthal et al., eds. 2007.

[5] This is the most comprehensive study on the subject so far; it contains a typology and lists many metaoperas.

[6] The section contains contributions by Yvonne Noble ("John Gay and the Frame Play"), Donald Bewley ("Opera within Opera: Contexts for a Metastasian Interlude"),

Metaopera now seems to get more and more into the focus of research; yet it still has not received the attention it deserves. Happily enough, the present volume, forming the proceedings of the 2007 WMA Edinburgh conference, contains no less than five articles on metaoperas (including the present contribution), articles that range from Offenbach to Strauss. The volume therefore also contributes to this development. In my paper I take up Fricke's, Danuser's and Halliwell's suggestion and treat metaopera as a distinctive genre, which in the following I shall examine both systematically and historically.

1.

In order to structure the field of metaopera – which is indeed a wide field –, I shall begin with the proposal of a definition and a basic typology[7]. It needs to be stressed in advance that with the term 'opera' I refer to all forms of musical theatre, be it Singspiel, musical, or works that are explicitly called operas; of course, this is not to say that an individual subform of 'opera' does not make a difference; a broad definition of the genre, however, seems to me to be more appropriate for the present purpose. For it permits me to define metaopera as follows: metaopera is an opera in which operatic matters of any kind are commented on (whether musically, verbally, or scenically), or otherwise, in which an opera or parts of an opera are performed, whether in a rehearsal or in a private or public performance. These two forms, however, are distinguished only for clarification's sake: of course, both types can appear in combination, and in fact they often do. Another distinction concerns the quantity of metaoperatic structures with-

---

and Theresia Birkenhauer ("Theatrical Transformation, Media Superimposition and Scenic Reflection: Pictorial Qualities of Modern Theatre and the Hofmannsthal/ Strauss Opera *Ariadne auf Naxos*").

[7] In his article, Fricke also proposes a typology of metaopera or rather on the mise en abyme of opera within opera; as different from mine, it is based on transmedial types of "Potenzierung" ('potentialisation', Fricke's term for mise en abyme), and differentiates between four basic categories: "gestufte Iteration" ('graded iteration'), "unendliche Iteration" ('endless iteration'), "rekursive Iteration" ('recursive iteration'), and "paradoxe Iteration" ('paradoxical iteration'; 2001: 226f.). It seems to me, however, that in addition to this a typology is needed which takes into account the specific structure of the medium opera.

in a given work: they may span the entire work (as, for instance, in *Capriccio*), or only parts of it (as in *Tosca*); in the latter case it is debatable whether one should indeed speak of a metaopera or rather of an opera containing metaoperatic sections or elements. As many, and especially current, opera productions show, operas which originally were not metaoperas can nevertheless be turned into such through the production, for instance – to name a frequent recent device – when the work is set in the stage design of an opera house; an example is Christian Wernicke's 2002 production of *Rheingold* in the Bavarian State Opera in Munich, the point of which is that the entire performance takes place at the Bayreuth Festspielhaus. This practice, which one could call 'secondary' or 'performative' operatic metaization, however, cannot be taken into account here[8]. A further differentiation distinguishes according to the question whether the comment on opera is implicit or explicit. Examples of implicit metaoperatic comments are Striggio and Monteverdi's *L'Orfeo*, in which "La Musica" herself announces the work and in which the aesthetic dignity the new genre had gained by this work is demonstrated through Orfeo's apotheosis by Apollo at the end; or Wagner's *Die Meistersinger von Nürnberg*, in which operatic aesthetics are negotiated indirectly via the early modern 'Meistersang'. An example of explicit metaoperatic comment is *Prima la musica*, in which librettist and composer discuss various operatic matters in great detail. This opera is at the same time an example in which an opera, or in this case, parts of an opera, are performed within the work. In *Prima la musica*, an aria from the popular contemporary opera *Giulio Sabino* is auditioned by the seria-singer Donna Eleonora, who is as vain as she is overtaxed by the part. Of course, Casti and Salieri used this scene to parody contemporary artists well-known in Vienna: the composer of *Giulio Sabino*, Giuseppe Sarti, and the castrato Marchesi, who had sung the part in the opera's premiere[9]. Other famous examples of this type are *Der Rosenkavalier*, in which Hofmannsthal and Strauss pay an ironic homage to the Italian opera by having a tenor sing an Italian aria – which was, of course, composed by Strauss – to entertain the Marschallin during her 'lever'; and *Don Giovanni*, in which Mozart makes a band on stage play parts of operas by his rival Antonio Soler and by himself in

---

[8]   For this aspect cf. the contribution of Simon Williams in the present volume.

[9]   For a detailed analysis of this work cf. Danuser 2005: 70–78.

order to entertain Don Giovanni and his guests at the festivity in his castle; and, of course, to make fun of Soler, and himself.

A special case occurs when an entire operatic performance takes place within an opera, as for instance in Hofmannsthal and Strauss' *Ariadne auf Naxos*, or in Britten's *Let's Make an Opera*. This type, which I call 'opera within the opera' – in analogy to the more common metadramatical form of the 'play within the play' – is my main concern here, for it allows me to address the fundamental question of generic distinctions most directly: what is, from a structural point of view, the specific difference between metaplay and metaopera? Obviously, it is the music. But which particular part music plays in metaopera, is indeed difficult to say. The reason, of course, lies in the polymorphous and polyfunctional, the protean character of music. It is worth attempting to find an answer, though. The example I will focus on is *Ariadne auf Naxos* – a sophisticated and complex, though highly rewarding case[10].

2.

As far as the examination of the *Ariadne* libretto is concerned, to use categories developed for the analysis of metaplays (cf. Pfister 1997: 299–307) seems appropriate. Accordingly, two levels can be distinguished: the primary level of the "Vorspiel", and the secondary, subordinate level of the "Oper", that is the opera within the opera. The "Vorspiel", which is set in the late 18th century at the palace of Vienna's richest man, presents the preliminaries of the private first performance of a young composer's opera seria, entitled *Ariadne auf Naxos*. However, a few moments before the rise of the curtain the heedless rich man demands the performance of an additional piece, a comical epilogue called *Die ungetreue Zerbinetta und ihre vier Liebhaber* (*The Unfaithful Zerbinetta and Her Four Lovers*), and this even simultaneously with the tragical *Ariadne*. It is this perverted double performance that is presented in the "Oper", which is about twice as long as the "Vorspiel". The "Vorspiel" thus provides a frame for the

---

[10] Research on *Ariadne auf Naxos* is quite extensive, see, for example, Könneker 1972, Kunze 1981, and, most recently, Zipfel 2007 and Birkenhauer 2007. Important issues, however, especially as far as the form and function of music and its relation to the text are concerned, have not yet been addressed.

"Oper". This frame, however, is not closed at the end; we do not see the reactions of either the characters from the "Vorspiel" or the fictitious audience. I shall return to this striking detail later.

With regard to the characters, the levels of "Vorspiel" and "Oper" are interlinked: some, like the composer and the dancing master, for instance, appear only in the "Vorspiel"; others, like the prima donna and Zerbinetta, appear on both levels. Stylistically, however, the levels are clearly distinguished. Hofmannsthal operates with strong contrasts: the "Vorspiel" is written in elegant prose; the characters use a style of conversation that indeed might have been used in late-18th-century Vienna, the only exception being a passage in which the composer is extemporising the text of an aria. In the "Vorspiel", the libretto thus pretends not to be sung but to be a spoken text. However, for the "Oper", that is for the opera within the opera, Hofmannsthal uses verse, metre, rhyme, stanzas, and a language of a highly artificial character. Thus, in the "Oper", the libretto pretends to be an operatic libretto of the 18th century – it is, as it were, a libretto's libretto, a metalibretto –, with the exception of the commedia dell'arte passages in which the libretto pretends to be a text extemporised by the comedians, and in which, accordingly, the language is less artificial.

To sum up: structurally, the libretto of *Ariadne auf Naxos* can be compared to metaplays such as Shakespeare's *The Taming of the Shrew* (a metaplay with a frame that is also not closed at the end), or Goethe's *Faust* with its "auf dem Theater" and "Prolog im Himmel", frames which equally remain unclosed.

But now the cardinal question needs to be asked: what is the music meanwhile doing?

First, a glance should be taken at the instrumental prelude, which is, in fact, the prelude to the prelude ("Vorspiel") and thus, in a way, a 'metaprelude'. Already here the intricacy of the piece becomes evident; at the same time, it is a wonderful example of metamusic:

Example 1: Ariadne auf Naxos, *"Vorspiel", mm. 1–21 (Strauss 1912/1996: 1f.).*

The leitmotivic density of those few bars is extreme. From the very beginning, two motifs appear in combination: the young composer's emotional, ambitious and aspiring motif, played by the violins, and the plain C major kettledrum motif related to the patron and his prosaic pseudo-patronage (see figure 53 [Strauss 1912/1996: 38]). These two spheres are in conflict with each other. The composer's motif tries to move away from its point of departure and to evolve freely, yet it is kept back, as it were, by the patron's motif. Actually, during the entire exposition the composer's motif is never set free: the ground bass on C is sustained for no less than twenty-six bars, until the next motif appears. Thus, the main conflict of the whole work is already contained in the opening measures: the insoluble conflict between the composer's aspirations towards unhindered unfolding – in short: his strife for autonomy; and his actual desperate dependence – in short: his heteronomous situation. This complex condition is presented in an especially vivid musical depiction.

The second motif in E flat major is again full of implicit meaning:

Example 2: Ariadne auf Naxos, *"Vorspiel", mm. 22–29 (Strauss 1912/1996: 2).*

At its next appearance in the "Vorspiel", this motif is related to the composer's following statement, in which he explains his opera's plot:

"Sie [i. e., Ariadne] gibt sich dem Tod hin – ist nicht mehr da – weggewischt – stürzt sich hinein ins Geheimnis der Verwandlung – wird neu geboren – entsteht wieder in seinen Armen!"[11] (Hofmannsthal 1985: 22) At its third appearance, however, the motif is related to the composer's following words: "Mein lieber Freund, es gibt manches auf der Welt, das läßt sich nicht sagen. Die Dichter unterlegen ja recht gute Worte, recht gute – *(Jubel in der Stimme)* jedoch, jedoch, jedoch, jedoch, jedoch! [...] Musik ist heilige Kunst [...]."[12] (Ibid.: 24) Thus the 'mystery of transfiguration' also refers to the relation between text and music: just as Ariadne is transfigured and reborn in the arms of Bacchus, the text is transfigured and reborn as soon as it throws itself, as it were, into the arms of music. The motif's first appearance in the instrumental prelude may thus be interpreted not only as a mere anticipation of what is to come, but also as a subtle and ironic comment on the notorious conflict between words and music, librettist and composer. And, in fact, this conflict is resolved musically before it even has been addressed in the text: the words may be quite valuable, but the real thing, which in the end saves the life of the half-dead libretto, is the music. Strauss makes clear that for him – to take up Casti's phrase – the 'music [comes] first, then the words'; ironically, he puts his librettist in his place. Whether Hofmannsthal was aware of this innuendo, one cannot know. What is clear, however, is that disagreements between Hofmannsthal and Strauss were particularly frequent during the gestation of *Ariadne*. But, maybe in order to offer recompense for Hofmannsthal, Strauss also embedded a hidden homage to him in the score: the words "[d]ie Dichter unterlegen ja recht gute Worte, recht gute" are to be sung on a sequence of notes which alludes to the famous fanfare with which their most successful coproduction so far – *Der Rosenkavalier* – begins:

---

[11] 'She [...] throws herself into the mystery of transfiguration – is reborn – renews life once more in his arms!' [My translation]

[12] 'My dear friend, there are many things in the world that cannot be put into words. Why, yes, poets set down quite good words, quite good ones – *(jubilation in his voice)* and yet, and yet, and yet, and yet, and yet! [...] Music is sacred art [...].' [My translation]

Example 3: Ariadne auf Naxos, *"Vorspiel", figure 110 (Strauss 1912/1996: 79).*

The instrumental prelude thus contains extensive musical comments on the opera itself as well as on operatic affairs in general. In fact, almost all is 'said' before the first word is even uttered. This also holds true for the other main conflict of the work: the seemingly insurmountable opposition of tragedy and comedy. It is exposed through the contrast of Ariadne's sublime motif played piano and 'getragen' ('measured') by the solo horn (mm. 46–48), and a vulgar waltz designating Zerbinetta and her sphere played by piano and flutes (mm. 48–50); at the end of the prelude, the motifs of the composer, of Ariadne, and of Zerbinetta are all brought together in conflicting combination, in a motivic 'imbroglio', anticipating the daring mixture of genres to come.

Another dramatic function of the instrumental prelude also deserves mentioning: its dealing with temporal levels. For the audience of 1916 – the year in which the second version of *Ariadne* was premiered in Vienna – the opera's music must have been quite a surprise. In comparison with *Der Rosenkavalier* of 1911, and even more so with Hofmannsthal and Strauss' first coproduction of 1909, *Elektra*, the style has indeed changed considerably. Strauss now employs only 36 musicians – which means a massive reduction of orchestral forces –, and he employs them in a sophisticated and sublimely anachronistic way. The reduced, chamber-music-like instrumentation differs remarkably from the typically luxuriant instrumentation of other early-20th-century German operas; it rather reminds one of an 18th-century orchestra. It is centered on strings, and is therefore also reminiscent of music from the classical period. Furthermore, the harmonic language, which emphatically keeps to tonality and even quotes traditional cadence structures, evokes the music of the late 18th century. However, as Hofmannsthal put it in a letter to Strauss, the music of *Ariadne* is no "sklavische Nachahmung" ('slavish imitation') of 18th-century music, but rather its "geistreiche Paraphrase" ('witty paraphrase') (Strauss/ Strauss, eds. 1955: 100). From the very first bar, the listener knows that he is listening to 20th-century music. Elements such as the pianoforte, dissonant chords, and fancy modulations serve as sources of friction, or – to use Brecht's term – of 'Verfremdung'. Thus the music vacillates between two temporal levels: late 18th and early 20th century. It is veritable metamusic: 'modern' music audibly and self-consciously grafted on 'classical' music. In view of the whole work one could put it this way: just as the genres of tragedy and comedy are combined in it, so are period styles. It is for this reason that *Ariadne* has later turned out to be one of the pioneering works of the neoclassical movement.

In this way, however, the music destroys the dramatic illusion –
even before such an illusion has been established; it lays bare the
plot's fictitiousness, and it situates the work in the present, that is, the
present of the early 20th century. From the beginning, the audience understands that the historical setting of *Ariadne* is only a masquerade,
and that the work is 'really' about the negotiation of contemporary issues.

With regards to the structure of the work, this means that the music
is an additional element of considerable semantic weight, which thoroughly alters the perception of what is set down in the libretto.
Throughout the work, this element adds another dimension to the
words and the actions on the stage. As Danuser points out, there are
musical links between "Vorspiel" and "Oper" (cf. 2001: 61–71); for
instance, motifs of the "Oper" are already prefigured in the "Vorspiel", and central motifs of the "Vorspiel" are later taken up in the
"Oper". Thus, the music can switch between the levels of the play-
within-the-play structure. It is not restricted to either the primary or
the secondary levels; it can link, but it can also separate them. All in
all, the music's form and function might be compared to a narrator's
comment in fiction; the musical quasi-narrator in opera, however, is
incorporeal and adaptable; he comments on that which is presented on
stage with or without being a part of it; he generates coherence and
connections along with or against the text; he speaks in different
voices and from varying places and perspectives, and, above all, in a
non-verbal, pre-conceptual language. Of course, this is the main difference between play and opera in general: in opera, music opens up
and expands the structure of dramatic communication. But for metaopera, this has crucial consequences, for it means that the complexity
of metacommunication in this genre can be further increased, and that
to a remarkable extent. It is the structural complexity resulting from
the hybrid nature of opera that makes up the specific feature of this
genre. And Hofmannsthal and Strauss knew very well how to exploit
this potential.

3.

The example of *Ariadne auf Naxos* is, of course, only one of many
that could be examined in the context of metaopera. Another would be
the aforementioned *L'Orfeo*, an elaborate case of metaopera at the

very beginning of the history of opera. Opera has thus reflected on it-self from the very start; and it has never since stopped doing so[13]. By referring to the specific artificiality of opera, as a consequence of which its structure and status had to be questioned and redefined again and again, Fricke has plausibly singled out a convincing reason for the strong and enduring metareferentiality of this genre (cf. 2001: 243). In addition, one could point out that opera – similar to the novel, but for different reasons – is a genre that was not discussed in the canonical early modern studies of poetics, as for example Julius Caesar Scaliger's *Poetices libri septem* (1561), or Martin Opitz' *Buch von der deutschen Poeterey* (1624). Unlike, for example, the cases of tragedy or heroic epic poetry, there was no extensive theoretical discourse dating back to antiquity existent for opera, for the simple reason that it had not been invented earlier than around 1600; it is for this reason, though, that librettists and composers had to find other ways of theo-retically negotiating their genre. Next to prefaces of librettos or scores, and letters, a place to discuss opera was opera itself. Therefore it was *L'Orfeo* which defined the state of the young art of opera long before the first treatise on this subject – Giovanni Battista Doni's *Trattato della musica scenica* of 1635 – was written.

In this respect, opera coincides significantly with a cultural phe-nomenon of a greater scope. Werner Wolf has spoken of "marked metatendencies" in Western culture "at least since the seventeenth century" which led to a "veritable 'metaturn', a genuine explosion of metareference in all kinds of media and discourses and on all levels" in our time (2007: 317). The history of opera seems to be in agreement with this: from the early-modern *L'Orfeo* through modern examples such as Schreker's *Der ferne Klang* and *Christophorus, oder "Die Vision einer Oper"*[14], or Janáček's *Osud*, to the 'opera to end all operas', *Europeras* by John Cage, or the recent postmodern piece *Schlachthof 5* by the German composer Hans-Jürgen von Bose, meta-reference in opera has become increasingly complex and dominant. All of these pieces present self-referential negotiations of the difficult genre of opera, or – to quote from a famous metaopera – of that "ab-

---

[13] Certainly it has not come to an end with *Capriccio*, as Fricke argues (cf. 2001: 243). On the contrary: Danuser (cf. 2005: 83–89) and Halliwell (cf. 2005: 54–77) have shown that metaopera is especially popular in avantgarde and postmodern contexts.

[14] On this metaopera see Walter Bernhart's contribution in the present volume.

surdes Ding" ('absurd thing'), opera (Krauss 1942/1987: 50), each in its respective cultural context – all this giving a good reason why metaoperas are particularly worthy of close study. Examined in relation to one another, metaoperas reveal the cultural history of opera: opera's history as told by opera itself.

Viewed from this perspective, Casti and Salieri's metaopera of 1786, *Prima la musica, poi le parole*, to choose an example, presents opera in a situation of conflict between heteronomy and autonomy. On stage, we see the librettist and the composer as victims of an act of 'aesthetic tyranny'; as mentioned above, a duke wants them to produce a new opera within only four days. The artists have no choice but to obey; they must practise their art in a state of extreme heteronomy. With regard to the historical situation of Casti and Salieri, however, one should better speak of an act of 'benevolent despotism', for Joseph II not only allowed but indeed asked them to make fun of aristocratic patrons and their misuse of opera. Obviously, this was not particularly cruel of him. That the emperor did so is, of course, part of his self-fashioning. In this way he distinguished himself from other aristocratic patrons less honestly interested in art, and demonstrated his taste and tolerance. The 'Festival of Metadrama' may therefore be best interpreted as a sophisticated case of self-flattery by Joseph II. But unlike the artists on stage, Casti and Salieri were not forced to produce under degrading circumstances; they could take their time and had the freedom to choose the way in which they wanted to fulfill the emperor's commission; one may thus indeed say that they were allowed to work in a state of relative autonomy.

Without the emperor having exerted influence on it in this respect, *Prima la musica* also reflects upon internal operatic problems relevant at that time: the status and hierarchy of text and music, or the increasing blending of opera seria and opera buffa, the latter being a tendency particularly typical of this period. Furthermore, *Prima la musica* and the entire 'Festival of Metadrama' are part of a cultural phenomenon one could describe as a first explosion of metareference, and particularly of metadrama, in the late 18th century. Many other metaoperas emerged around that time: in 1786, the same year, Diodati and Cimarosa's *L'impresario in Angustie* was premiered in Naples; in 1797, the libretto was again set to music by Fioravanti. In 1789, Da Ponte wrote *L'ape musicale*, and, in 1798, Bretzner and Dittersdorf wrote *Die Opera Buffa*. Examples of metaoperas written before 1786 are, among others, Metastasio and Sarro's *L'impresario delle Canarie*

(1724), Metastasio and Gluck's *Le Cinesi* (1754), Macchia and Haydn's
La Canterina (1766), Calzabigi and Gassmann's *L'opera seria*
(1769)[15], and Saint-Alphonse and Grétry's *Les trois d'âges de l'opéra*
(1778). Also, metaplays were written in great number: Tieck's *Ein
Prolog, Der gestiefelte Kater*, and *Die verkehrte Welt*, or Goethe's
Faust I (which shares many features with metaoperas of the time,
e. g., *L'impresario delle Canarie* [cf. Hartmann 2004: 345f.]), to name
but a few[16]. This 'meta-explosion' might be interpreted as being a
symptom of the increasing emancipation and new positioning of literature and the other arts that occurred in those years on the verge of the
modern age.

All of these aspects of opera in the context of late-18th-century
Vienna – from internal operatic problems to cultural developments of
epochal significance – are thus contained in a nutshell in this one
metaopera, *Prima la musica*.

Ariadne auf Naxos as a work of the early 20th century shows a
different picture. This metaopera is, as Danuser has shown (cf. 2001),
an emphatic manifesto of artistic autonomy – a declaration of inde-
pendence –, and, as such, also a manifesto of modernism. This becomes especially apparent upon interpreting *Ariadne* in relation to
Prima la musica; the connection suggests itself as Hofmannsthal and
Strauss themselves seem to have had this earlier metaopera in mind.
One even gets the impression that they decidedly tried to take up the
tradition and emulate their predecessors: with a patron who orders two
operas to be performed simultaneously, *Ariadne* presents an act of
aesthetic tyranny that is even worse than the one shown in *Prima la
musica*. Also, the motifs of the rivalry between librettist and composer, seria and buffa singers and genres are taken up and resolved
differently. Thus, as in a palimpsest, the earlier metaopera becomes
visible in-between the lines of the new one. *Ariadne auf Naxos* could
therefore well be regarded as an example of meta-metaopera, of opera
on opera on opera, thus illustrating operatic metareferentiality to the
highest degree.

The fact that *Ariadne* is a rewriting of an older metaopera allows
one to determine clearly the aesthetic positions represented in it. The
motif of tyrannical patronage, for example, is employed by Hof-

---

[15]   For a close analysis of this piece cf. Danuser 2005: 78–83.

[16]   For other examples cf. the list of plays in Schöpflin 1993: 690–695.

mannsthal and Strauss in order to demonstrate that they, unlike Casti and Salieri, are completely free to choose subject and style of their productions. As genuinely modern artists, they are not dependent on noble patrons anymore, neither on dukes nor on emperors. For them, there is one authority only: the audience. This, too, is reflected in *Ariadne*. As mentioned above, Hofmannsthal and Strauss conspicuously did not make use of the opportunity to close the frame of the "Vorspiel". Unlike in other metaoperas such as Leoncavallo's *I Pagliacci* or Britten's *A Midsummer Night's Dream*, the fictitious audience does not intervene with the opera within the opera either; it does not even appear on stage. The real audience is thus not confronted with another audience on stage, but directly with the opera within the opera. I consider this gap in the opera's structure a significant detail: thereby Hofmannsthal and Strauss highlight the fact that the only standard to measure success or failure of a modern opera is the (real) audience, and that the audience's reaction is unpredictable. And indeed, the first version of *Ariadne*, which was premiered in Stuttgart in 1912, was a failure. In this version, the opera within the opera was still an opera within a play: *Ariadne* served as an operatic interlude in Hofmannsthal's translation of Molière's *Le Bourgeois gentilhomme*. Yet, as Strauss wrote in his autobiography: "Man hatte für den hübschen 'Zwitter' kein kulturelles Verständnis" ('there was no cultural understanding of this pretty "hermaphrodite"'; qtd. Hofmannsthal 1912/1985: 237). Moreover, the local monarch, King Karl of Württemberg, disturbed the performance by interrupting it with a reception which lasted for almost an hour. These experiences seem to be literally inscribed in the revised version of 1916. One could even argue that the "Vorspiel" is a subtle form of taking revenge for the humiliation Hofmannsthal and Strauss had to endure in Stuttgart.

Ariadne also shows that generic conventions – in the late 18th century still very powerful – have by now completely lost their normative power. In fact, they only serve as material to play with for librettist and composer. The combination of genres, which for the fictitious 18th-century composer was still impossible, is child's play for Hofmannsthal and Strauss: *Ariadne* is a genuine synthesis of tragedy and comedy, truly original and not repeatable, a unique work instead of a mere representative of its genre. And this holds true for any other joint opera by Hofmannsthal and Strauss.

As far as the rivalry between librettist and composer is concerned, *Ariadne*, as shown above, contains a hidden musical commentary on this matter already in the instrumental prelude, and then discusses it explicitly, in music and words, in the "Vorspiel". The most insistent commentary on this subject, however, is the ending of the work: the duet of Ariadne and Bacchus and the concluding instrumental passage, which together form an emphatic, overwhelming ending, a true operatic finale. In its course the music carries the listener away on waves of great, ever increasing power. Correspondingly, the words of the final duet are, in contrast with earlier parts, barely understandable for the listener. Thus the ending not only hints at (as did the real composer in the instrumental prelude), or claims (as did the fictitious composer in the "Vorspiel"), but indeed carries out that music takes the lead over words. In short: the finale demonstrates and enacts the supremacy of music over words. With this it is only consistent that the last measures of the opera are given to the orchestra alone; music, as it were, 'has the last word'.

To interpret this as a musical realization of Nietzsche's concept of the Dionysian does not seem to be far-fetched, especially if one considers that Nietzsche had developed his concept under the impression of Wagner's operas, that Strauss knew his writings very well[17], and, most importantly, that it is in fact Dionysos who is presented on stage as a character, which Strauss indicated through a particularly exotic and intoxicating music. Thus the finale of *Ariadne* is a glorification of the Dionysian without reserve: it presents and performs music as the true Dionysian art and marks Strauss as its archpriest. In this light, the missing frame closure gains yet another dimension: for, in the realm of Dionysos, there is no place for intellectual discourse, and, especially, for metareferentiality; therefore, the frame must not be closed in the end. Music has crossed the boundaries, and this cannot be undone.

I want to add one last thought: as mentioned above, Ariadne was premiered in 1916 in Vienna. Viewed from a historical point of view, a striking connection becomes apparent: the meta-metaopera *Ariadne* emerged at a time when the Habsburg Monarchy, which had also produced the 'Festival of Metadrama' more than a century earlier, was

---

[17] In 1925, in a letter to Hofmannsthal, Strauss mentioned that he was just again reading *Die Geburt der Tragödie*, "mit genießender Freude" ('with relishing pleasure'; Strauss/Strauss, eds. 1955: 467). For Strauss' reception of Nietzsche see Bayreuther 2005 and Youman 2005.

about to decline in World War One. The fact that in the face of the approaching end of an era its cultural tradition is once again conjured up, seems to be no coincidence; it appears that the self-referential reflection in *Ariadne* is not limited to opera and metaopera, but also involves the entire culture that had made opera possible in the past. However, *Ariadne* also looks forward into the future. And this specific temporal ambiguity, as I have tried to point out before, is already contained in the opera's instrumental prelude; it tells the whole story more beautifully than I ever could.

References

Bayreuther, Rainer (2005). "Der Held des Heldenlebens". *Archiv für Musikwissenschaft* 62: 286–302.

Bewley, Donald (2007). "Opera within Opera: Contexts for a Metastasian Interlude". Fischer/Greiner, eds. 335–346.

Birkenhauer, Theresia (2007). "Theatrical Transformation, Media Superimposition and Scenic Reflection: Pictorial Qualities of Modern Theatre and the Hofmannsthal/Strauss Opera *Ariadne auf Naxos*". Fischer/Greiner, eds. 347–357.

Braunbehrens, Volkmar (1989). *Salieri: Ein Musiker im Schatten Mozarts*. Munich: Piper.

Bretzwieser, Thomas (1995). "Komponisten als Opernfiguren: Musikalische Werkgenese auf der Bühne". Annegrit Laubenthal, Kara Kusan-Windweh, eds. *Studien zur Musikgeschichte: Eine Festschrift für Ludwig Finscher*. Kassel: Bärenreiter. 511–522.

Danuser, Hermann (2001). "Selbstreflexion bei Richard Strauss". Bernd Edelmann, Birgit Lodes, Reinhold Schlötterer, eds. *Richard Strauss und die Moderne: Bericht über das Internationale Symposium München, 21. bis 23. Juli 1999*. Berlin: Henschel. 51–77.

— (2005). "The Textualization of the Context: Comic Strategies in Meta-Operas of the Eighteenth and Twentieth Centuries". Karol Berger, Anthony Newcomb, eds. *Music and the Aesthetics of Modernity: Essays*. Cambridge, MA: Harvard University Press. 65–97.

Fischer, Gerhard, Bernhard Greiner, eds. (2007). *The Play within the Play: The Performance of Meta-Theatre and Self-Reflection*. Amsterdam/New York, NY: Rodopi.

Fricke, Harald (2001). "Oper in der Oper: Potenzierung, Ipsoreflexion, Mise en abyme im Musiktheater". François Seydoux, ed. *Fiori Musicologici: Studi in onore di Luigi Ferdinando Tagliavini nella ricorrenza del suo LXX compleanno*. Bologna: Pàtron. 219–245.

Hager, Manuela (1986). "Die Opernprobe als Theateraufführung: Eine Studie zum Libretto im Wien des 18. Jahrhunderts". Albert Gier, ed. *Oper als Text*. Heidelberg: Winter. 101–124.

Halliwell, Michael (2005). "'Opera about Opera': Self-Referentiality in Opera with Particular Reference to Dominick Argento's *The Aspern Papers*". Suzanne M. Lodato, David Francis Urrows, eds. *Word and Music Studies: Essays on Music and the Spoken Word and on Surveying the Field*. Word and Music Studies 7. Amsterdam/New York, NY: Rodopi. 51–80.

Hartmann, Tina (2004). *Goethes Musiktheater: Singspiele, Opern, Festspiele, 'Faust'*. Tübingen: Niemeyer.

Hauthal, Janine, et al., eds. (2007). *Metaisierung in Literatur und anderen Medien: Theoretische Grundlagen – Historische Perspektiven – Metagattungen – Funktionen*. Berlin: de Gruyter.

Hofmannsthal, Hugo von (1912/1985). "Ariadne auf Naxos: Oper in einem Aufzuge nebst einem Vorspiel. Neue Bearbeitung". *Hugo von Hofmannsthal: Sämtliche Werke. Vol. XXIV. Operndichtungen 2*. Ed. Manfred Hoppe. Frankfurt/M.: Fischer. 7–48.

Kokott, Jörg Henning (1968). *Das Theater auf dem Theater im Drama der Neuzeit: Eine Untersuchung über die Darstellung der theatralischen Aufführung durch das Theater auf dem Theater in ausgewählten Dramen von Shakespeare, Tieck, Pirandello, Genet, Ionesco und Beckett*. Cologne: Gouder & Hansen.

Könneker, Barbara (1972). "Die Funktion des Vorspiels in Hofmannsthals *Ariadne auf Naxos*". *Germanisch-Romanische Monatsschrift* 22: 124–141.

Krauss, Clemens (1942/1987). *Capriccio: Ein Konversationsstück für Musik in einem Aufzug*. Mainz: Fürstner.

Kunze, Stefan (1981). "Die ästhetische Rekonstruktion der Oper: Anmerkungen zur *Ariadne auf Naxos*". Wolfram Mauser, ed. *Hofmannsthal und das Theater: Die Vorträge des Hofmannsthal-Symposiums Wien 1979*. Vienna: Halosar. 103–123.

Noble, Yvonne (2007). "John Gay and the Frame Play". Fischer/ Greiner, eds. 321–333.

Pfister, Manfred (1997). *Das Drama: Theorie und Analyse*. 9th ed. Munich: Wilhelm Fink.

Schmeling, Manfred (1977). *Das Spiel im Spiel: Ein Beitrag zur vergleichenden Literaturkritik.* Rheinfelden: Schäuble.

Schöpflin, Karin (1993). *Theater im Theater: Formen und Funktionen eines dramatischen Phänomens im Wandel.* Frankfurt/M.: Peter Lang.

Strauss, Franz, Alice Strauss, eds. (1955). *Richard Strauss – Hugo von Hofmannsthal: Briefwechsel. Gesamtausgabe.* Zurich: Atlantis.

Strauss, Richard (1912/1996). *Ariadne auf Naxos: Oper in einem Aufzuge nebst Vorspiel von Hugo von Hofmannsthal. Op. 60 (II). Study Score.* London: Boosey & Hawkes.

Voigt, Joachim (1955). "Das Spiel im Spiel: Versuch einer Formbestimmung an Beispielen aus dem deutschen, englischen und spanischen Drama". Ph.D. dissertation, University of Göttingen. Typescript.

Weisstein, Ulrich (2006). "'Die letzte Häutung': Two German *Künstleropern* of the Twentieth Century: Hans Pfitzner's *Palestrina* and Paul Hindemith's *Mathis der Maler*". Walter Bernhart, ed. *Selected Essays on Opera by Ulrich Weisstein.* Word and Music Studies 8. Amsterdam/New York, NY: Rodopi. 229–272.

Wolf, Werner (2007). "Metafiction and Metamusic: Exploring the Limits of Metareference". Winfried Nöth, Nina Bishara, eds. *Self-Reference in the Media.* Berlin: de Gruyter. 303–324.

Youman, Charles (2005). "The Role of Nietzsche in Richard Strauss's Artistic Development". *The Journal of Musicology* 22: 309–349.

Zipfel, Frank (2007). "'Very Tragical Mirth': The Play within the Play as a Strategy for Interweaving Tragedy and Comedy". Fischer/Greiner, eds. 203–220.

Christophorus, oder "Die Vision einer Oper"
Franz Schreker's Opera as a Metareferential Work

Walter Bernhart, Graz

Schreker's late opera, *Christophorus, oder "Die Vision einer Oper"*, is the document of a creative crisis experienced by the composer in the 1920s at a time of decisive changes in the world of music and the arts in general, which Schreker felt unable to share or accept for himself. *Christophorus* reflects these changes and the composer's attitudes to them and thus forms a prime example of a metareferential work in which the focus is on selfreferential considerations about its own status as a work of art. Metareferential awareness finds reflection both in the texture of the music itself, which introduces stylistic parodies of contemporary musical practices ('music on music'), and on the generic or art-philosophical level. Here interestingly the opera proves – despite its subtitle – to be not so much specifically an 'opera on opera' (on the issue of how – or whether at all – to write an opera at the given time) but more generally a work about 'drama on drama', or 'theatre on theatre', demonstrating an (ultimately self-defensive) struggle of the highly theatrically oriented composer with criticism from advocates of 'absolute music'.

Franz Schreker's (1878–1934) last but one opera, *Christophorus, oder "Die Vision einer Oper"* (*St Christopher, or "The Vision of an Opera"*, 1924–1929), has not been in the limelight of critical attention, just as Schreker in general has not been of central concern in the otherwise lively and hotly debated world of twentieth-century opera. Yet more recently we can observe a modest Schreker revival taking place, as witnessed, for instance, by the Schreker cycle at Kiel Opera from 2001 to 2003, or by the highly acclaimed production of *Die Gezeichneten* (*The Stigmatized Ones*) at the Salzburg Festival of 2005. The reception of Schreker's works is a particularly interesting story. One should keep in mind that Schreker was the most highly acclaimed opera composer from around 1917 to 1921. A veritable Schreker wave swept over Austria and Germany at the time, based on the sensational success of *Der ferne Klang* (*The Distant Sound*, 1917) and *Der Schatzgräber* (*The Treasure Seeker*, 1920), and due to the judgement of Paul Bekker, the influential Frankfurt critic, who, in a seminal article of 1918, propagated Schreker as the only true and worthy successor of Richard Wagner who by far surpassed the other operatic

heroes of the time – Pfitzner, d'Albert, even Strauss (after *Salome* and
Elektra!). The German/Austrian trauma of having lost the war left its
mark on the psyche of the two nations and led them to find
compensation in achievements in the world of music, where
traditionally they had undisputed strengths. Thus the issue had
extreme political and cultural relevance, and to have found in
Schreker a "Messiah of German Opera" (as proclaimed even in America, cf. Hailey 1993: 85) became of crucial importance. This was at a
time when Schreker still lived in Vienna, a city that suddenly lacked
scope in a drastically shrunken country. Yet everybody's darling,
Schreker – who was also a highly successful teacher – was lured away
to Berlin to become the director of the city's prestigious Musikhoch-
schule. Although the first few years there were a period of continued
success, it soon became clear that Berlin was not really Schreker's
world and that the drastic changes of the time were not to his mind.
The new aesthetic tendencies of 'Neue Sachlichkeit' ("new objec-
tivity", or "new sobriety"; ibid.: 168) and neoclassicism, as well as
American jazz, were ultimately alien to Schreker, and the new
'Zeitoper' ("opera of the times"; ibid: 241, or "topical opera"; ibid.:
358) was a profound challenge to the fastidious opera composer.
Schreker, who had always been admired for the opulent 'sound magic'
('Klangzauber') and alluring timbral qualities of his refined orchestral
palette, was now faced with a world of hard and dry sounds where
"rhythm […] seems to dominate" and "motor impulse replaces
passion", as Schreker himself observed in an essay of 1928, significantly called "Stilwende" ('change of styles'; qtd. ibid.: 155). As a
recent *New Yorker* article has put it in a nutshell: the "foxtrotting
nineteen-twenties" stood against Schreker's "gossamer textures"
(Ross). Particularly bitter for Schreker was the fact that his own
colleagues and students played a prominent role in this change of
taste: Hindemith, Busoni, Krenek, Hába, Toch, Weill – they all enthu-
siastically welcomed the new tendencies, which, ironically, was partly
a consequence of Schreker's own characteristic style of teaching: he
never took a dogmatic stance by asserting a specific style of writing and
establishing a 'school' of his own – quite in contrast to Schoenberg,
who became a very welcome colleague and friend of his in Berlin.
Schreker rather believed in encouraging his students to help them find
their own individual styles. Even more disappointing for Schreker
than his students who avidly embraced the new trends were the attacks
by influential critics of the time. They condemned Schreker on moral

grounds, censuring his "artistry (*Artistentum*)" (Hailey 1993: 170) and immoral subjects ('sittenlose Stoffe') treated by "a 'soulless nerve artist'"[1]. Schreker was blamed for being a writer of "sexual kitsch operas" (ibid.: 146) and romantic "Schwulst"[2]. Above all, Adolf Weißmann from the *Berliner Zeitung* diagnosed music as being in a world crisis[3] and attacked Schreker's "'[...] weibliche, weichliche Natur ... Ja, es fehlt der zuckende, doch männliche Rhythmus einer kraftvollen Persönlichkeit [...]'"[4]. All this led to a veritable creative crisis in Schreker, a crisis which was aggravated by the fact that Nazi propaganda machinery started to push forward and targeted at Schreker, whose father had been identified as a Jew.

All these observations are very much in place for my topic as they form the background for *Christophorus*, which was written between 1925 and 1929 and directly reflects the critical situation just outlined. In fact, Christopher Hailey, president of the Franz Schreker Foundation and profoundest Schreker scholar, sees the composer's problems with his students as the ultimate trigger of the opera[5], as witnessed by the opera's framing situation of a composition teacher with his students. An additional point is made by Frank Harders-Wuthenow, who considers Weißmann's criticism, quoted above, of Schreker's "feminine, soft nature" the main spring of the composer's choice of subject matter, namely the legend of Saint Christopher.

The political cataclysm of 1933 had a direct impact on Schreker: the premiere of *Christophorus*, scheduled for the spring of that year at Freiburg, did not take place, prohibited by Hitler's 'seizure of power' ('Machtergreifung'), and the composer himself, totally shattered, did

---

[1] Harders-Wuthenow 2005: 27, quoting Alfred Heuß in *Zeitschrift für Musik*, 1921 ("seelenloser Nervenkünstler"; qtd. ibid.: 11).

[2] Hailey 1980: 115 ('bombast', 'magniloquence').

[3] Cf. *Musik in der Weltkrise*, the title of a book by Weißmann, published in 1922 (misquoted by Harders-Wuthenow as *Die Weltkrise der Musik*; 2005: 30).

[4] Qtd. Harders-Wuthenow 2005: 14. ("Schreker is a feminine, soft nature ... Yes, the twitching but masculine rhythm of a powerful personality [...] is lacking"; ibid.: 30.)

[5] "Das Unbehagen über seine unbändige Kompositionsklasse der frühen zwanziger Jahre [...] war wohl der Ausgangspunkt für CHRISTOPHORUS." (Hailey 2002a: 14. 'It is most likely that uneasiness about his ungovernable composition class of the early twenties was the starting point for CHRISTOPHORUS.') Here and in the following all unquoted translations are my own.

not long survive the historical watershed: he died in March 1934. A Schreker revival after the war, which could naturally have been expected, did not take place because the composer, in spite of his personal friendship with Schoenberg (*Christophorus* is dedicated to him), was not accepted as a member of the so-called Second Viennese School. The deathblow came from Adorno, who saw in Schreker a "Romantic" and "Impressionist" writing "music of puberty" and "hopeless sterility", lacking reflection and "disregard[ing] constructive discipline" (Adorno 1963, qtd. Hailey 1993: 317–319). Adorno's 'modernist' asceticism allowed for no appreciation of Schreker's orchestral sensualism and essentially paratactic syntactical logic based on the principle of sharp contrasts and strong theatrical effects. Christopher Hailey argues that only the 'postmodernist' age brought a rediscovery of Schreker (cf. ibid.: 320), signalled by two seminal symposia, in Graz (1976)[6] and Berlin (1978)[7], and by the belated world premiere of *Christophorus* (at Freiburg, as originally planned) in 1978, this time on the occasion of the centenary of Schreker's birth. Schreker criticism, despite some substantial individual contributions, is still in its infancy, as Hailey affirms in his groundbreaking *Cultural Biography* of the composer of 1993. This is particularly true for *Christophorus*, which is clearly Schreker's most complex opera, but, as asserted by Sieghart Döhring, "eines der Haupt- und Schlüsselwerke"[8] and, according to Gösta Neuwirth, "die Summe seiner Intentionen"[9].

The complexity of *Christophorus* is due to the fact that it is – far more so than any other Schreker opera – "Geheimwerk und Lebensbeichte"[10], the composer's assessment of his self-understanding as a musician at a time of distress, when his artistic value system was critically challenged and the composer desperately tried to come to grips with a radically changed situation. This accounts for the fact that the opera – unusual for Schreker, who generally was a fast worker – had a long gestation period and saw a great number of revisions. (Hailey lists as many as six different versions of the opera; cf. 1980: passim.)

---

6   See Kolleritsch, ed. (1978).

7   See Budde/Stephan, eds. (1980).

8   Döhring 1978: 29 ('one of his main and key works').

9   Neuwirth 1978: 109 ('the sum of his intentions').

10 Harders-Wuthenow 2005: 14 ("Secret Work and Life's Confession"; ibid.: 30).

This reflects both the composer's uneasiness with, and fundamentally ambivalent attitude towards, his subject, and accounts for its opacity and difficulty, which have led to occasional criticism and discontent.

The first version of the opera was called *Christophorus – eine moderne Legende*, and its intention was to retell the old legend of St Christopher for the modern world. It is the story of the giant who wants to serve only the mightiest authority and thus enters the service of the Emperor. But when he discovers that the Emperor is afraid of the Devil he follows the Devil, until he finds out that the Devil shuns away from a crucifix, which tells Christopher that Christ must be more powerful than the Devil. So he starts searching for Christ but does not know where to find him until he is told by a hermit that he should give up wasting his enormous strength in warfare and fighting and should rather put it to a peaceful service by carrying people across a dangerous river, which he does. One day a child asks to be carried across but when passing, the river gets terribly rough and the child becomes an extremely heavy burden: Christopher is terrified and realizes that he is carrying the Christ child and with him the burden of the world. He sinks and is swallowed up by the river but when returning to the surface the river has become perfectly calm and peaceful.

To understand the plot development of the opera it is essential to know well the details of this story since the legend is told only very briefly in the Prelude of the opera. In this Prelude we find the framing situation already referred to, where a master composer, Meister Johann, requires his students to write string quartets based on this legend. However, one of the students, Anselm, declines to do so: he prefers writing an opera on the subject and thinks this form to be more appropriate for the modern times. He opts for updating the plot and dramatizing the story. The equivalencies between the old legend and its modern rewriting by Anselm are made little explicit in the text, only a private "Introduction" given by the composer (not found in the score nor otherwise published by Schreker himself) offers a few hints. This Introduction was written at the request of Joseph Marx, his Styrian composer-friend, who confessed of not having understood the story. The Introduction explains that the mighty 'Emperor' of the legend is "heute die Kunst und die Schaffende [sic], zeugende Liebe in ihrer primitivsten Gestalt, der bürgerlichen Ehe"[11], to be overcome

---

[11]   Schreker 2005b: 67 ("today art and creating, engendering love in its most primitive form, the bourgeois marriage"; ibid.).

by the more powerful "'Teufel'" ("'Devil'"), in the modern shape of
"Laster" ("vice"), which is in turn overcome by the "'Jesuskind'"
("'Christ child'") in its modern version, namely, "das Gottähnlichste
im Menschen, das reine Auge des Kindes" and, musically, "die
reinste, keuscheste Form der Musik, das Streichquartett"[12]. What is
not particularly apparent in this Introduction, however, is the fact that
the final childlike stage is also represented in the opera by a quotation
from Laozi's *Daodejing*, which appears at the beginning of the
opera's Postlude, again indicating a more contemporary religious
sphere than the old legend's Roman Catholic sainthood.

Anselm thinks that St Christopher is an undramatic character, that
the story is "langweilig [...] und sentimental über die Maßen", and for
his operatic dramatization he thinks that one essential element is
missing: "das Weib, / das süße, lockende, / teuflische Weib"[13]. This
woman, for Anselm, is Lilith from the Old Testament, the serpent,
who in his version of the legend becomes vice, the modern form of the
Devil. (Schreker, like many of his illustrious contemporaries such as
Schoenberg, Adolf Loos, or Karl Kraus, were deeply impressed by
Otto Weininger's misogynist theories, a typical product of the 'ner-
vous age', which became a main spring for the famous 'wicked' eroti-
cism in Schreker's works; cf. Harders-Wuthenow 2005: 29.) Lilith is
introduced into Anselm's story as Lisa, who – and this contributes significantly to the complexity of the opera's plot – is Meister Johann's
daughter and Anselm's object of love. Lisa, however, is engaged to be
married to Christoph, one of Meister Johann's other students. So what
happens is that the 'real-life' situation of Anselm in the frame story
becomes the trigger for the central constellation in his framed story,
that is, the operatic version (or 'vision') of the legend of St Christopher. The frame's Christoph turns into the opera's St Christopher, also
called Christoph, and the frame's Lisa marries Christoph, in the
planned opera, and has a child. Yet she turns into a Lilith when
shocked about her vanishing beauty as a consequence of child-bearing
(which is an ingenious idea with reference to the legend!), and she
succumbs to the temptations of Dionysiac artistic dancing, and to
those of Anselm. At this, the jealous Christoph shoots Lisa, and

---

[12] Ibid. ("[...] the most godlike in man, the child's pure vision [...] the purest, chast-
est form of music, the string quartet"; ibid.).

[13] Ibid.: 75 ("Boring [...] and exceedingly sentimental"; "the sweet, tempting, / dev-
ilish woman"; ibid.).

Anselm hauls off Christoph, whom he confesses to be in love with, to rescue him. One should keep in mind, though, that all these dramatic events are elements only of Anselm's 'vision of an opera', and it is a main structural point to be made that the two plot levels of the frame and the framed cannot be disentangled in the opera – they develop concurrently. It is no coincidence that the central character is called Anselm, alluding to E. T. A. Hoffmann's novella "The Golden Pot" with its typically Hoffmannesque plot situation of the mingling of dream and reality. To finish the story: in the second act we find Christoph and Anselm on the run, hiding as bar musicians at an opium den, with the drug addicted Christopher trying to conjure up Lisa at a séance. Yet who appears, 'real-life', instead of the expected spectre is Christoph and Lisa's child guided by Meister Johann, both as beggar musicians. Christoph is devastated and (mentally) 'sinks under the weight of the child', which marks the end of the second act. Yet in the Postlude Anselm is equally in distress because he finds himself unable to finish his opera. All characters – including the 'real-life' Lisa – are gathered to encourage him, and the child asks his father, Christoph, to carry him home, at which Anselm finally hears "Stimmen" ("Voices") and the "Pulsschlag der Stille" ("Pulsebeat of silence") within himself: "Musik und nichts weiter –" ("music and nothing more –") – a string quartet (Schreker 2005b: 136f.). This is in perfect keeping with the peaceful ending of the legend and finally replaces Anselm's illusionary 'vision of an opera'.

The complexity of the drama in *Christophorus* consists, for one, in the simultaneity, with identical characters, of a frame story and a framed story, which, further, is itself a modern adaptation of an old story. This structural complexity is additionally enhanced by the fact that the frame story contains still another story, namely that of a conflict between musical forms and styles, represented by the dispute between Meister Johann's several students, a conflict which – as the frame and framed stories are inseparably intertwined – is continued in Anselm's framed story, so that the conflict of musical styles becomes also an element of Anselm's 'vision of an opera', which is basically the opera that we, as external observers, experience on the stage. Schreker seems to have been aware of the intricacy of this structural situation, which comes out in a remark he makes in his Introduction for Joseph Marx: "Sie werden sehen und hören, vielleicht auch ohne Hinweis entdecken, wie der Konflikt der musikalisch getrennten Welten seinen Lauf neben dem Drama nimmt."[14] This is an unusually explicit reference to the metamusical level of the work, which appears – even more explicitly – in the sub-title of the opera (*"Die Vision einer Oper"*). As already mentioned, this metareferential sub-title was not there from the beginning: the first version said *"eine moderne Legende"*. Christopher Hailey has closely traced the genesis of the opera libretto (see 1980) and has shown that the further the text evolved the more Anselm became the central character, over the Christopher of the legend and the main title of the work. This is reminiscent of the genesis of a typical Henry James story, where the emphasis also tended to shift from the story itself to the circumstances of its telling, that is, where the metareferential element became an increasingly dominant feature. When Schreker had originally chosen the subject of St Christopher – if we follow Harders-Wuthenow's argument referred to above – in order to defend himself against Weißmann's charge of effeminacy, he later shifted his focus more and more to the aesthetic and compositional issues of the time, whereby Anselm's dilemma of a conflict of styles became central to the work, which, in turn, clearly reflected Schreker's own artistic dilemma. It is for the first – and only – time that we find in Schreker's works a "self-conscious stylistic awareness", a "'constructive' principle", as Hailey perceptively notes, which is clearly distinguished from Schreker's otherwise "unconscious stylistic assurance" (1993: 175). As a consequence, we detect in *Christophorus* a 'stylistic mosaic' (cf. Denut 2009: 57), which Schreker himself refers to in his Introduction by naming the following items: "klassizistische Symphonie", "die Leidmusik von der Tragödie der Frau", "künstlerischen Tanz", "Jazzmusik", "die volksliedartigen Weisen des Kindes", and finally "absolute Musik"[15]. (Significantly, Schreker does not talk about any particular form or style of opera, or opera in general, a point to be taken up later.) H. H. Stuckenschmidt has identified an even greater number of styles in the opera and lists them as contrastive pairs:

---

[14]   Schreker 2005b: 67 ("You will see and hear, perhaps also discover without having it indicated, how the conflict of the musically divided worlds runs its course next to the drama."; ibid.).

[15]   Schreker 2005b: 67 ("classicistic symphony", "the grief music of the tragedy of a woman", "artistic dance", "jazz music", "the child's melodies resembling a folk song", "absolute music"; ibid.).

[...] polytonale Symphonik neben archaisierendem Quartettklang, gelehrte Kontrapunktik neben einfachem, harmonisch begleitetem Chanson, das Modeinstrument der Singenden Säge neben Klavier, Saxophon und Schlagzeug, arioser Gesang neben rhythmisch und im Tonfall fixierter Sprechstimme, melodramatische Strecken neben reinem Singspieldialog[16].

It is clear that some of the stylistic experiments in the opera are satirical and serve to parody styles that were propagated in the early 1920s. This is particularly true for the music that accompanies Starkmann, the critic of the *Neutöner* journal, who is a figure parodying Weißmann. In Scene 2 of Act I we hear five bars of fugue-like, 'linear' music in C major, Hindemith-like, ironising contemporary tendencies to turn away from old-style "Verstiegenheit" ("extravagance"; Schreker 1931: 13f.; Schreker 2005b: 80). Hilarious is the kind of 'wedding chorus' sung by the students, "frisch und burschikos": "Starkmann blickt etwas unsicher in das Blatt und kräht mit"[17] – a parody of 'Neue Sachlichkeit'. This chorus is, in Hailey's words, "of imbecilic simplicity" (1993: 249) and develops, musically, into a scene reminiscent of the 'thrashing scene' ('Prügelszene') from Wagner's *Meistersinger*.

While such cases are clearly parodies and meant to be appreciated as such, other passages which introduce 'modern' styles are less obviously ironic. This is true for the dance music at the beginning of Act II, which comes in the ragtime/cakewalk rhythm (familiar by Debussy's "Golliwog's Cakewalk" from *Children's Corner*, 1906–1908), and for the "Tragisches Couplet" ("tragic couplet"; Act II, Scene 3), which is Anselm's chanson called "'Das Gift'" ("'The Poison'") and sung by Rosita, Starkmann's escort (Schreker 2005b: 119). She is, significantly, announced as "uns'rer Oper / gefeierte Diva –"[18]. The satire is obvious: this operatic diva is prepared to do modern 'light' music in

---

[16] Stuckenschmidt 1970: 50 ('polytonal symphonic style next to archaic quartet sound, learned counterpoint next to simple, harmoniously accompanied chanson, the fashionable instrument of the singing saw next to piano, saxophone and percussion, arioso singing next to rhythmical and melodically fixed speaking voice, melodramatic passages next to pure *Singspiel* dialogue'). The spirit of Adorno is lifting its head when Stuckenschmidt adds that the opera 'touches most dangerously on the realm of the operetta' ("streift am gefährlichsten das Reich der Operette"; ibid.) – which it nowhere actually does.

[17] Schreker 2005b: 93 ("in a fresh boyish manner"; "Starkmann looks somewhat unsurely at the page and croons along"; ibid.).

[18] Schreker 2005b: 118 ("the acclaimed diva / of our opera –"; ibid.).

the style of Kurt Weill. Yet what further happens is that the voice of Rosita "sich allmählich in die Lisas zu verwandeln scheint"[19], and, in a dialogue which takes place parallel to the chanson, Christoph confesses his drug addiction and his desire to conjure up Lisa: the sense of parody is totally lost, and the 'feel' of the new style – in musical terms – is never truly established. Eric Denut, discussing self-referential (or rather, more specifically, metareferential) elements in *Christophorus*, makes the perceptive remark that, when introducing new styles into his work, Schreker never had problems of technique, which Schreker was in full command of, yet it was his sensibility that ultimately stood against true innovation (cf. 2009: 57f.). So, although Schreker, when starting on his new opera *Christophorus*, was optimistic as usual about his new style, he was soon annoyed by the 'topicality' of the work[20] and seems to have realized that he should not prostitute himself, as he was wont to do due to his well-established obsession with public success. Thus, the anti-illusionist, metamusical elements of parody in the opera – in the context of its general self-referential stylistic multiplicity – are basically only of an episodic character.

A more central metamusical element of the opera is the fact that it addresses the issue of opera already in its title. Thus, *Christophorus* is regularly called an 'opera on opera'[21], which, of course, to a certain extent it is. Clearly, Anselm wants to write an opera, in spite of his master's wish for a string quartet. Anselm, however, fails in his attempt, and what we hear instead at the end is – a string quartet. This course of events has been read, somewhat rashly, as a direct response to the crisis of opera as witnessed in the 1920s, answering contemporary doubts about whether in such times it would still be possible to write operas – the suggested answer being: no. It is a misconception, however, when, as a consequence, Gösta Neuwirth, for example, talks

---

[19] Ibid.: 119 ("gradually seems to change into Lisa's voice"; ibid.).

[20] "Das Aktuelle des *Christophorus* stört mich." (Letter to Paul Bekker, 24 January 1927; qtd. Hailey 1980: 18.)

[21] For example: "Die Handlung der Oper dreht sich um drei Komponisten, doch ist *Christophorus* weniger ein Künstlerdrama als eine Oper über die Operngattung selbst." (Hailey 2002a: 15. 'The plot revolves around three composers, yet *Christophorus* is less an artists drama than an opera about the genre of opera itself.')

about a 'transformation of the opera into a string quartet'[22] as a sign of turning away from opera. Schreker himself anticipated such a reaction yet clearly rejected criticism such as: "Warum aber [...] schreibe [sic] Sie denn selbst noch eine Oper?"[23]. The reasons Schreker gives for his denial are not particularly convincing[24], but the fact is that he wrote not only *Christophorus* obviously as an opera – and indeed a fine opera – and that another one was soon to follow, *Der Schmied von Gent* (*The Blacksmith of Ghent*, 1929–1932). So, Anselm's failure to write an opera does not imply a failure of opera at large. Opera as a genre is not put into question; however, an artistic approach, which is represented by opera, is put up for inspection in the 'conflict of the musically divided worlds' that Schreker addresses in *Christophorus*.

A close look at the libretto – as always written by Schreker himself – surprisingly shows no direct verbal references to opera, apart from the sub-title and Rosita being called a "diva of our opera" (Schreker 2005b: 118), as already mentioned. Anselm's references to his visionary work consistently use other terms from the world of theatre: "Dies ist *dramatisch*! / Doch fehlt das Weib"[25], or: "wähl ich zum *Drama*: / Lisa, Lilith, die Schlange"[26]. He plans the '*acts*' of his work (cf. ibid.: 81) and hands over to Lisa as a wedding present "[e]iner Tragödie erste[n] Akt"[27]. Later he says: "Die große *Szene* hebt an"[28], and: "Die *Szene*, von der ich dir sprach, / ist fertig"[29]. "Die *Komödie* endet. / Die *Szene* bricht ab –"[30]; "Die *Komödie* ist aus"[31]; "Es war doch nur *Spiel* ..."[32]; and

---

[22] "Wandlung der Oper zum Streichquartett" (Neuwirth 1978: 109; 'the transition from the opera to the string quartet'). Cf. similarly: "Soll das denn heißen, dass die ganze Opernidee zuletzt nichts mehr taugt?" (Eberhardt & Horst 2003. 'Does that mean that the whole idea of opera is no longer of any use?')

[23] Schreker 2005b: 67 ("But why [...] do you yourself still write an opera?"; ibid.).

[24] One reason Schreker gives is that authors need not share their characters' opinions (which, of course, is true but contributes little to the metareferential issue of the opera), another that a time will come when opera will "be saved by a drawing on its original shape" ("Zurückgreifen auf seine ursprüngliche Art"; 2005b: 67).

[25] Schreker 2005b: 75. ("This is *dramatic*! / But the female element is lacking"; ibid.). This one and all subsequent emphases in quotations are my own.

[26] Ibid.: 76 ("I choose for the *drama*: / Lisa, Lilith, the snake"; ibid.).

[27] Ibid.: 94 ("The first *act* of a *tragedy*"; ibid.).

[28] Ibid.: 101 ("The great *scene* begins"; ibid.).

[29] Ibid.: 104 ("[T]he *scene* I told you about / is ready"; ibid.).

[30] Ibid.: 109 ("The *comedy* ends. / The *scene* breaks off"; ibid.).

finally Christoph realizes: "[ich] hab doch gelebt nur, / mehr schlecht als recht, / [...] ein *Bühnen*leben"[33]. These quotations show that the artistic alternative to a string quartet on which Anselm is working is never referred to as an 'opera' at any point, the references are always to drama and theatre in far more general terms. The fundamental aesthetic issue of the work, thus, is not the contrast between opera and string quartet, but more generally the contrast of drama/theatre and – in Schreker's own words – "absolute Musik" ("absolute music"; 2005b: 67). Schreker was "above all a man of the theater" (Hailey 2002b: 5), and theatricality was one of his major 'vices', according to Adorno. Schreker never reflected thoroughly on his craft, and also his small essay called "Meine musikdramatische Idee" of 1919 is not a very profound document of self-reflection. Yet it at least honestly makes sure from the beginning that he does not really have a clearly expressed 'musico-dramatic idea'. What Schreker asserts is that the general aim of his works is "[e]ine Art 'Verismus', wenn man will"[34], and the most interesting notion to cull from this essay is the following: "Klang [ist] eines der wesentlichsten musikdramatischen Ausdrucks-mittel [...] in entscheidenden Augenblicken des Dramas"[35]. Yet he grants that the world which is thereby brought to stage life is only a world of appearances ('Schein'), and not that of pure being ('Sein'). There was an aesthetic debate going on at the time about the 'natural-ism' of the vocal tone as in contrast to the 'illusionism' of the instru-mental tone, discussed, among others, in Paul Bekker's *Klang und Eros* (*Sound and Eros*) of 1922[36]. Schreker increasingly realized that his own world of the theatre – as a sensual, naturalistic, vocalizing, dramatic manifestation of subconscious spheres of the psyche – is only a world of appearances and not the 'real thing'. It is only instrumental music that he conceived of as giving access to pure being, a conviction which

---

[31]   Ibid.: 110 ("The *comedy* is over"; ibid.).

[32]   Ibid.: 111 ("It was only a *game* ..."; ibid.). A more appropriate translation of the German "nur *Spiel*" would be "only *playing*".

[33]   Ibid.: 133 ("[I have] lived / more wrongly than rightly, / [...] only a *stage* exis-tence"; ibid.).

[34]   Qtd. Zibaso 1999: 43 ('a sort of "verismo", if you want').

[35]   Qtd. ibid. ('sound is one of the most essential means of musico-dramatic expres-sion in decisive moments of the drama').

[36]   "Bekker stellt dem 'Naturalismus' des Vokaltons den 'Illusionismus' des Instru-mentaltons gegenüber." (Molkow 1980: 89)

Schreker precisely presents on stage at the end of *Christophorus*. It is a particularly moving passage when the child, "im Fiebertraum" ("in a feverish dream"), craves of his father, Christoph: "Trag mich heim / [...] woher wir kamen – / dort hinaus, / dort hinaus –"[37]. The phrase 'trag mich hinaus' ('out there') replaces what the old legend says, namely, 'trag mich hinüber', i. e., 'across' (the river). It is Hailey's very persuasive reading of the passage that this 'hinaus' (replacing 'hinüber') means 'hinaus aus dem Theater' ('out of the theatre') (cf. 1980: 132), in other words, out of this world of mere appearances – and what we hear following this is the string quartet and the concluding C major to end the opera. Of course, such an ending is in perfect keeping with the idea of the legend, but we need to be aware of the fact that only a sixth attempt in the long gestation of the opera produced this ending. Schreker's struggle with it seems to mirror his existential crisis about his self-understanding as an artist of the kind he was – a man of the theatre. The hostilities and neglect which he faced and which seriously undermined his self-esteem, would induce him to write such an ending to his opera to serve him as a means of mental relief and compensation by vicariously acting out an escape from the pressures – an escape which he was consciously and in real life not prepared to take. One should, significantly, add that this ending of the opera is a perfect ending for an opera, opening up an Edenic 'secondary world' which, if we follow W. H. Auden, is the essence of opera (cf. 1968; just as the whole Epilogue of *Christophorus* with its gripping orchestral interlude is a magnificent operatic achievement – in Hailey's words, "one of the most haunting scenes in twentieth-century opera"; 1993: 246).

Thus, the major metareferential aspect of *Christophorus* is not so much opera as a particular musico-dramatic genre, or the question of which kind of opera should be written at the given historical moment. Rather, the discussion focuses more generally on the central aesthetic issue of dramatic representation. An earlier essay by Wolfgang Molkow has demonstrated that in all of Schreker's operas we find aesthetic metareference, 'art on art', in the form of what he calls "'tönende Symbole'" ('sounding symbols'; 1980: 83). They sometimes already appear in the title (*Der ferne Klang* [*The Distant Sound*], *Das Spielwerk* [*The Carillon*]), in other works we find centrally placed musical

---

[37] Schreker 2005b: 135f. ("Carry me home / [...] whence we came, / out there, / out there. –"; ibid.)

instruments, like the lute in *Der Schatzgräber* or the organ in *Der singende Teufel* (*The Singing Devil*). As Molkow asserts, Schreker's sound visions in his operas are always already prefigured in their subjects[38]. It is interesting to note, however, that the form of aesthetic self-reflection which Schreker chose for *Christophorus* is of a character different from his earlier works. While the earlier ones manifest the composer's famous obsession with sound, in *Christophorus*, the emphasis has shifted and is now put on dramatic presentation: 'sound on sound' is replaced by 'drama on drama', where the musical genres of the opera and the string quartet represent forms of 'drama' and 'non-drama', respectively. This is in keeping with the development of Schreker's late style of writing, which acquired a far more 'reduced' orchestral quality (as Hermann Danuser's careful analysis of Schreker's *Whitman Songs* – its orchestral version was written at the same time as *Christophorus* – has shown; cf. 1980: 50). An additional metareferential element of *Christophorus* can be found in its several parodies of musical styles of the time, as discussed. These, again, are not specifically operatic styles, they are more general cases of 'music on music'. So, while it is convincing when Denut asserts that *Christophorus* is the 'culmination of Schreker's self-referentiality'[39] – if one grants that Denut is in fact talking about metareferentiality (cf. Wolf 2009: passim) – a closer investigation of the work can show that, interestingly, it is hardly an 'opera on opera' in any more specific sense. The fact that the opera shows forms of operatic presentation which Schreker had not used before does not, as yet, turn the work itself into a metareferential one; otherwise any work showing stylistic innovations would directly become metareferential: merely implied reflections of an author on how to write his work do not as yet turn the work into a metareferential one. To the extent that *Christophorus* goes beyond this stage and actually does contain metareference to a considerable degree, it is a particularly instructive case of self-reflexivity. Harald Fricke, in his 2001 survey of 'opera in opera', is quite right in grouping *Christophorus* with *Die Meistersinger von Nürnberg* and *Palestrina* as an art-philosophical, aesthetic-

---

[38]   "[…] in allen Opern geht es um eine Klangmetaphorik, bei der die Schrekersche Klangvision bereits im Sujet vorgezeichnet ist" (Molkow 1980: 83).

[39]   "[…] ist die Oper *Christophorus* der Höhepunkt der Schrekerschen Selbstreferentialität" (Denut 2009: 53).

theoretical drama of ideas[40]. As such it deserves more critical attention than it has received so far, as it also deserves more stage productions than it has been granted in the past.

References

Adorno, Theodor W. (1963). "Schreker". *Quasi una fantasia. Musika-lische Schriften II.* Frankfurt/Main: Suhrkamp. 181–200.

Auden, W. H. (1968). "The World of Opera". *Secondary Worlds: The T. S. Eliot Memorial Lectures 1967.* London/Boston, MA: Faber and Faber. 76–102.

Bekker, Paul (1922). *Klang und Eros.* Stuttgart/Berlin: Deutsche Ver-lagsanstalt.

— (1918/1923). "Franz Schreker: Studie zur Kritik der modernen Oper". *Neue Musik. Gesammelte Schriften 3: Sammlung kleiner Schriften.* Stuttgart/Berlin: Deutsche Verlagsanstalt. 41–84.

Budde, Elmar, Rudolph Stephan, eds. (1980). *Franz-Schreker-Symposion.* Schriftenreihe der Hochschule der Künste Berlin. Berlin: Colloquium.

Danuser, Hermann (1980). "Über Franz Schrekers Whitman-Gesänge". Budde/Stephan, eds. 49–73.

Denut, Eric (2009). "Der Kompositionslehrer und der Komponist: Selbstreferentialität in Schrekers Oper *Christophorus*". Markus Böggemann, Dietmar Schenk, eds. *"Wohin geht der Flug? Zur Jugend": Franz Schreker und seine Schüler in Berlin.* Hildesheim/ Zurich/New York, NY: Olms. 53–62.

Döhring, Sieghart (1978). "Der Operntypus Franz Schrekers". Kolleritsch, ed. 19–30.

Eberhardt & Horst (2003). *Christophorus, oder "Die Vision einer Oper".* Tonkunst online. [On the Opernhaus Kiel production 2003] http://www.die-tonkunst.de/dtk-archiv/eh_pdf/0303_christophorus. pdf. [17/06/2007.]

Fricke, Harald (2001). "Oper in der Oper: Potenzierung, Ipsoreflexion, mise en abyme im Musiktheater". Francois Seydoux, ed., in collab-

---

[40] "[…] in der Reihe ästhetisch-theoretischer Ideendramen […] durch Wagners kunstphilosophisch-räsonnierende *Meistersinger von Nürnberg* begründet" (Fricke 2001: 241; 'in the series of aesthetic-theoretical dramas of ideas founded on Wagner's art-philosophically argumentative *Mastersingers of Nuremberg*').

oration with Giuliano Castellani and Axel Leuthold. *Fiori Musico-logici: Studi in onore di Luigi Ferdinando Tagliavini*. Bologna: Pàtron editore. 219–245.

Hailey, Christopher (1980). "Zur Entstehungsgeschichte der Oper *Christophorus*". Budde/Stephan, eds. 115–140.

— (1993). *Franz Schreker, 1878–1934: A Cultural Biography*. Cambridge: CUP.

— (2002a). "Franz Schreker, Christophorus und der Weg des Anselmus Lu". *Franz Schreker: Christophorus oder "Die Vision einer Oper"*. Programme booklet. Kiel: Bühnen der Landeshaupt-stadt Kiel. 9–16.

— (2002b). "Franz Schreker and the Pluralities of Modernism". *Tempo*, New Series, No. 219 (January 2002). 2–7. http://www. jstor.org/pss/946695. [26/09/2006.]

Harders-Wuthenow, Frank (2005). "The Birth of Tragedy from the Spirit of Decadence: Franz Schreker's Opera *Christophorus*". CD booklet [Schreker 2005a]. 25–32. (German version: "Die Geburt der Tragödie aus dem Geist der Décadence: Zu Franz Schrekers Oper *Christophorus*". 9–16. Orig. publ.: "Die Geburt der Tragödie aus dem Geiste der Décadence: Zu Franz Schrekers Oper *Christo-phorus*". *Franz Schreker: Christophorus, oder "Die Vision einer Oper"*. Programme booklet. Bühnen der Landeshauptstadt Kiel, 2002. 23–33.)

Kolleritsch, Otto, ed. (1978). *Franz Schreker: Am Beginn der Neuen Musik*. Graz: Universal Edition/Institut für Wertungsforschung.

Molkow, Wolfgang (1980). "Die Rolle der Kunst in den frühen Opern Franz Schrekers". Budde/Stephan, eds. 83–94.

Neuwirth, Gösta (1978). "Der späte Schreker". Kolleritsch, ed. 106–110.

Ross, Alex (2005). "All About Schreker". *The New Yorker* (August 22). http://www.therestisnoise.com/2005/08/schreck.html. [26/09/2006.]

Schreker, Franz (1919). "Meine musikdramatische Idee". *Merkblätter des Anbruch* 1 (November). 6–7.

— (1931). *Christophorus, oder "Die Vision einer Oper"*. Oper in 2 Akten (3 Bildern), Vorspiel und Nachspiel von Franz Schreker. Klavierauszug mit Text von Erwin Stein. Berlin: Edition Adler/ Magdeburg: Heinrichshofen's Verlag.

— (2002). *Christophorus, oder "Die Vision einer Oper"*. Oper in 2 Akten (3 Bildern), Vorspiel und Nachspiel von Franz Schreker.

Libretto, reprint (in German). Programme booklet. Bühnen der Landeshauptstadt Kiel. 37–63.

— (2005a). *Christophorus, oder "Die Vision einer Oper"*. CD. Live recording, Opernhaus Kiel, June 2002 – March 2003. CPO 999 903–2.

— (2005b). *Christophorus, oder "Die Vision einer Oper"*. Oper in 2 Akten (3 Bildern), Vorspiel und Nachspiel von Franz Schreker. Libretto, reprint (in German and English). CD booklet [Schreker 2005a]. 64–137.

Stuckenschmidt, Hans Heinz (1970). "Schreker und seine Welt". Haidy Schreker-Bures, H. H. Stuckenschmidt, Werner Oehlmann. *Franz Schreker*. Wien: Lafite/Österreichischer Bundesverlag. 39–52.

Weininger, Otto (1903). *Geschlecht und Charakter: Eine prinzipielle Untersuchung*. Wien/Leipzig: Wilhelm Braumüller.

Weißmann, Adolf (1922). *Musik in der Weltkrise*. Stuttgart/Berlin: Deutsche Verlagsanstalt.

Wolf, Werner (2009). "Metareference across Media: The Concept, its Transmedial Potentials and Problems, Main Forms and Functions". Werner Wolf, ed., in collaboration with Katharina Bantleon and Jeff Thoss. *Metareference across Media: Theory and Case Studies. Dedicated to Walter Bernhart on the Occasion of his Retirement.* Amsterdam/New York, NY: Rodopi. 1–85.

Zibaso, Magali (1999). *Franz Schrekers Bühnenwerke: Eine Biographie in Selbstzeugnissen und Analysen seiner Opern*. Saarbrücken: PFAU.

'The Play's the Thing'
Self- and Metareference in Contemporary Operatic Adaptation of Twentieth-Century Drama

Michael Halliwell, Sydney, NSW

A strong element of metareference is a characteristic of much contemporary English-language opera. This paper examines this phenomenon through the discussion of two recent operatic adaptations of twentieth-century drama: *A View from the Bridge* (William Bolcom) and *The Silver Tassie* (Mark Anthony Turnage). It is, in particular, the use of 'traditional' operatic structures such as arias, ensembles, and, most notably, pre-existing songs characteristic of much recent opera, in which elements of self- and metareferentiality in opera are foregrounded.

> Nochmals [...] stellten sich mir Mythos und Geschichte gegenüber, und drängten mich dießmal sogar zu der Entscheidung, ob ich ein musikalisches Drama oder ein rezitirtes Schauspiel zu schreiben hätte. (Richard Wagner)[1]

This paper investigates self- and metareferential elements in two recent operatic adaptations of twentieth-century drama: *A View from the Bridge* (William Bolcom; based on Arthur Miller's play) and *The Silver Tassie* (Mark Anthony Turnage; based on Sean O'Casey's play). The use of arias, ensembles, and, in particular, pre-existing songs within the selected operas demonstrates the way in which elements of self- and metareferentiality in opera are foregrounded while simultaneously illustrating a trend towards what might be considered pre-Wagner formal structures. Both plays upon which the operas are based require the performance of pre-existing songs, and it is instructive to note how composers and librettists engage with this challenge, thus sometimes even unintentionally emphasising the artifice of the art form. While neither of the operas have the pronounced ontological, self-interrogatory qualities of early-twentieth-century works such as Strauss' *Ariadne auf Naxos* or *Capriccio*, or later examples such as Dominick Argento's *The Aspern Papers* or John Corigliano's *The*

---

[1] 1851: online ("Once again [...] Myth and History stand before me with opposing claims [...] forcing me to decide whether it was a musical drama, or a spoken play, that I had to write." Wagner 1966: 357).

Ghosts of Versailles, through the very nature of the dramaturgical and musical choices made by composer and librettist aspects of self-and metareferentiality are inevitably present[2].

The development of the wide range of orchestral resources by composers, Wagner in particular, has given later composers the tools whereby they can even more strongly than before suggest an impression of interiority and depth in their creation of operatic character. I have argued elsewhere that opera exhibits essential features that ally it more closely with fictional structures than with conventional spoken drama (cf. Halliwell 2005a: passim). In a sense opera 'narrates' the action through the orchestral music rather than having that action presented in an unmediated form, as happens in drama. This music 'tells' us about the characters as does the narrator in a novel, rather than the dramatic action 'showing' us the characters in action as in spoken theatre. Opera's narrative mode can be seen more as diegetic (in the literary sense of 'telling') rather than mimetic ('showing'): the singer is not simply an autonomous character and does not 'speak' directly to the audience, but is part of a more complex narrative process.

This raises interesting issues when a dramatic work is adapted as an opera; in particular, which elements in the original work translate most effectively into opera? Does the transformation of spoken drama into opera create the equivalent of a novelistic interiority and density that cannot be conveyed to anywhere near the same extent in the spoken theatre? In the novel we are able to enter the mind of a character through the narrator or through other often complex narrative modes, and the analogous musical resources available to composers allow a similar process to occur in opera. Therefore, perhaps can we talk about the 'novelisation' of drama in its adaptation into opera[3]?

---

[2]   See my earlier discussion of self-referentiality in opera (2005b). In the present essay I use the term 'self-referential' generally when referring to moments in the particular opera under discussion and when attention is drawn to the actual opera itself as a 'performance'. 'Metareference' is more broadly used to describe moments in these operas where the attention is drawn to a wider view of opera as a genre.

[3]   Opera has plundered literature for the whole of its over-four-hundred-year history. From sources that have their origin in Greek and Roman mythology, composers and librettists have drawn on the works of classical writers and adapted them freely for their own purposes. Of course spoken drama has always been a fruitful source for librettos, and the 19th century saw a great increase in the use of spoken drama as a source for opera librettos, with the plays of Shakespeare, Schiller, Hugo and others, often in translation, finding an afterlife in their operatic transformation.

In adapting a play into opera there are some essential features that characterise operatic dramaturgy that have a profound effect on the process of adaptation. Dahlhaus asserts that the "story underlying an opera does not exist independently of the music; and the story in the libretto as such is not the story of the opera as a musical drama" (1989: 101). He argues that one cannot actually 'tell' the story from the libretto alone as the dramatic thrust of an opera occurs in the music and not in the verbal text. One of the major issues is the fact that music exists in the present; it "isolates" a given situation and "lifts it out if its context" (ibid.: 102)[4]. In this sense, what can be adapted effectively is that which can be adapted into music: "the determining element is the action realised in music, not the action that can be read in the text alone" (ibid.)[5]. In drama an event which occurs in what could be called 'real time' might have a very short duration but it can be substantially extended in opera, which often confers upon it a ritualistic quality[6].

It is in the arias and ensembles in particular where time can be suspended and this ritualisation can have free reign, and this is something that even the most highly rhetorical monologue in drama cannot achieve[7]. One can legitimately ask whether the return to arias

---

[4]   One of the major issues that will confront the operatic adaptor is the reality of the different timeframes that operate in opera. Dahlhaus notes that time in opera "is not to be measured by the clock that governs external reality – and governs the spoken play, insofar as it observes the rules of reality" (1989: 106). In this sense the operatic adaptations of stage plays will differ substantially from the original work.

[5]   Dahlhaus provides a concise summary of the salient issues in the adaptation of drama into opera: "(...) the idea of drama was always conditioned by the prevailing ideas of the time; it had to be realised with musical means that satisfied the dramatic purpose without offending the prevailing ideas of musical form to such an extent that the work was experienced as musically amorphous. The history of opera, to do its subject justice, must become a history of dramaturgical ideas in relation to principles of musical form; each element in the equation is as changeable as the other, and in no epoch is it possible to assume the existence of a 'prestabilised harmony' between the two, created by a power of Reason working in history." (Ibid: 110)

[6]   These are moments that are linked to Verdi's idea of the 'parole sceniche', which are words or phrases that can immediately make a scene comprehensible as well as offering the necessary colour.

[7]   Dahlhaus describes the "tragic undercurrents" which can appear in the "cracks of the conversation" in the plays of Ibsen and Chekhov, and he sees an analogous tension in the operatic aria through the "manifestation of an emotional state – sometimes

and ensembles which is so characteristic of recent opera indicates a return to a pre-Wagner quasi opera seria form where the dramatic imperative is driven by and within the musical forms as much as by the stage action. What has in fact developed is a range of operatic structures which lie somewhere between the flexible, free-ranging interiority of Wagner and the more formal structures of pre-Wagnerian opera.

Opera, by its very nature, is a genre that often has well-defined elements of self-consciousness. Herbert Lindenberger, in discussing the use of discrete song in opera as well as the extreme self- and metareferentiality of those moments where opera reflects on its own status such as Mozart's *Der Schauspieldirektor* or Strauss' *Ariadne auf Naxos*, or where the phenomenon of the opera-within-an-opera occurs, observes that these are elements illustrative of the

> self-referentiality that opera displays whenever a character breaks through the bounds of ordinary singing to burst literally into song. At such times the performing that singers do when they pretend to "really" sing becomes an emblem of the artifice and exaggeration of the more spacious song we call opera. (1984: 141)

The primary perspective of this investigation is the use that the two composers under discussion make of traditional operatic forms such as songs, arias and ensembles. By focusing on these forms and, particularly, on pre-existing songs in the selected operas, some conclusions can be drawn about aspects of intentional and sometimes unintentional self- and metareference. However, of most importance for the essential thematic concern of this paper is the use of actual song.

Carolyn Abbate makes a useful distinction between two kinds of operatic discourse, one being what she describes as 'phenomenal' music in opera which is produced "by or within the stage world" (1991: 119). This is music which is heard by the characters in the opera, as well as, of course, by the audience. The most obvious form this takes is when characters actually 'sing' a song of some kind which is heard and accepted as such by the other characters on stage. At moments such as this we are alerted to the self-conscious, 'performance' aspect of opera through this strategy. However, Abbate's term is perhaps somewhat limiting, and a more useful terminology in this context would be music mise en abyme.

---

unacknowledged by the character himself – that is at odds with the dialogue which gave rise to the aria" (1989: 100).

The second kind of music which characterises operatic discourse is what Abbate calls 'noumenal' music. This is music which she describes as "for our ears alone" (in effect, for the audience's ears). This music "emanates from other loci" which are generally the orchestra as well as the voices of the singers. Of course this is only possible if we accept the fundamental operatic convention that the characters on stage do not hear 'their' music. As Abbate notes, operatic characters are 'deaf' to the music which

> is the ambient fluid of their music-drowned world. This is one of the genre's most fundamental illusions: we see before us something whose fantastic aspect is obvious, since the scenes we witness pass to music. At the same time, however, opera stages recognizably human situations, and these possess an inherent 'realism' that demands a special and complex understanding of the music we hear. We must generally assume, in short, that this music is not produced by or within the stage world, but emanates from other loci as secret commentaries for our ears alone, and that characters are generally unaware that they are singing. (Ibid.)

Perhaps a more useful term than 'noumenal music' would be 'extra-diegetic music', similar to the description of the predominant use of music in film. This is, of course, the standard locus of operatic music: at the level of discourse, as opposed to music mise en abyme which is the use of music at the story level. Of course, the distinction between these two kinds of music is not always so clear-cut and what is of great interest occurs when the distinctions between these two modes blur, when music mise en abyme is appropriated by extra-diegetic music or, less frequently, as Abbate notes, when moments of "fabulous contradiction" occur, when a character has a similar awareness as the audience, hearing "beyond realistic song to that other music surrounding him" (ibid.).

Opera has always made use of forms of songs as mise en abyme from the songs of shepherds in early baroque works, to ballads in German Romantic opera, to pop and jazz songs in contemporary opera[8]. These strategies have, if anything, increased in late-20th- and

---

[8]   Gary Tomlinson observes: "From the late eighteenth century on, the prominence of stage songs in opera [...] poses a dualism that had not been an issue in early modern operatic expression [...]. In seventeenth-century opera a lullaby functioned as a code that might carry the reassurance of a stable if arcane representational connection. A narrative ballad in romantic opera instead invokes the specter of a split between two kinds of music, one transcendent to the sensibilities of the characters on-stage and one immanent to them [...]. The diegetic distance established by the

early-21st-century opera with its characteristic postmodernist eclecticism, including its deliberate appropriation of operatic and other styles from earlier or contemporary traditions. Popular song in many forms plays an important role in many post-war operas and is sometimes used with great complexity and subtlety. One of the most important results of this 'intrusion' is that aspects of the metareferentiality of the genre are often foregrounded[9]. This perspective supports Abbate's argument that 'phenomenal' music consists of moments when "opera flaunts itself, representing within itself those who watch it and hear it, who write it, and who perform it, even as it blurs the distinction between these three functions" (ibid.)[10]. However, another aspect of the significance of the use of real song is highlighted by Lindenberger, who remarks that literal songs in an opera "generally mark those moments of high intensity" during which "we are made to feel that the opera is briefly revealing its emotional center to us" (1984: 85). One is aware of a similar phenomenon in the use of song in many of Shakespeare's plays; however, not with the same element of self-referentiality. What may on first appearance be a simple use of a song for immediate dramaturgical effect can sometimes have much larger thematic importance. Abbate observes that song in opera frequently produces an "exaggerated musical simplicity", which is not a musical failure but "a musical gesture whose meaning must extend beyond the notes of the song itself to the song as performance (heard by the operatic characters) and narration". She cites many examples of songs recomposing "(in an alternative way) the plot of the opera that it inhabits" (1999: 138). It is in this sense, too, not only in the formal mirroring of vocal music, that the use of phenomenal song is a form of

---

irruption of the phenomenal voice forces the issue of the distinction between the two realms." (1999: 92)

[9]   One should never forget that opera's founding figure, Orpheus, is a singer, and thus establishes the fundamental self-referential aspect of opera from the outset.

[10]   Carolyn Abbate further defines this distinction in terms of an "oscillation" between the performative and the narrative modes, as a "shift between performing narration on one hand and enacting dramatic events on the other, defining a move across a discursive space. Phenomenal narrative song in opera is a (heard) musical performance set against the unheard operatic music that functions (in part) as accompaniment to action, to the unwinding of a simpler form of time [...]. Any operatic narrative [...] creates such a node, a layering of time, in which real elapsed time, the time it takes a performer to perform, is laid over the time represented by the narrative." (1999: 123)

mise en abyme. As we shall see, both operas discussed in this paper each use a particular pre-existing song in a highly-charged and significant fashion.

While the operas to be examined in this paper are not explicitly self-interrogatory as such, they use a range of operatic forms in an often self- and metareferential way. Through the often self-conscious and deliberate use of these forms, new works adumbrate famous examples of the occurrence of these forms in previous works in the canon. The audience is frequently alerted to this by the clearly apparent preparation of these self-referential moments and the emphasis on their 'stand-alone' quality. Thus the audience is made aware of the composer's deliberate and calculated use of particular operatic conventions, which is often achieved (or prepared) by a sudden or very obvious change in the musical discourse (for example, from chromatic or atonal harmonic language to a diatonic one, or from complexity of rhythmic structure into simpler and often repetitive rhythmic patterns). This creates moments where actual musical structures themselves within the opera can become self-referential and, indeed, metareferential; e. g., the deliberate and readily apparent preparation of a musical quartet can allude to this as a peculiarly operatic form, perhaps a form which is unexpected in the discourse of the particular opera, thus emerging as a particularly self-referential moment. But the use of this structure can, on another level, point metareferentially to famous examples in earlier operas such as Verdi's *Rigoletto*. Luciano Berio remarks on the pervasive presence of convention in opera, observing that the composer

> should always be aware that most of the operatic conventions, characters or ingredients on which he is so keen to turn his back are unavoidably present, in more or less explicit form, on stage. Whatever they may do, say or sing, the figures that come and go on the operatic stage, be they never so experimental, will always bear the mark of operatic associations. Those figures, those 'characters' that advance towards us, seem to have already sung arias, duets, cavatinas and ensembles. Even if still and silent or employed in unexpected vocal behaviour, they seem all to be 'singing' because, whatever they may do, they implicitly carry about them the signs of operatic experience. They are inhabited by them and themselves inhabit a space – the opera house – that is never empty because it throngs with memories and ghosts (operatic ones, of course) that impose their presence and their model. Every form of musical theatre played out within an opera house is also, inevitably, a parody. (1997: 298)

Of course much of this recent self- and metareferential trend is related to the rejection of many of the elements of modernism, of which Berio was a celebrated exponent, and which has been characteristic of much opera since the 1970s. How far this has been driven by audience demand is an interesting question, and certainly the innate conservatism of mainstream opera audiences must be a major factor. But many would argue that current opera production is experiencing an almost unprecedented boom in popularity, and although this is still largely made up of a relatively small range of 'canonical' works, there is a surprising amount of new operas being performed, of which the two discussed in this essay are highly successful examples[11].

* * *

As previously mentioned, the two operas to be examined are Bolcom's *A View from the Bridge* and Turnage's *The Silver Tassie*. However, a brief discussion of another recent opera relevant to the focus of this essay is useful. *The Great Gatsby* (John Harbison) is an exemplary instance of the contemporary use of music mise en abyme which, at times, becomes fully integrated into the extra-diegetic music of the opera, thus 'normalising' its self-referential elements. *The Great Gatsby* was premiered in 1999 at the Metropolitan Opera in New York and subsequently revived by the Met. It was also staged by the Lyric Opera of Chicago in 2000. The reviews of the opera were generally very positive, but somewhat surprisingly, the opera has received no further productions. Permeating the whole score is a jazz idiom which Harbison employs to help create the aural equivalent of the striking ambience of the novel's setting during the early 1920s.

The main devices he uses are a small jazz band with singer, as well as in several scenes a radio, which, in fact, plays music created by this jazz band but with suitable apparently 'electronic' distortion. Interspersed throughout are 'recreations' of songs typical of the period but which have been newly composed by Harbison with lyrics by Murray Horwitz. Characters also sing along with the band at various points, but the intersection of the music mise en abyme and the extra-diegetic music becomes most interesting when the music arising out of the orchestra seems to have elements of mise en abyme, despite emerging from what must be regarded as an extra-diegetic source. These are

---

[11]   In North America, the number of new operas being produced is particularly impressive – with probably a similar rate of enduring success when compared with previous periods – and this trend shows no sign of lessening.

moments such as the sound of jazz music coming from a hotel ball-
room through the open window of the hotel suite in the crucial scene
where Gatsby threatens to take Daisy away from Tom, which then
precipitates the tragic accident and its equally tragic consequences[12].
Brody asks an interesting question in regard to the different levels of
discourse in *Gatsby* which is directly relevant to the two operas to be
examined in this paper:

> In what other opera is background music so persistently thematic and shifting
> relationships of background and foreground so crucial to the dramatic effect?
> From the characters' viewpoint, the entertaining music they hear in their
> environment is unlikely to be the focus of their undivided attention. It is a large
> part of their world, but they are busy with each other. For the audience, privy to
> the opera's noumenal music, this background music is woven into a comprehen-
> sive harmonic and rhythmic design and an intricate pattern of similarities and
> distinctions that echo back and forth between onstage entertainers and 'unsung'
> music. Following this pattern, we not only hear sounds along with the characters
> inside *Gatsby*'s stage world; we also hear them paraphrased in noumenal music
> that they do not hear but that nonetheless may seem to emanate from them –
> music that carries traces of their memories or habits of thought and self-
> presentation. (2001: 423)

Brody does not explore issues of self-reference per se, but implicit in
his comment above is the issue of the opera drawing metareferentially
attention to its own essence: its music. We are forced to pay attention
to the music *as music*, emanating from different, identifiable loci rather than being immersed in the extra-diegetic sound world of music
with its prime source in the orchestra pit. In a sense the music's
production and its formal qualities become the focus of attention
rather than the 'transparent' means by which the drama is propelled,
and, consequently, the self- and metareferential elements in the opera

---

[12] Brody notes that Mendelssohn's wedding march from *A Midsummer Night's
Dream* is the opera's only "quotation of pre-existing music" which is "paraphrased
(also uniquely) in directly chronological stage time and with both phenomenal and
noumenal music". The complexity of the moment is increased when a jazzy version is
heard: "For the first time, phenomenal music is paraphrased phenomenally, as the
characters onstage and the audience alike hear a shift from solemn rite to secular
party." (2001: 443f.) Brody makes the further point that what Harbison achieves
through "comprehensively intertwining noumenal and phenomenal music" with "the
'inner' noumenal music that the orchestra plays or the characters sing (but do not
hear)" and which "mingles most ambiguously with the 'outer' music of their
environment" is the "distinction between social and psychic spaces" which seems to
"evaporate" (ibid.: 448).

are foregrounded. There is a complex interweaving of audience focus and narratorial point of view in changing combinations between these different discourse levels.

William Bolcom's adaptation of Arthur Miller's 1955 play, *A View from the Bridge*, was premiered in 1999. Bolcom had the playwright as co-librettist together with Arnold Weinstein. Miller remarked that he always considered this play to be good operatic material, stressing its theatricality and describing it as

> a kind of contemporary Greek play, which means there is a lot of open, naked emotion, right on the surface. There is no attempt to make events 'natural.' It's a very *theatrical* approach to this subject. Consequently, from the first page, it is telling you what the emotional stakes are, rather than letting you gradually infiltrate them into your awareness – which is an operatic approach, I think, with the emotions being wide open. Long before I ever thought of it as being operatic, it was more of a Greek tragedy. In those plays, the characters more or less tell you what it is they are feeling. It didn't need a whole lot of shuffling around to be made into an opera. (2001: 18)[13]

The original play underwent substantial revision after the first performance in New York. Miller reworked his one-act play with its many passages of free blank verse intended for a non-naturalistic performance style into a two-act form for its British premiere in 1957, increasing the number of 'extras' who were there to portray the neighbourhood. When revisiting the play some forty years later it was a simple matter to turn these non-speaking characters into a chorus. Miller maintained that he always saw these non-speaking characters in a quasi-operatic sense, pointing out that although they had no "written lines", they "came close to singing, in the sense that they were reacting onstage. That chorus has been there from the beginning." (Ibid.: 20)

The influence of Greek drama is also apparent in the character of Alfieri, the lawyer, who, Miller observes, "acts as a form of choral leader, as in Aeschylus" (ibid.), and he is also the frame narrator. This narrative device is expanded in the operatic adaptation with his narrational and linking role extended and integrated into that of the chorus[14]. The one-act version of the play was found the most amenable in

---

[13]   There is another, Italian operatic version of the play, by Renzo Rossellini, *Uno squardo del ponte* (1961).

[14]   As Bigsby notes of the play, "the action is summoned into being by a man able to look back on the events and see them entire. Alfieri places the frame, deciding where the story begins and ends and what, therefore, that story is. His narration is in the

terms of the actual text used, although the opera generally uses the dramaturgy of the two-act version[15]. Although in the basic shape and sequence of events in the opera there is much similarity with the original, the collaboration with the playwright to imaginatively re-engage with the play allowed the composer the freedom to move away from the original work[16]. However, the opera only uses text from the play. The use of the first, more stylised version of the play accords very well with operatic aesthetics. What the composer and librettist have done is to 'graft' particular operatic structures, sometimes extremely self-consciously, onto what is, in a sense, already an 'operatic' play.

This becomes most apparent in the several instances of dialogue scenes between two characters which become arias of self revelation for one of those characters who might address the second character[17]. The calculated use of aria in this opera is striking and provides significant moments of self- and metareference. Miller, as a playwright, offers some penetrating analysis of this most operatic of forms:

> In an aria you're considering something, rather than being swept along by it. In effect, it gives a moment of pause. It can be a moving pause, it can be conveying story as well, but it's the *emotional* story: "What is happening to me as a result of this dilemma we're in." It's the flowering of emotions of the individual. An aria can propel an action, and reveal the depths of the character's feelings about it. Marco's aria is a good example: You realise what the stakes are for him, for Eddie, for the whole story. The aria displaces a whole dialogue from the play. It also makes it possible to see the size of the character; he defines himself to some degree in that aria, which wouldn't happen had it just been dialogue. (2001: 19)

---

present, the action in a factitious past, factitious because lifted out of time, with no past and no future. The tense is the present but the action has already been completed. Alfieri knows what went before and what comes after but chooses not to tell us." (2005: 188)

[15]   Bolcom remarks that they found "the first version could in many cases be set musically just as it was. In working with sections of it, we did go back to a much more extended kind of language, which is natural for singing." (2001: 15)

[16]   Bolcom notes that there was "no sense that his text was sacrosanct. He was willing to have cuts [...]. He allowed change, welcomed it, nurtured it, encouraged it. We did no violence to the subject, and he knew it." (1999: 1132)

[17]   For the later production at the Met, Bolcom added an aria for Beatrice with new words by Miller in which the words, "When am I gonna be a wife again", are the impetus for a moment of torment for her. He also added a new aria for Eddie. Bolcom regarded the changes as substantial enough to talk of the 'New York Version' of the opera.

Interestingly, this could be argued as fundamentally an opera seria view of the function of the aria. Miller, in fact, wrote a new text for an aria for the character of Marco, described above, which occurs near the end of the opera. Arnold Weinstein, the co-librettist, commented on the use of arias from his perspective. Discussing the power of the images that many of the lines in the play contain, he describes the arias as "composites of those images" which

> have different colors, different emotional rhythms that are distributed in scenes where that material does not appear in the play. These arias intensify the building and the peaking of the scenes, and are lifted from longer, more dialogical scenes in the play. Balance and shaping have a purely musical function in opera, offering an intrinsic excitement in the use of forms. (2001: 23)

This view accords with Dahlhaus in that it is the musical imperatives which determine the structure as well as propel the drama.

The creation of a chorus is perhaps the most substantial change from the play, and is employed frequently to comment on the action, but also as a link between scenes and to provide commentary on what has happened or to express its forebodings as to what will come[18]. Sometimes the chorus becomes more individualised with solo voices emerging from the choral texture. Inextricably linked with the chorus is Alfieri, and his role as frame narrator varies: sometimes he is part of the chorus, at times the narrator, and occasionally a character directly intervening in the story. The chorus also functions as the subconscious of the characters, expressing thoughts and fears that they cannot or will not acknowledge. Many of the scenes with Alfieri and chorus occur 'in limbo', and this further undercuts the naturalism of the presentation, emphasising a ritualistic quality.

One of the aspects of the way in which the chorus is employed is their frequent use of atavistic Italian words and phrases which are analogous to Verdi's concept of the 'parola scenica', adding more than just local colour but a larger sense of the Italian background and flavour to the Brooklyn neighbourhood of the opera's setting. This is first intimated in Alfieri's musings in the opening passages of the

---

[18] Bolcom, when questioned about the turning a literary classic into opera, remarked that "if you can't add something new, what's the point? I thought that music could help in our case by adding the role of the chorus [...]. By having a real chorus, I thought I could increase the claustrophobic feeling of the tenement setting – enormous crowds in small places, people around all the time." (1999: 1130)

opera where he universalises the work that is to follow with the chorus chanting in the background:

> Alfieri
> When the tide is right the ocean breeze floats in from Italy ... where this neighbourhood began.
>
> Chorus
> Italia! Sicilia! Siracusa!
>
> Alfieri
> On those distant rocks we fought the Carthaginians ... Caesar whipping us on in Latin.
>
> Chorus
> But this is Brooklyn. Red Hook. New York Bay. Today!
>
> Alfieri
> Still, sometimes when the tide is right you smell the Mediterranean air, and you stare at Brooklyn sky, and you see Roman eagles there.
>
> (Bolcom 2002: 3–7)

Interestingly, this gives the opera an intensely veristic colour. The events that follow deliberately have much of the quality of those two celebrated examples of verismo opera, *Cavalleria rusticana* and *I Pagliacci*, even if the musical idiom is very different; there is the same sense of small-town claustrophobia, inflexible codes of honour, insularity and suppressed emotions even though this is 'big city' New York. This certainly has the effect of self-consciously situating the opera in a particular tradition, and illustrates aspects of the opera's meta-referentiality.

Of course this 'Italian' idiom is often supplemented by Bolcom's extensive use of a wide range of distinctively American musical idioms. These two strands fuse most memorably in the song, "Paper Doll", which achieves great symbolic and thematic importance in the opera. Bolcom seizes on this song, which is sung by Rodolpho in the play and considerably expands its occurence in the opera. It occurs firstly in the chorus immediately after Rodolpho has sung his first 'motorcycle' aria, soon after their arrival, telling of life in their small Italian town. This theme then 'introduces' Catherine's line: "Rodolpho, are you married too, like Marco?" (Ibid.: 88) This snatch of melody becomes linked with the relationship between Catherine and Rodolpho, and the song itself is, both in terms of its lyrics and melody, important in the unfolding of the triangular relationship between Catherine, Rodolpho and Eddie.

Immediately after this first quotation the song is sung by Rodopho, who has already been identified as a singer:

> I am also a singer ...
> One night last year
> the tenor got sick.
> And I took his place
> in the garden of the hotel.
> Three arias I sang without a mistake ...
> Thousand lire notes
> they threw from the tables.
> Six months we lived
> on that one night. (Ibid.: 89f.)

The change from baritone to tenor from the play is significant. Apart from the expected 'standard' casting of the lover as a tenor in conflict with the older rival baritone (Eddie), the music for this character is lyrical and ingratiating. The kind of sound, both in terms of voice and musical idiom, that is being striven for is that of a typical 'Neapolitan tenor' of the 'old world', which contrasts with the sometimes 'new world' 'jazzy' and even 'bluesy' quality of much of Catherine's music. Indeed, Rodolpho is instructed to sing it, alla napolitana, molto rubato. However, he only sings the chorus of the song, not the verse as in the play.

During the unfolding of the events of the opera, Rodolpho's characteristic music undergoes a stylistic change reflecting his acculturation, and his 'big' aria later in the act ("Those New York Lights") when he and Catherine have returned from the movies after having been in Brooklyn for some weeks, has much more of a 'Broadway' feel to it, although still with some of the tenorial, Neapolitan inflections of his performance of "Paper Doll"[19].

Miller describes the reasons for his choice of this song in the play:

> I felt that it's the kind of song that, at the time, would have been adored in Sicily, because of that rhythm. I'm sure the Mills Brothers' version must have made it to Sicily. That's really one of the most exciting moments of the play to me – I love that music! Bill [Bolcom] made it an operatic "Paper Doll," which at the same time sustained the original impulse behind the music. I guess it was the acme of

---

[19]   This is probably the 'hit song' of the opera and has been anthologised as such. As many of the stand-alone numbers in the opera, it is written expressly so that it can be performed separately. Bolcom, in a number of instances, composes alternative introductions and endings to these numbers to facilitate their concert performance.

pop music at that time, and Bill really seized on it. It's funny, and very touching at the same time. (2001: 19)

Here Miller touches on the potency of pre-existing song in opera where what seems on the surface to be the fairly unexceptional use of a well-known song can carry so much extra weight and significance. As Lindenberger notes, it can be seen as a moment when an opera reveals its emotional core (cf. 1984: 85).

Ironically Rodolpho introduces "Paper Doll" with the phrase "I sing jazz too", which, after he has sung the first couple of phrases, including a very Neapolitan 'sob' in the first phrase, elicits the scornful comment from Eddie (as music critic and expert): "Hey, that ain't jazz" (Bolcom 2002: 91f.), a particularly metareferential moment drawing attention to the song as well as the 'performance' of the song. Rodolpho's performance of the song is very much in the Neapolitan idiom, rising to a high, sustained B flat in the first phrase and accompanied with warm strings. Here we have a direct intersection and blending of music mise en abyme and extra-diegetic music. The song and its performance on one level is strictly music mise en abyme – he sings what he thinks is and knows they will all recognise as a typical popular 'American' song with all that this implies. However, the style in which he sings it is inappropriate for what might be considered an 'authentic' performance of the song. His understanding of American culture at this stage, as reflected in this 'performance', is understandably limited[20].

Significantly, this is a moment when the border between music mise en abyme and the extra-diegetic becomes blurred. The orchestral accompaniment, which, of course, neither Rodolpho nor the others can 'hear', is extra-diegetic, but is 'inauthentic' as it consists of a lush, quasi operatic string accompaniment (à la Puccini), and not the more expected contemporary popular style. All on stage are aware that he is singing a song – it is a moment of pure 'performance' – but none are aware of the 'unheard' (to them, not us) music surrounding and accompanying this song. The song is thus enveloped in a musical web which has significance for the larger audience, but not for the 'audience' on stage who do not hear it. What seems in effect a simple,

---

[20] Bolcom has discussed his strategy in how the song is used: "[Rodolpho] doesn't sing it like an American pop singer, but like someone who would have learned the tune in Sicily or Naples in that very lyrical, popsy style popular throughout southern Italy." (1999: 17)

if somewhat 'inauthentic' or inappropriate performance of the song, carries a much larger weight of 'meaning' for the audience, encapsulating the multivalence of this 'performance'[21].

While Eddie, Catherine and Beatrice comment, Rodolpho continues undaunted by them and finishes the verse with another sustained B flat including (on the recorded performance) another typical tenorial 'sob' so characteristic of this genre. Immediately after Rodolpho has finished, Marco addresses Eddie as "Eduardo", the Italianisation of his name emphasising the Italianate quality of what has just transpired. Later in the scene between Eddie and Beatrice, Eddie again complains about the singing: "He sings on the ships! On the dock, he sings! All of a sudden a whole song comes out – with motions" (ibid.: 104f.). Rodolpho's self-referential mode of singing thus becomes emblematic for Eddie of the threat that Rodolpho poses to him, as well as his exoticism and what Eddie considers his effeminate nature.

The singing thematic reoccurs in the scene when Rodolpho and Catherine return from the movies. This is introduced by a brief orchestral quotation of "Paper Doll", which leads into a discussion between Catherine, Eddie and Rodolpho, who mentions that he wishes to see the opera, the theatres, and the lights of New York. This sets up the 'New York Lights' aria where there is a curious mixture of music mise en abyme and extra-diegetic commentary, similar to, but also somewhat different from Rodolpho's performance of "Paper Doll". Although Rodolpho is expressing his wishes and desires about his new life in America, and this is 'supported' by the colourful and descriptive extra-diegetic orchestral accompaniment, there is a strong sense of 'performance', not only in the formal structure of the aria, but the quality of Rodolpho as singer and performer that has been established previously. Here the audience is aware more of the singer's rather than the character's 'performance'. This is emphasised by the very theatrical, 'Broadway' ending to the aria with its pianissimo sustained F sharp and open harmonies. We, the audience, are forced to focus on the performance of the song rather than the song itself.

Bolcom has explained his attraction to these kinds of metareflexive moments in this opera:

---

[21] Brody, discussing analogous moments in Harbison's opera, describes music that the characters "do not hear but that nonetheless may seem to emanate from them – music that carries traces of their memories or habits of thought and self-presentation" (2001: 423f.).

> I wanted the major characters to have tunes with the same accessibility that a good Broadway tune had, in the days when there were good Broadway tunes (which unfortunately is a very long time ago!). Certainly there are moments when you think, "Gee, here I am, right in the center of an aria." I couldn't avoid the feeling of Verdi, Puccini, Boito. So I decided, "I'll *absorb* it," since it fits many of the situations in this story. But I also decided that another way to deal with this need for "Italian-ness" would be to absorb one of the things that the people of Red Hook themselves, as Italian immigrants, would have absorbed: popular music of their time in America. (2001: 17)

It is at the same time another multivalent moment where it is difficult to separate the vocal 'performance', the mise en abyme, from the extra-diegetic music surrounding it: the singer appears to step out from behind his role as a character and becomes a performer.

Brody describes the many moments in Harbison's *Gatsby* where the "relationships between realistic background music, its paraphrases, sung dialogue, and noumenal (extra-diegetic) orchestral music incessantly recombine under the pressure of these collisions" (2001: 428). There is a similar moment here, where the music Rodolpho sings sounds almost as if it is a pre-existing Broadway song. In fact, since the premiere of the opera the aria has become popular in its own right as a stand-alone number similar to the situation with many songs from the Broadway shows[22].

The aria seems to invite the audience to listen to it in this way with its applause-inducing ending, emphasising its capacity as music mise en abyme. Bolcom deliberately structures the aria in a metareferential way which has the effect of inviting the audience to consider not only a long operatic tradition but also the contemporary Broadway 'show-stopper', which, itself, has operatic influences and its own inherent metareferentiality. Paradoxically, it is at the same time a much more (hetero-)referential moment than Rodolpho's earlier performance of "Paper Doll" even though it seems to occur strictly in the extra-diegetic discourse level, and despite that song being presented as a 'performance'. Thus the usual way of linking these two discursive levels through motivic or harmonic allusion is not utilised here; meta-referential, structurally 'traditional' strategies anticipate and, indeed, generate audience response.

---

[22] Indeed, what is becoming relatively common in contemporary opera is for what are considered potentially 'hit' moments from the score to be 'released' in some form immediately prior to the premiere, very much in the Broadway tradition.

This is a moment that well illustrates the duality at the heart of stage performance[23]. This fundamental aspect of stage performance is even more apparent in opera where the cult of the singer *as singer* rather than representing a character has been an essential aspect of the art form virtually from its inception. Contemporary opera, in moments such as that described above, continually re-contextualises itself as part of an on-going tradition without any parodic intentions, perhaps looking back to operatic practice before the overwhelming paradigm-shift of Wagnerian aesthetics and its later evolution into musical modernism.

A further crucial use of "Paper Doll" occurs towards the end of the first act where an instrumental version of the song is played twice on the record player in the apartment[24]. It occurs as Rodolpho and

---

[23] Bert States, describing performance on the spoken stage, observes that "we see that the *I* of the actor is not at all the *I* of the character he is playing, the voice that keeps saying, 'I', 'I', 'I' throughout the play. The actor's first person is what appears before us *as* the character, the being that has, in effect, no voice of its own but whose very presence and way of appearing constitute the act of direct speech within the indirect speech in the enacted event. It is visible in the effortless hard work that produces on the actor's brow beads of perspiration that do not belong to the character. But the *I* is not simply the actor's real body. It is rather the unnatural attitude of the body, the thousand different means and behavioural peculiarities by which the actor unavoidably remains just outside the character he is playing. He is always slightly quoting his character, though not as Brecht's actor practises quoting – that is, not as a consciously estranged style. Even if he is quoting in the Brechtian sense, there is a quotation beyond this quotation. No matter how he acts, there is always the ghost of a self in his performance (not to be confused with egotism). Even the most unsophisticated theatergoer can detect something else in the characterisation, a superconsciousness that could be nothing other than the actor's awareness of his own self-sufficiency as he moves between the contradictory zones of the illusory and the real, vraisemblance and vrai, seeming and being – between Hamlet and what of himself he has allowed to be displayed as Hamlet. It is not a statement made by the body or the eyes, but an intentional edge in the performance, signified by the aura of style and concentration, or by the submission of the body to a certain rigor, or absence of excess, that relieves the most naturalistic performance of a completely convincing realism. It is something that could not be found in any other form than that of art." (1985: 124f.)

[24] Bolcom explains his strategy for the version of the song he uses at this point describing it as a combo on tape with Bolcom himself on the piano: "We'll do a real Fifties, twelve-to-the-bar, early rock-and-roll version [...]. I have made a simple, small recorded version for a sort of bargain-basement-sounding combo that will be

Catherine attempt to deflect Eddie's rising anger at their developing relationship. Catherine actively defies Eddie by getting Rodolpho to dance with her to the recorded music, which he does rather reluctantly as he is very much aware of Eddie's hostility. Rodolpho finally takes the 'record' off and the extra-diegetic music resumes. Brody remarks of similar moments in *Gatsby* where

> the radio confounds the characteristic theatrical fiction of disembodied song. It is a realistic source of music in *Gatsby*'s stage world [...]. But the onstage radio also mimics the disembodied, invisible sound of operatic music emanating from an orchestra pit. Lacking the symbolic or acoustic punch or noumenal music, it functions ironically – as a conspicuously inadequate, even fraught, source of music for scenes of glamour or romance. (2001: 422f.)

The situation is similar, but not identical in Bolcom's work. It is a distorted version of a song we have already heard in a discursive combination in its 'first' performance in the opera. On one level it seems similar to orchestral snatches of the "Paper Doll" melody, but, in this case emanating from an identifiable source. However, it 'silences' the lyrics which gave Rodolpho's performance much of its power and in this sense could similarly be seen as an 'inadequate' source of music.

The recording is repeated a few moments later after Eddie has goaded Rodolpho into sparring with him. Rodolpho is reluctant to hit Eddie who takes advantage of this and lands a punch. Rodolpho, somewhat stunned, then starts the record again and this time invites Catherine to dance, thereby deliberately taunting Eddie. Marco has been watching this unfold and finally places a chair in front of Eddie and stops the record. This is the climax of the act in which Marco demonstrates his superior strength at lifting the chair while Eddie is left looking defeated and foolish.

The song has undergone a transformation in its use from a brief orchestral and purely extra-diegetic quotation, to the 'Neapolitan' performance by Rodolpho with its mixture of discursive levels, to its use as music mise en abyme as a recording. In a sense the most 'inadequate' performance has become the most potent in terms of plot significance and brings to a head the open rivalry between Eddie and Rodolpho and the not-so-subtle threat from Marco at the end of the act.

---

playing the tune for the dance sequence; you could have bought something like it at Woolworth's at the time, on a 45-rpm doughnut disc." (2001: 16)

Another interesting instance of the blurring of discursive levels occurs in the opening of the second act. The setting is the wharves with
longshoremen unloading crates of whiskey just before Christmas, an
open crate lying on the ground. Eddie is grouped with Tony, Mike and
Louis, characters with whom Eddie interacts throughout the opera.
The stage directions indicate that they are grouped together "almost
like a barbershop quartet" (Bolcom 2002: 193). Then thirteen bars of
barbershop music in a "Doo-Wop tempo" occur. This brief fragment
is completely unaccompanied by the orchestra apart from a discrete
cymbal providing a rhythmic pulse. The interlude is introduced by a
typical, close-harmony four-voiced sustained chord which then leads
into the expected typical barbershop quartet in 12/8 with a rhythmic
bass line supporting the close-harmony upper parts. After about eight
bars the orchestra quietly enters with sustained chords in the strings
and woodwinds and the mood is abruptly broken as Tony alerts Eddie
to the fact that the foreman is looking.

The way this moment is presented is complex. The impression
created is that this is a self-referential doubling of performance as
such by these four men, isolated by lighting on the stage, engaged in a
spontaneous, slightly inebriated performance of a popular form of music that might realistically occur in this situation, but it is self-reference with wider metareference to this non-operatic performance
genre. This impression is underlined by the fact that it sounds unaccompanied, apart from the discrete rhythmic pulse of the cymbal. The
(hetero-)referential probability of the performance is initially somewhat undercut by the albeit unobtrusive entry of the orchestra, which
adds a feeling of foreboding as the orchestral sound thickens. This is a
moment almost of alienation in the Brechtian sense and certainly has
the effect of shattering the illusion of realism that had been created at
the beginning of this scene. However, the moment also feels 'natural'
as this could be a light-hearted expression of happiness on the part of
the characters at the impending holiday period. We have a moment of
music mise en abyme which is undercut and finally obliterated by the
extra-diegetic, 'unheard' (to those on stage) music of the orchestra and
thus metareferentially points to music-making as such.

There are no more intrusions of self-referential music in the second
act and the opera moves rapidly towards its tragic climax. There are
two large-scale arias, one for Catherine immediately prior to the sexual encounter with Rodolpho which occurs offstage. A little later
Marco has an extended, 'formal' aria in the sense that the introduction

to the aria has the main theme that will be developed in the aria itself. The aria is a distillation of elements from several scenes in the play and has a similar 'number opera' quality like several of the other arias in the opera. This, as has been suggested, emphasises the 'operatic' quality of the opera at the expense of its verismo quality and thus may be seen as another instance of self-referential reflection of the opera on itself as opera. Bolcom has described his aesthetic in regard to these formal structures:

> Yes, there are set pieces [...] this opera isn't one with a seamless, continuous musical fabric, what I call the 'paved asphalt' style. There are places where people might think, "Gee, I'd like to clap", and I hope they will. I'd like them to relate to it like a Verdi opera. (1999: 1132)

Another device which emphasises non-naturalistic and self-referential qualities in the opera is the use of the frame narrator Alfieri. Of course, this character is taken directly from the play but what the opera is also able to do is to musically establish this frame by using the same music and similar text at the opening and ending of the opera to create both a verbal and aural reinforcement of this device[25]. Alfieri has a final verse speech in the play which again situates the events that the audience has just witnessed on a more universal plane. His concluding words, "This is the end of the story. Good night." (Bolcom 2002: 567), undercut the naturalism of the death of Eddie and emphasise the 'performance' nature of what has just taken place. This further distances the action and works strongly against the naturalistic scenes that precede it; a 'Verfremdungseffekt' with clearly self-referential function[26]. We are made aware once more that what we have witnessed has, on one level, been summoned by the memory of Alfieri, and while this process has lent these events an almost mythical quality, we are also aware that what we have witnessed remains a 'performance', framed by Alfieri's commentary[27].

What these devices as well as the other changes and additions to the score also achieve is to further emphasise the closed 'number'

---

[25] This is reminiscent of Britten's strategy with Vere as prologue and epilogue in *Billy Budd*.

[26] The two-act version does not have these words, or the final verse speech of Alfieri, indicating that Miller strove for a more naturalistic mode in this version.

[27] The use of Alfieri as frame narrator might be compared with how Harbison uses Nick in his opera, but he is much less of a constant 'judging' and participatory presence as Nick.

characteristics of the opera. Virtually all the arias in the opera have alternate endings as appendices which are to be used if performed as 'stand-alone' pieces, and this suggests that Bolcom's idiom tends towards more traditional 19th-century operatic structures as well as the development of 20th-century musical theatre. Through its use of traditional operatic set pieces the opera transforms what is already a stylised play into an even more ritualistic form[28]. This is particularly apparent in the ending of the opera where the movement from the particular to the universal is striking as Alfieri, the frame narrator, expands the events just concluded into a much larger context[29]. On a purely practical level, this shows a composer aware that suitable moments in the opera will be excerpted by singers for concert performance, but it also reveals a composer not overburdened by the anxiety of influence, but one who regards the 400-year history of opera as a limitless resource. Bolcom's eclectic musical background has obviously influenced and enriched his aesthetic, and this opera is a good example of the trend in recent years towards the employment of many formal operatic structures in a self- and metareferential way while mostly, if not always completely, avoiding the danger of becoming pastiche.

---

[28] Dialogic scenes in the play are often transformed into solo arias in the opera, and perhaps the best example of this occurs in the aforementioned aria for Marco near the end of the work. In both versions of the play, Alfieri, accompanied by Catherine and Rodolpho, pleads with Marco to promise not to seek revenge on Eddie for his betrayal of him and his brother to the Immigration Service. Alfieri will arrange bail for Marco in return for this promise, which he finally receives. In the opera this scene is cut and replaced by a solo moment for Marco. The text, by Miller, is new, and in effect transforms what is a naturalistic conversation between the four characters in the play into a more universal meditation on the immigrant experience. The aria's trajectory moves from a generalised reflection on the reasons for emigration and then personalises Marco's own experience with its focus on the betrayal by Eddie. It ends with a move towards the universal once more.

[29] As Bigsby notes of the play, Alfieri "sees in the desperate and uncomprehending actions of one man an echo of other times and other places, thereby conferring significance on the actions of a marginalized man. He understands what Eddie Carbone cannot. He sees in the events he recalls something more than an anecdote. To him it is a myth, a fable. The immediate, the physical, the real are absorbed for him, and hence for us, into something whose significance extends beyond mere fact." (2005: 189)

* * *

In their adaptation for the English National Opera in 2000 of Sean O'Casey's play *The Silver Tassie* (1928), composer Mark-Anthony Turnage and librettist Amanda Holden have retained most of the origi-nal dialogue and the opera has a structure and sequence similar to the play[30]. Both works are searing indictments of the First World War and its aftermath, with the action occurring in Dublin and on the Western Front[31]. The play has four acts of roughly equal length while the opera further divides each act into several scenes. Both composer and libret-tist have described their conception a four-movement symphonic struc-ture[32]. In effect the division of each of the four acts into discrete scenes adds a cinematic fluidity to the opera which is absent from the play, with acts one and two and three and four being linked by orches-tral 'War' interludes, much as Britten has done in several of his operas[33].

The first act of the play sets up the departure of the young Harry Heegan to the front after just having led his football team to their third cup victory, which has allowed them to retain the cup: the 'Tassie' of the title. The frenetic pace and restless musical idiom of the first act

---

[30]   The play was a new direction for the playwright and he felt it was his best work to date. It is charactcrised by a blend of realism and expressionism and subsequently has taken a central position in O'Casey's output, yet it was famously refused by W. B. Yeats and the Abbey Theatre in Dublin. This resulted in O'Casey effectively turning his back on his homeland. However, Shaw sprang to his defence. The play was first performed in London, has remained highly-regarded and has been staged many times in subsequent years.

[31]   Holden described her strategy: "I stripped away all non-operatic phrases and words, keeping only those that clearly defined the characters and the plot" (2000: 177).

[32]   Holden maintains that the four acts "suggested a classical symphonic symmetry" with the first act "setting up the drama", and the second being a "slow movement". The third act would be "a kind of scherzo macabre", and the "finale a dance" (2000: 177). She moreover remarks that she could "easily start to fashion the opera by omitting the lengthy comic episodes without losing the essentially tragi-comic flavour and main characters" (ibid.: 176).

[33]   This is one of several aspects of the adaptation that suggests the influence of Britten, in particular his 'James operas', *The Turn of the Screw* and *Owen Wingrave*, which both have scenes linked by musical interludes and in the case of *Wingrave* was written for television. *Peter Grimes*, of course, has the famous scene-linking 'sea interludes'.

moves effectively towards the climax, which is the departure of the men to the front after some leave, and this moment is given poignant effect with the use of the Robbie Burns song, "The Silver Tassie". Out of what is a jaggedly chromatic, often atonal and sometimes confronting musical idiom comes this highly effective moment of stasis and pathos which has the effect of heightening the emotion of the men's departure as well as achieving a sense of foreboding as to what awaits them[34]. Turnage skilfully blends the simple folk-like melody of the song – the singer is instructed to sing this "without vibrato" – with a discretely astringent orchestral commentary.

The highly-contrasting second act is set in the trenches and is an expressionistic mixture of dialogue, rhythmic chanting and snatches of songs. It is largely choral and is dominated by the eerie figure of a soldier known as "The Croucher", whose voice "rings out as if from another world" (Turnage 2002a: 141). Almost like a figure from Greek drama, he intones sonorous musical passages of sometimes misquoted Biblical gloom, and his baleful presence and deep bass voice further suggest impending tragedy. Undercutting this are the often deliberately banal comments and music of the men, including a 'Corporal' and 'Officer'. In the play this act has the effect of a macabre combination of Greek drama and music hall, and Turnage exploits this overall structure very effectively[35]. However, he makes sparing use of the actual chants and songs that O'Casey intended to be performed and had printed as an appendix to the play, although those that Turnage does use are integrated very effectively. Librettist Amanda Holden declared the play to be "perfect operatic material" and remarked that O'Casey's son "confirmed to [her] that his father always regarded this play as operatic, having filled it with songs" (2000: 177). This comment links O'Casey's play very strongly with Miller's *A View from the Bridge*, in which Miller himself identified its prominent operatic qualities.

The third act is set in a hospital ward back in Ireland where Harry, after being severely wounded in France, is awaiting an operation. He is visited by his parents, a blinded Teddy, as well as Barney, who has

---

[34] An added element of pathos is the later discovery that when he returns wounded from the front, Harry will be deserted by his 'faithful Jessie', who takes up with his friend Barney, the man who won the VC for saving Harry's life.

[35] There are occasional echoes of the Richard Attenborough 1969 film, *O What a Lovely War*, both musically and in the satirical characterisation of the Officer.

been awarded the VC for saving Harry's life. However, his act one sweetheart Jessie refuses to come up to the ward. The act makes plain the complete change in Harry's circumstances, and the only genuine sympathy he receives is from Susie, now a nurse in the hospital. This act is swift-moving and was conceived in symphonic terms as a 'scherzo'.

The musically inventive final act blends the sounds of a stage band playing period music with a mixture of jazz, Irish jigs, tangos and other popular dance forms[36]. This music accompanies six swiftly-moving, linked scenes during which Harry finally discovers Jessie and Barney in a compromising situation and his final realisation of the handicapped life that he will henceforward be forced to lead. As Harry and Teddy leave the stage the others reflect that life goes on for those who have been physically untouched by the war.

As suggested above, one of the crucial metareferential moments in the opera is Harry's singing of the Burns song, "The Silver Tassie". The song is first briefly quoted in the orchestra after which it is sung by Harry with Teddy joining in the chorus. The song is important in terms of its thematic content as well as its direct reference to the silver cup that Harry has won. Similar to Bolcom's opera, the use of a pre-existing song is significant in this opera. Harry's singing ability is frequently mentioned, and as part of the celebration for the football victory and their imminent departure for the front, Barney calls on Harry to sing the song, "Will ye no come back again". Harry replies: "No, no, the one we all used to sing", to which Barney replies, "The Silver Tassie" (Turnage 2002a: 83). Harry replies: "And here it is; The Silver Tassie", holding up the cup (ibid.: 84). However, he does not immediately sing the song, first describing the bad sportsmanship of their football opponents, and then the course of the game they have just won. A brief three-note theme in the orchestra is taken up by their words "play the game", and then "referee", and this theme is developed into a duet for Barney and Harry. It will return with great poignancy as the men go 'over the top' at the end of act two while

---

[36] The play has Harry accompany himself with the ukulele while singing "Swing low, sweet chariot". Turnage chose not to use this moment. He remarks that his "two biggest fears were to be bad Britten *War Requiem* in the second act and bad *Riverdance* in the fourth" (2002b: 16).

kicking a football ahead of them[37]. This is the military action that in-
capacitates Harry. Harry then grabs a bottle of wine and reaches for
Jessie with the words: "Now a kiss while our lips are wet" (ibid.: 106).
    A large ensemble develops and out of the general bustle of depar-
ture, Harry finally calls for one last drink. The moment before he
starts the song the stage direction states: "During the song Harry finally becomes a soldier, buttoning up his coat, putting on his helmet"
(ibid.: 122). The song itself is essentially unaccompanied apart from a
slowly-changing sustained chord in the orchestra. Each verse, however, is interrupted by a jagged, extra-diegetic orchestral outburst which
immediately subsides into the sustained chords once more over which
Harry, then with Teddy, sings. Each ensuing orchestral interruption
between verses becomes softer and less angular, and the final refrain,
"It's leaving you my bonnie lassie!", is sung by the three men with
Teddy's words full of irony as his fraught relationship with his wife
has been shown in this first act[38].
    In effect, then, the song appears to occur as music mise en abyme
as the orchestral accompaniment is discrete and unobtrusive and it has
the unaccompanied freedom typical of folk song. The fact that it is a
well known song with its own nostalgic metareferential elements gives
it more significance and poignancy in the context of leave-taking. Of
course one of the great ironies that will become apparent during the
course of the opera lies in the words: "But my resolve will yet be
strong 'til I come back to my faithful Jessie" (ibid.: 124). Jessie will not
prove faithful and will 'betray' Harry for the man that saves Harry's
life.
    Direct quotation of the song occurs once more in the final act of
the opera in an orchestral interlude prior to scene three where Harry,
now in a wheelchair, is given the cup by his father. Harry has been
shadowing Barney and Jessie who attempt to elude him during the
dance. Through his exertions, Harry feels faint and collapses. He calls
on his father to give him some wine and then sings the words: "Oh
bring to me a pint of wine and fill it in a silver Tassie" (ibid.: 381),

---

[37]   Turnage uses motivic material to suggest the strong football theme running
through the opera. Indeed, "the football game is made much more of in the opera than
in the play, and the football music provides a link and a transition" (2002b: 12).

[38]   Turnage remarked on the difficulty integrating the song into his idiom: "[...] to go
from quite harsh dissonant harmony to something in B flat major was quite hard to
do". However, he "hung onto it because it is a very beautiful tune" (ibid.: 16).

this time completely unaccompanied. In a sense he has completely 'silenced' any orchestral commentary and the full poignancy of the song is now apparent without any extra-diegetic commentary.

This leads rapidly on to the final scene where Harry flings the cup away and he and Teddy leave the stage. Even though he does not sing the song again and there is no direct quotation, 'traces' of it remain. His "Slow Air", which is sung to the accompaniment of an off-stage band, has a similar poignant feel to it, and ends in a brief duet with Teddy, much as the performance of "The Silver Tassie" in act one. Even Harry's final 'aria' has a similar 'poetic' feel to it. The words link it directly with the song: "The cup I won is all that is left, the cup that I won, you take it away forevermore" (ibid.: 442f.), this time with much deeper resonances. The now broken cup, after he has flung it on the ground, is reflected in his words: "Mangled and broken. There is your cup." (Ibid.: 443) Harry, of course, refers more to himself now 'mangled and broken', both physically and psychologically.

This intricate linking of the song and cup, both charged with great emotional resonance, is consistent with the end of the opera. The brightness of both the cup and the physical and vocal elation of Harry at the end of act one, despite the fact that he is going back to the front, are linked, and his youthful vigour and strength is emphasised, but is tempered by the poignancy of the song with its unstated but very present sense of sorrow to come. The situation has come full circle in act four where Harry's future is bleak at best, and the cup lies broken and tarnished, much like his life. Of course this suggests his particular situation, but also more broadly the lives of the generation destroyed by the war, both those who have lost their lives, but also those who live on, physically and psychologically maimed and broken. The song carries a great deal of symbolic weight, both through its metareferential significance as well as its thematic centrality, and, as with "Paper Doll" in *A View from the Bridge*, represents the emotional core of the opera.

However, this is by no means the only use of music mise en abyme in this opera. Mention has been made of the surreal musical chants that O'Casey incorporated in act two of his play. Turnage specifically referred to the difficulties he saw this device as presenting:

> They're a problem! They work wonderfully in the play, but they aren't necessarily helpful in an opera, because he uses musical moments as a complete contrast to the dialogue [...]. O'Casey has rhythmic chanting, set out almost like a poem, which is very attractive to a composer. When I actually saw the play, I found that

with actors chanting it was quite weak – not that the actual language is weak, but the solution was tame. You need a chorus, an overwhelming presence on stage. (2002b: 12)

What Turnage does is to use the chorus in act two as this "overwhelming presence", and, indeed, the act is almost completely choral in texture. The brooding figure of The Croucher functions almost like a cantor intoning doleful chants, which are taken up by the various groupings within the chorus. However, a variety of different textures emerge which give individuality to what is seen as the collective predicament of the soldiers. O'Casey's dialogue is extremely stylised throughout this act and Holden alters it little, but Turnage has the men frequently sing this dialogue to new melodies yet with a similar effect to that in the play. The famous song from the war: "We're 'ere, because we're 'ere" (2002a: 171), is sung in unison (to the melody of "Auld Lang Syne") by the men to virtually no accompaniment apart from strummed chords in the strings. This moment is introduced by The Croucher's repeated chant: "And let them die" (ibid.: 151), which is accompanied by a wordless melisma by the tenors and basses in the chorus which then changes to:

> In the pissing rain and whistling wind [...]
> And all the shirkers safe at home [...]
> They're warm and dry and happy [...] (ibid.: 166–170)

with a gradually more intrusive orchestral commentary. This dies out to just the menacing strummed chords which are suddenly interrupted by extra-diegetic orchestral commentary. Again, the 'unadorned' song emerging from the commentary is most effective, the voices in unison suggesting the shared experience.

A second mixing of discursive levels occurs a little later when the men sing what appears to be song as mise en abyme:

> Thirty days hath September,
> April, June and November. (Ibid.: 181–184)

This is a mnemonic verse known to all school children to enable them to remember the number of days in each month, and is transformed, however, in the next lines to the highly charged:

> Shall we die at the start
> or in the middle of November?
> We have beaten out the time upon the duckboard,
> we have watched the sunrise from the firestep;
> cursing the barbed wire up there on the top. (Ibid.: 183–188)

This choral section has the musical instruction "Sweet and Mournful" and gradually builds from its unison vocal line and sparse orchestral accompaniment into a large-scale ensemble with four-part divided chorus and full orchestral accompaniment. Again the effect is of a song as mise en abyme being transformed by orchestral extra-diegetic 'intervention' into a fully extra-diegetic passage.

Another effective and somewhat similar passage occurs with a small boys' chorus who depict a group of stretcher-bearers, which immediately follows this extended choral moment with its *fff* climax to The Croucher's words, "and their bones fell asunder" (ibid.: 216) with full chorus and orchestra. This is one of the chants from the play that Turnage has used, including the melody notated by O'Casey[39]. Similar to previous music mise en abyme passages, it has virtually no accompaniment, apart from sustained low strings, with unchanging harmonies and a subdued military snare drum. The banality of the words and rhyme is counteracted by the poignancy of the sound of the unison boys' voices and the simple melodic line:

> Oh, bear him gently, carry him softly,
> a bullet or a shell said stop, stop, stop;
> he's had his day and left the play,
> since he gamboll'd over the top, top, top. (Ibid.: 217f.)

This emerges from some of the thickest orchestral and vocal texture in the opera, and the fragility of the boys' voices emphasises the vulnerability of the men's (and boys') lives in this situation. Similar in structure to the previous large ensemble, the boys' chorus is interspersed with chants from The Croucher: "The Lord giveth and the Lord taketh away. Blessed be the name of the Lord" (ibid.: 218–220), with increased orchestral comment. His intervention then changes the boys' line to the more lyrical:

> Oh carry him softly, bear him gently,
> the beggar has seen it through, through, through;
> if it hadn't been him,
> it might have been me or it might have been you. (Ibid.: 220f.)

The melody is transformed by a much slower tempo. After a brief interlude of men's voices the boys come back to their original melody and the bitter chant:

---

[39] Turnage remarks that it is a "poignant, silly little tune, and I felt it contrasted well with the rest" (2002b: 17).

> Carry on, to the house of pain
> where the surgeon spreads his aid, aid, aid,
> and we show man's wonderful work, well done
> to the image that God has made, made, made. (Ibid.: 223–226)

The poignancy now has a much harsher edge. This then develops again into a large ensemble. The same pattern emerges: what starts ostensibly as a song as mise en abyme is gradually transformed by extra-diegetic commentary into large-scale ensembles for the combined forces on stage and in the pit where all the choral elements are incongruously juxtaposed.

However, the final act of the opera sees the most sustained use of self-referential music, largely in the form of a dance band (which generally consists of three violins with a changing array of wind and brass instruments) that 'accompanies' the various events. Its function as a music mise en abyme becomes blurred as it is transformed and absorbed into extra-diegetic music at various points, only for its self-referentiality to emerge strongly again. Many of the scenes in this act have a dance-like accompaniment. The title of the act is "Dance", and some of the musical instructions for sections of the score include "Jessie's Jig" (ibid.: 344); "Waltz for Teddy" (ibid.: 357); "Slow Air" (ibid.: 378); "Slow Air 2" (ibid.: 392); "Tango" (ibid.: 407), and "Another Tango" (ibid.: 417). Turnage describes his use of these forms not as "direct quotations" but as "deconstructed versions of a jig, a waltz, and so on" (2002b: 15). In fact, Turnage does not use one of the major musical clues from the play: the song "Swing low, sweet chariot", which Harry sings in the play[40].

In many ways the use of the dance band parallels the use of the jazz band in *The Great Gatsby*. The prominence of the band fluctuates according to the nature of drama taking place and at times recedes completely into the background and is subsumed by extra-diegetic music, whereas at other times it is foregrounded. In Harbison's *Gatsby*, as Brody notes, "[j]azz pours into half of the opera's scenes", but it also is "easy to miss the nuances in its agreeable period songs and take the work as a whole for a 1920s pastiche held together with high-toned, illustrative modern music" (2001: 442). On one level *Gatsby*

---

[40]   Turnage argues that the musical elements in the play are used by O'Casey as "a complete contrast to the dialogue". The song "Swing low, sweet chariot" was a "problem" where "in opera you are in song all the time anyway, so you have to find a different solution" (2002b: 12).

could be seen as pastiche and thus consistently metareferential, but the integration of the jazz elements is subtle and often undercuts this metareferentiality. Turnage's employment of his band is perhaps at times even more integrated into the texture of the music, but at others emerges from the extra-diegetic commentary as a distinct self-referential musical source: it functions on one level like a directorial camera lens, as if one is moving visually and aurally in and out of the room where the band is situated in terms of its fluctuating prominence in both the visual and aural 'actions'. Of course a stage band is not uncommon in opera: one can think of outstanding examples from operas as diverse in style as *Rigoletto* and *Wozzeck*, and Turnage remarked on his difficulty in finding the right kind of music for the band to play so that the music in this act would not sound like what he terms "bad *Riverdance*".

> The band in the football club play a lot of jazz, but I would have thought they would have also played a few jigs. So there's a tango, an Irish jig, a slow air which is almost an Irish tune, filtered through and under what I'm doing. I wanted to be subtle about it in the same way as when I work with jazz musicians – more integrated, not suddenly stuck on top. I didn't want to have something so obviously Irish and indeed tonal, because the score is chromatic, and at times atonal. It's more vague inflections. You'll get a feeling that it's a jig: they're not specifically Irish but they are often in 6/8 or 9/8, so they have that lilting feel. (2002a: 16)

This final act is similar to act two: characterised by a dominant musical colour and idiom (act two had a pervasive choral texture), and it ends as it begins with a final plaintive solo violin above the other strings, clarinet and trombone of the band; this complements the circularity apparent in both the play and opera in terms of Harry's journey. While not specifically stated in the stage directions, it is likely that the band is visible throughout the action and thus functions as a clear music mise en abyme (just as the record player in *A View from the Bridge*).

Another blurring of the discursive levels occurs with a song that Harry sings to the accompaniment of the band. Harry is called on by Susie in scene four of this act to sing while accompanying himself on the ukulele. The stage directions state: "As Harry takes the ukulele and begins to tune it, the off-stage band starts up again. Harry listens and occasionally hums along to himself" (2002a: 407). The music is a 'tango' and there is a drunken chorus (not in the score but on the recording) which sings along to the melody played by the clarinet and violin. Harry at first hums along to this melody, and then sings:

> Why do I watch while they live?
> Why do they need to be kind?
> Life has no favours to give.
> Let them dance!
> I'm leaving the fray.
> Let the men with the girls dance again,
> and the girls go and dance with the men.
> I'll hurry out of the way. (Ibid.: 408–412)

Turnage acknowledges that this melody is based on a song called "Spain", which O'Casey referred to in the first edition of the play but which he left out in later editions. According to Turnage, O'Casey left "a couple of verses that look like they could be grafted onto 'Spain'", and what he has done is to "allude to it, rather than quote directly" (2002b: 15).

The harshness of the sentiments Harry expresses is juxtaposed with the rather banal dance-band melody and the stylistically predictable phrasing of both band and singer. However, interspersed in the dance-band accompaniment are violent extra-diegetic outbursts from the orchestra, much as in act one with "The Silver Tassie" performance, which adds a further layering to the scene. It is not immediately apparent whether what Harry is actually singing is song as mise en abyme. What sounds like it could be a pre-existing song in terms of the melody, and which Turnage confirms is the case, is undercut by the words which reflect Harry's feelings and are not the rather conventionally trite words of a typical romantic song of this style and period. The prominence of the band emphasises the self-referential quality of the 'performance' with Harry's smoothly limpid vocal line further suggesting this, but the words of his 'song' and the orchestral interjections undercut this perception. It is another moment when discursive planes intersect and the distinctions between them blur. It is also a conspicuous moment where words and music deliberately 'collide': the sentiments expressed by the words are subverted by the music. This is illustrative of moments where the self- and metareferential elements in the opera emerge strongly, but then become 'naturalised' in the performance as experienced by the audience.

The opera's ending sees the different dramaturgical imperatives of the genre provide the opportunity for a moment of great intensity as well as dramatic truth. In an opera where formal arias are not nearly as clearly defined as in Bolcom's work, there is one such moment for Harry which immediately follows Barney's flinging him to the ground from his wheelchair. While this cannot be seen as song as mise en abyme, it mirrors the performance of "The Silver Tassie" in act one, including a discrete and slow-moving orchestral accompaniment. It also ends with a unison passage, this time, naturally, without Barney, but with Teddy. The final ensemble of the opera has an almost ritualistic quality, and this ending is perhaps more life-affirming and has less of the violent contrast between the mixture of banality and trage-dy of the play's ending. The formality of the musical structure has more of a ritualistic quality, but perhaps less of a visceral impact when compared to the play[41].

Both Bolcom's *A View from the Bridge* and Turnage's *The Silver Tassie* use a particular pre-existing song as well as other musical and structural self- and metareferential elements with great effect to convey the emotional core of each work. However, it must be borne in mind that each composer approaches the original dramatic work with a sharply differing operatic aesthetic. Bolcom leans unashamedly on an operatic tradition of 'number' opera within a largely tonal idiom, whereas Turnage's musical roots most obviously lie in modernism. Significantly, however, both use the device of frequently metareferential performance, and both exploit the formal structures of 'traditional' opera consistently and to great effect.

These devices are employed for a variety of dramatic purposes, often presented initially as the performance of pre-existing material, but which is a self-referential 'performance' that soon becomes transformed by extra-diegetic orchestral commentary where the emotion at the core of the song takes on a wider significance. These are significant moments when the distinctions between discursive levels become blurred and where the emotional charge contained in the song functions as a mise en abyme, not necessarily in terms of the events that occur in the opera, but in defining its psychological and emotional dramaturgy. What for the context of the present volume, however, is most important is the fact that the deliberate use of metareferential musical performance emphasises the elements of self-consciousness

---

[41] The opera received generally good reviews when it was premiered in 2000, and the reaction was even more positive when it was revived in London in 2002. It has subsequently been staged in Dortmund and Dublin. Several reviewers compared Turnage to Britten, and the influence can certainly be felt at times. There is evidence of a sure feel for operatic dramaturgy and his musical idiom has a vitality and flexibility that suggest a new operatic talent is emerging.

and self-reflection that characterise both works, unambiguously situating them in an on-going and vibrant operatic tradition.

References

Abbate, Carolyn (1991). *Unsung Voices: Opera and Musical Narrative in the Nineteenth Century*. Princeton, NJ: Princeton University Press.

Attenborough, Richard, dir. (1969). *O What a Lovely War*. Film. UK: Accord Productions.

Berio, Luciano (1997). "Of Sounds and Images". Trans. David Osmond-Smith. *Cambridge Opera Journal* 9/3: 295–299.

Bigsby, Christopher (2005). *Arthur Miller: A Critical Study*. Cambridge: CUP.

Bolcom, William (1999). "A View from the Composer". *Opera* (Oct.): 1129–1133.

— (2001). "A Note by Composer William Bolcom". *A View from the Bridge*. CD booklet. New World Records B00005M998. 15–17.

— (2002). *A View from the Bridge* [piano score]. Milwaukee, WI: Hal Leonard.

Brody, Martin (2001). "'Haunted by Envisioned Romance': John Harbison's *Gatsby*". *The Musical Quarterly* 85/3: 413–455.

Dahlhaus, Carl (1989). "What is a Musical Drama?". Trans. Mary Whittall. *Cambridge Opera Journal* 1: 95–111.

Halliwell, Michael (2005a). *Opera and the Novel: The Case of Henry James*. Word and Music Studies 6. Amsterdam/New York, NY: Rodopi.

— (2005b). "'Opera about Opera': Self-Referentiality in Opera with Particular Reference to Dominick Argento's *The Aspern Papers*". Suzanne M. Lodato, David Francis Urrows, eds. *Word and Music Studies: Essays on Music and the Spoken Word and on Surveying the Field*. Word and Music Studies 7. Amsterdam/New York, NY: Rodopi. 51–80.

Holden, Amanda (2000). "A Librettist's View". *Opera* (Feb.): 175–179.

Holland, Bernard (1998). "To a Southerner, a Belle and a Butterfly are Different". *New York Times* (24 Sept.): 23.

Lindenberger, Herbert (1984). *Opera: The Extravagant Art*. Ithaca, NY: Cornell University Press.

Miller, Arthur (2001). "A Conversation with Playwright/Co-Librettist". CD booklet. New World Records 80588–2. 18–20.

States, Bert O. (1985). *Great Reckonings in Little Rooms: On the Phenomenology of Theater*. Berkeley, CA: University of California Press.

Tomlinson, Gary (1999). *Metaphysical Song: An Essay on Opera*. Princeton, NJ: Princeton University Press.

Turnage, Mark-Anthony (2002a). *The Silver Tassie* [piano score]. Mainz: Schott.

— (2002b). "Turnage on Tassie". *The Silver Tassie*. CD booklet. ENO Alive B0001KL5BC. 10–17.

Wagner, Richard (1851: online). "Eine Mittheilung an meine Freunde". Projekt Gutenberg-De. http://gutenberg.spiegel.de/?id=5&xid=4100&kapitel=3&cHash=da589a9260chap003#gb_found. [12/09/2007.]

— (1966). "A Communication to My Friends". *Richard Wagner's Prose Works*. Trans. William Ashton Ellis. New York, NY: Broude Brothers. 269–393.

Weinstein, Arnold (2001). "A Note by Co-Librettist, Arnold Weinstein". *A View from the Bridge*. CD booklet. New World Records B00005M998. 22–23.

Robert Carsen's Production of *Les Contes d'Hoffmann*
An Exercise in Theatrical Self-Reflection

Simon Williams, Santa Barbara, CA

Robert Carsen's 2001 production of *Les Contes d'Hoffmann* at the Bastille Opera in Paris is set in the very opera house in which the production is being performed, with Mozart's *Don Giovanni* being used as a foil to the action. This meta-referential approach complements one of the most constant themes in E. T. A. Hoffmann's stories, that of the space between reality and the imagination, in which many of his most striking characters reside. The climax of Carsen's pro duction comes in the Antonia scene, which is staged as if in the orchestra pit of the theatre, with Antonia's mother returning to life as a ghostly Donna Anna. In the confrontation between mother and daughter the perils of a life lived between reality and imagination are powerfully represented, as too are the seductive pow ers of opera.

Like Bizet's *Carmen*, Offenbach's *Les Contes d'Hoffmann* is one of those works that have been so frequently performed that its popularity hides the unique qualities that initially made it so prominent in the repertoire. Since its first performance at the Opéra comique in 1881, it has acquired a performance tradition that situates it in the popular imagination somewhere between the gothic excesses of German Ro manticism and the pratfall-laden farce of English pantomime, with touches of science fiction in some productions. It is also, like *Die Zauberflöte* and *Hänsel und Gretel*, one of those works often thought of as an occasional opera, as something to take the family to for a di version during a festive occasion, and perhaps little more than that. But *Les Contes d'Hoffmann* is more than that. One of the significant virtues of Robert Carsen's celebrated production of the opera, first staged at the Opéra de la Bastille in 2001 and since then frequently revived, has been to challenge this somewhat maudlin tradition.

While few would claim that Carsen is a post-dramatic director, whose main concern has been to reject what Hans-Thies Lehmann has called "the theatre of sense and synthesis" (2006: 25), in his produc tion of *Les contes* he does show himself to be preoccupied with one of the key concerns of the postdramatic theatre – the problematics of theatrical presentation. His production opens onto a large, empty stage in the middle of which is Hoffmann, frantically scribbling on the floor. Soon this space is transformed into a bar, not the homely German tavern prescribed by Jules Barbier, Offenbach's librettist, but a replica of the very bar that the audience in the stalls has just left, the long bar that runs the complete length of the Bastille foyer. The theatrical context of the action is kept in the forefront throughout the production. The Olympia episode is set as if the action takes place on a stage, but viewed from the back wall, so that we see the reverse sides of the wings, while the backdrop of the actual stage is the reverse of a proscenium curtain. The Antonia episode is set, memorably, in the orchestra pit of the theatre, not in the actual orchestra pit of the Bastille, but in an orchestra pit constructed on stage, with a proscenium arch and curtain towering above it. At a crucial moment in the action that curtain will rise to give us a front view of the set that we had seen from the rear in act 1. The Giulietta episode is set once again on a stage, but right by the footlights looking out into the auditorium, and the action takes place both on the narrow strip of stage by the footlights and among the audience, which is played by the chorus, seated in the bank of seats that occupies the rear part of the actual stage. The Epilogue returns to the theatre bar and then back to the bare stage. In this strikingly self-referential, in fact metareferential, production, in which the audience is forced to reflect on the medium of its presentation, normal perspectives are reversed and, like Hoffmann himself, we are not always sure what it is we are seeing, nor where the boundaries lie between what is and is not theatre.

Carsen's decision to use the theatre as the setting for his production is, given the interests of E. T. A. Hoffmann, entirely appropriate. Hoffmann's dramatic works, primarily his operas, have not proved to be lasting – though *Undine* is still given the occasional airing in Germany today – but he was consistently engaged in theatre, either as an innovative stage director during his years in Bamberg or as drinking companion and muse to Ludwig Devrient, the great German romantic actor. But Hoffmann's main contribution to our understanding of theatre resides less in the operatic works he produced, more in the stories in which he wrote about the theatre, which suggests that as a writer he was concerned less with theatre per se and more with the phenomenon of theatricality.

Hoffmann's stories almost define the term 'romantic irony'. They are not seamless narratives, but tales in which a plenitude of various

sources is made abundantly clear through fragmentation, shifts in narrative viewpoint, and disruptive changes in genre, from letters to narration to dialogue to official documents to press reports. Many of
Hoffmann's characters, his narrators and his grotesquely comic, fan-
tastical creations, do not dwell easily in the material world. They, and
along with them the reader, are frequently uncertain as to what is
reality and what is hallucination, to the degree that these categories of
perception are called into question. The bizarre antics that many of
Hoffmann's characters engage in arise from the clash between the
wild realms in which their imaginations are embroiled and the con-
stricted bounds of bourgeois life within which their physical bodies
are grounded. The magnificently contorted figures that teemingly pop-
ulate the prints of Jacques Callot struck Hoffmann as being the aptest
visual counterparts to the products of his own literary imagination,
which led him to publish the first four collections of his stories under
the general title *Fantasiestücke in Callots Manier* between 1814 and
1815. Hoffmann saw in the Breughelesque Callot a kindred soul, in
whose work, like his own, "das Gemeinste aus dem Alltagsleben [...]
in dem Schimmer einer gewissen romantischen Originalität [erscheint]"
(c. 1980: I/27)[1]. Among the most celebrated of Callot's pictures were
his series of figures from the commedia dell'arte, which Hoffmann
especially admired; these magniloquent, flamboyant, strutting actors,
singers, and acrobats suggested that it was in theatrical performance
that the often violent incompatibility of the mundane and the imagina-
tive could most effectively be represented. Hoffmann's great novella
of the theatre, "Prinzessin Brambilla", is his most detailed literary
exploration of this terrain, and it is a work that oscillates between
weird melodrama, excessive farce, and symbolic visions of spellbind-
ing beauty. In some regards, the production tradition of Offenbach's
Les Contes d'Hoffmann seems to have been informed by this view of
Hoffmann as a writer of wildly mixed genres.

Carsen's production at the Bastille seems, initially at least, to turn
its back entirely upon this tradition; for a start, all characters are deci-
sively of the 21st century and realistically presented. However, absolute contemporaneity is not the only point of reference. At the start of
the action, prior to her planned rendezvous with Hoffmann, Stella is
performing in an opera by Mozart. While Offenbach and Barbier do

---

[1]   '[...] the commonest thing from everyday life [...] is clad in the lustre of a certain
romantic originality'. [This one and all further translations are mine.]

not specify the work, Carsen does; it is *Don Giovanni*, and in the opening scene on the bare stage, he has a full tableau of the banquet scene from that opera – complete with statue, Stella in the costume of Donna Anna, and a chorus of Spanish guitarists and dancers – wheeled across the stage. It is a striking moment which establishes a motif that runs through the entire production. In each of the three central acts, scores of *Don Giovanni* are displayed prominently on stage and are often handled by the principals; the Commendatore's statue features prominently in all but the Giulietta sequence; and members of the Spanish chorus at the banquet sing in the Prologue, the Olympia scene, and the Epilogue.

The persistent reference to *Don Giovanni* recalls one of Hoffmann's most celebrated stories, "Don Juan", which was published in the first volume of the *Fantasiestücke*. In this story, the narrator, an opera composer, wakes up in the bedroom of a hotel where he is staying and hears the sound of instruments tuning-up. He learns from the waiter that, oddly enough, adjoining his room is a box to the local theatre, where, he is told, a performance of *Don Giovanni* is about to take place. A great *Giovanni* enthusiast, our narrator instantly takes his seat prepared to be mesmerized by Mozart's "dramma giocoso". During the performance, however, his rapt attention is disturbed by a person who has entered the box behind him. "Schon oft glaubte ich dicht hinter mir einen zarten, warmen Hauch gefühlt, das Knistern eines seidenen Gewandes gehört zu haben" (Hoffmann [c. 1980]: I/42)[2]. In the interval he turns to find out who the interloper is and is amazed to see Donna Anna, who has been present both in his box and in the singer on stage. After a brief and troubled conversation she leaves and the story continues with a description of the second act followed by satirical comments on obtuse and tasteless audiences. At midnight, the narrator returns to the box, the theatre now being empty, and meditates on the unearthly power that possesses Don Giovanni and Donna Anna. At two o'clock he leaves and as he does he thinks that he hears echoes of the orchestra strings in the pit. Next day it is reported that the singer who played Donna Anna died at two o'clock that morning.

"Don Juan" is a characteristically Hoffmannesque story; the supernatural ambience is gripping while the ambiguities of the tale are never explained. The narrative contains a critique, indeed one of the most

---

[2]   'Often I thought I felt a delicate, warm breath close behind me and heard the rustle of a silken garment.'

influential critiques ever written, of *Don Giovanni*, and the singer's death is reported at the end in a conversation between comic characters. Frustratingly though, the central event, the conversation between the narrator and Donna Anna, is presented only in summary form, ostensibly because the narrator is unwilling to translate her Italian into German, a language which, he claims, is too stiff and insipid: "jede Phrase ungelenk, das auszudrücken, was sie leicht und mit Anmut Toskanisch sagt" (Hoffmann [c. 1980]: I/43)[3]. Nevertheless, in one of the two of her speeches he quotes, she reveals that singing disturbs her profoundly. Singing reveals to her

> manches im Innern geheimnisvoll Verschlossene, was keine Worte aussprächen, singend zu begreifen. "Ja, ich begreife es dann wohl", fuhr sie mit brennendem Auge und erhöhter Stimme fort, "aber es bleibt tot und kalt um mich, und indem man eine schwierige Roulade, eine gelungene Manier beklatscht, greifen eisige Hände in mein glühendes Herz! Aber du – du verstehst mich, denn ich weiß, das auch *dir* das wunderbare romantische Reich aufgegangen, wo die himmlischen Zauber der Töne wohnen." (Ibid.)[4]

Donna Anna stands on the dangerous border between imagination and the physical world, and while some of Hoffmann's creations flourish in this terrain, she succumbs.

Offenbach's *Les Contes d'Hoffmann* does not offer a complete dramatization of any of Hoffmann's stories; each of the central acts is based merely upon one or two incidents from those stories – the Olympia act is taken from the long, celebrated tale of demonic possession, "Der Sandmann"; the Antonia act is adapted, quite radically, from the closing pages of "Rat Krespel"; while the Giulietta act, the least developed of the three, is assembled from fragments of "Die Abenteuer der Silvesternacht". The opera was in fact based primarily on material that was at least once removed from Hoffmann's stories, a previously successful boulevard play. Not surprisingly, therefore, much of Hoffmann's characteristic grotesquerie, rapturous romantic vision, and demonic horseplay have been toned down so as to devise

---

[3] '[...] every phrase is too clumsy to express what she said so lightly and with Tuscan grace'.

[4] '[...] some things mysteriously locked up in her, which no words could express, or singing comprehend. "Yes, I understand it well", she continued with burning eyes and raised voice, "but all around me is dead and cold, and while people applaud a difficult roulade, successful grace notes, icy hands grasp my glowing heart! But you – you understand me as I know that to *you* too that wonderful romantic kingdom has been revealed where the heavenly magic of music dwells".'

an action more in accord with the tastes of mid-19th-century Parisian bourgeois theatregoers. Nevertheless, as Heather Hadlock has pointed out in her monograph on the opera, Offenbach's tastes were far from alien to those of E. T. A. Hoffmann, and the stylistic variety of the music complements Hoffmann's literary diversity, so that *Les contes* has the feeling of a 'Hoffmannesque' opera. Hadlock comments on how, uncharacteristically for a 19th-century opera, much of the music is not assumed to be the natural speech of the characters. Instead, she continues,

> it is striking that the inhabitants of *Les contes d'Hoffmann*'s world perform and hear each other's performances, almost continually. The score of *Les contes* comprises a catalogue of types of performed song in 19th-century opera: drinking songs, a narrative ballad, an oracular voice, a serenade, festive choruses, and a music lesson scene [...]. Indeed, approximately half the opera's music is presented as music that the characters are consciously *singing*, and that they and the others on-stage can *hear*. (2000: 36f.)

She draws parallels between this performed music and to the frequency of performed occasions in Hofmann's own works. And it is the theme of performance, theatrical as well as musical, and of its impact upon the performer that is the central concern of Carsen's production at the Bastille[5].

Each act in the production is centred on a performance; in the Prologue, Hoffmann's performance of "Klein Zach" includes a quite striking and very funny impersonation of Hoffmann's dwarf, in a style reminiscent of Callot's figures; in the Olympia act, Olympia's song is, of course, the pivotal event, as is Antonia's outburst of song in response to the appearance of her mother. Offenbach and Barbier did not construct the Giulietta scene around a performance, but Carsen has Dapertutto serve as a stage director, who manipulates each one of the figures until in the septet they form a pattern that he has carefully constructed throughout the playing of the episode. In the Epilogue, the performance is not seen; it has just taken place off-stage, in Stella's rendition of Donna Anna.

Carsen's constantly shifting viewpoints of the stage and its relationship to the auditorium allows him to adopt a Pirandellian perspective on the action, which works best in the Olympia episode. Here, the

---

[5] My discussion of the production is based both on a performance seen at the Opéra de Bastille in May 2001 and on the DVD recording of the production issued by TDK, no. 5450270008438.

performance by Olympia of her song refers to a theatre of marionettes, her jerky movements being akin to the stiff-limbed gesticulations of a puppet, although there are hints that strata of a more human spontaneity lie beneath her artificial exterior. But the act is most striking to the degree that it seems to reverse the passionate complaint uttered by Donna Anna in the "Don Juan" story. Here when Olympia performs a 'difficult roulade' or 'successful grace notes', the applause of the audience does not work like cold-hands on the heart of Hoffmann; on the contrary, they make it glow ever more warmly, and, in a moment of particularly inspired lunacy, his passion even leads Olympia to feign an orgasm as she perches on top of him. Coppelius' fascination with eyes, rather luridly enacted through his picking an eyeball out of a massive jar filled with the things, sets up a theme for the act, that through performance our imagination can give life to what is dead, but the subsequent destruction of Olympia, carried out with pronounced violence by Coppelius, trashes the entire idea. In the Olympia act, *Don Giovanni* is constantly to the fore, through the Commendatore's statue that dominates the scene with its back to the audience, through the Spanish chorus from the initial tableau, who are now Spalanzani's guests, and through the physical presence of Mozart's actual score, to which for a time Olympia clings; furthermore, her white dress alludes to the one that had been worn by Donna Anna in the tableau during the Prologue, as if she is a maladroit reflection of her. As the entire act is, from the audience's point of view, seen from the back of the stage – in reverse, as it were – one can also read it as a satiric reversal of the values contained within performance.

The centrepiece of the entire production is the Antonia scene, which climaxes upon a quite stunning coup-de-théâtre that recalls more directly the plaints of Donna Anna in the "Don Juan" story. Moreover, at the moment it occurs, it throws the entire operatic enterprise into a disturbingly questionable light. Crespel's house is not Barbier's 'oddly furnished room' with violins and an uncanny portrait of Antonia's mother hanging on the wall; instead, we see on the stage floor an orchestra pit, with orchestral stands, a conductor's podium, and stage right a piano. Not surprisingly, the score and orchestral parts for *Don Giovanni* are placed on the podium and the stands. Neither the pit nor the curtain literally simulate the ambience of the Bastille, but it is unmistakable that the vast proscenium arch filled by a plush red curtain, which towers several feet above the pit, is emblematic for the grand opera house. The act opens with Antonia grabbing the score of *Don*

Giovanni off the conductor's podium and clinging to it as one ob-
sessed, establishing at once the theme of mania with music as the food
of life and with opera as the means by which it is supplied. The
turtledove about whose abandonment Antonia sings is not, as Barbier's
libretto suggests, Hoffmann, but opera itself and, more specifically,
Don Giovanni. Music is constantly on the minds of the characters; the
servant Frantz fantasizes on how well he sings, while executing comic
numbers with a broom in front of the curtain; Niklausse self-
consciously conjures images of pure sonic beauty from the violin; and
Antonia and Hoffmann, in their love duet, sing of music as if it is a
source both of solace and jealousy.

The proscenium arch that dominates the orchestra pit acquires a
notably forbidding presence as the action advances, so that the unseen
stage that we know lies behind takes on an increasingly disturbing
presence, and when Dr. Miracle suddenly steps through the curtains
our sense of the stage as site of danger and potential destruction is
augmented. Dr. Miracle is a creation of Barbier's not Hoffmann's, but
he has Hoffmannesque characteristics. He is a mesmerist who can lure
the mind from limited bourgeois reality to the realms of the imagination where categories are broken down and mysterious vectors and
impulses threaten the mesmerized. In Carsen's production, he is also a
performer: when we first see him he is a figure from burlesque, playing with a spotlight and eliciting peals of song from Antonia as if he
were conjuring them out of her. The realm from which he has come
seems a threat to one's very existence, an embodiment of everything
that Donna Anna had feared about singing in "Don Juan". A precise
rendering of this threat is delivered at the climax of the act, in the
staging of the great trio in which Dr. Miracle makes the picture of
Antonia's mother sing, leading to Antonia's death. In the trio, the
theme of "Don Juan" that performance can be the purveyor of death
rather than life, is brought to fruition, while the 'icy hands' that Hoffmann's Donna Anna spoke of are displayed as agents of the 'wonderful romantic kingdom' of music. Only, while Offenbach and Barbier
envisaged this message being purveyed through the portrait alone,
Carsen spectacularly employs the entire theatre.

At the point where Dr. Miracle summons Antonia's mother to lure
her daughter to death by singing, the curtain in the onstage proscenium rises to reveal the scenery that we had seen from the rear in act 1,
a mistily romantic, single perspective set. In the centre of this vast
stage stands Antonia's mother, clad as Donna Anna, but in a costume

that is decayed and yellowing with age, a dress that was once a ball gown, but is now a shroud; like Mrs. Havisham's wedding dress, it is composed as much of cobwebs as it is of lace. Antonia, transfixed at the sight of her mother, sings her part in the trio from the orchestral pit, but as the trio ends and her mother sweeps from the stage after delivering an elaborate and ironic bow to the audience, Antonia herself rushes on to the stage to deliver the rapturous solo that will lead to her death. It is a remarkable scene, not only because of its stunning theatricality but because of the strangely ambivalent impact it has upon the audience, because while it celebrates the raw power of theatre, it also makes the audience aware that it might itself be complicit in the death of Antonia, even perhaps that a passionate love of opera is itself akin to a longing for death.

One of the odd and potentially perilous aspects of Carsen's staging of this scene is that it can only be done if the audience interrupts the music with its applause. To allow Antonia time to run off-stage from the orchestra pit and to reappear on the proscenium stage, which is several feet higher than the stage floor, it is necessary for the audience to applaud and for some time; otherwise this transition would have to be accomplished in total silence. This reminds us that among the classical arts, opera is particularly noted for a following that frequently verges upon fanaticism. Fanaticism involves surrender, in the instance of opera to the majestic sweep of the spectacle and the plangent appeal of the music. Opera, perhaps more than others of the arts, requires total emotional surrender; if one gives less than that, its action can all too easily strike one as forced and lacking in credibility, while its musical language will sound orotund, inflated, and rhetorical. Opera can only work if one willingly abandons, for however brief a time, control over one's emotions. In witnessing and applauding the surrender of Antonia to her mother in the guise of Donna Anna, we share in, or even enable, the romantic death against which Donna Anna in the story so passionately objects.

After the theatrics of the Antonia act, the less developed and essentially static Giulietta episode is faintly disappointing, though Carsen's staging of this act serves as a metaphor for the entire production and, in a way, for Hoffmann's own view of the theatrical. The actual stage space is extremely narrow and backed by footlights; behind them are banks of seats, which rather disconcertingly move in time to the barcarolle and then become the site for an elegant orgy among the chorus which is also the 'audience' for the intrigue among the principals. As characters move easily from the stage into the stage audience – in fact, when Giulietta departs, she goes out through the actual audience – the barriers of the stage dissolve. In the course of the evening, the four villains, sung by a single singer, have become progressively more and more dominant, and Dapertutto is the most powerful of all; he literally becomes the stage director when he rehearses Giulietta to execute his stratagem on Hoffmann and eventually takes over the entire stage, moving characters at will and shaping their gestures, as if they were marionettes. The effect is to highlight the artificiality of theatre, to ask, ultimately, about the ontological status of what it is we have been seeing. In addition, the humiliation of Hoffmann reminds us how unlike Hoffmann is to Don Giovanni, and how defeat rather than victory is the lot of the romantic poet.

Carsen's production of *Les Contes d'Hoffmann* cannot be seen as evidence of a postdramatic theatre. While Carsen does everything to highlight the theatricality of the event he is staging, he sustains the narrative flow of the opera's action and creates a production in which, ultimately, the various elements of music, song, word, gesture, movement, and blocking all cohere into a unified work rather than compete against each other. But while aesthetically his production remains within the familiar bounds of the Gesamtkunstwerk, thematically it takes up issues that have rarely been applied to Offenbach's opera. Throughout the production those self-referential aspects of the action that draw our attention to characters performing are given such prominence that, as Dapertutto stage-manages the septet toward the end of the Giuletta episode, we are prepared to see the human social condition itself as a performative one. But at the production's climactic moment, the appearance of Antonia's mother on the set of *Don Giovanni*, we are not only encouraged to adopt a metareferential perspective on the work through witnessing Antonia's death by singing on a stage, but whatever insight we gain from this moment is unnervingly directed back to ourselves. It asks us to examine our own predilection, enthusiasm, or obsession for operatic performance. In so doing, Carsen not only rescues Offenbach's opera from the theatrical clichés that have smothered it, but he offers his production as a basis from which we may chose to re-evaluate the entire project of opera.

References

Hadlock, Heather (2000). *Mad Loves: Women and Music in Offenbach's* Les contes d'Hoffmann. Princeton, NJ/Oxford: Princeton University Press.

Hoffmann, E. T. A. ([c. 1980]). *Werke in fünf Bänden*. Cologne: Luzia Prösdorf.

Lehmann, Hans-Thies (2006). *Postdramatic Theatre*. Trans. Karen Jürs-Munby. London/New York, NY: Routledge.

Leoncavallo's *Pagliacci*
Operatic Metareference on Stage and on Film

Bernhard Kuhn, Lewisburg, PA

This article discusses textual, musical, as well as visual self-references and meta-references in Leoncavallo's opera *Pagliacci* (1892). It first considers the opera as an intermedial combination, analyzing the use of self-references separately in libretto and score. It then reflects on metareferences in the realization of the opera (understood as an intermedial fusion) by examining and comparing selected elements of Costa's (1947) and Zeffirelli's (1982) filmic interpretations.

The analysis of text and score of *Pagliacci* illustrates that the opera incorporates numerous textual and musical self-references, some of which ought to be classified as metareferences. Specific examples of metareferences in *Pagliacci* include the opera's prologue, the commedia within the opera, as well as the ending of the opera. Considering the interplay of the different media employed in an opera performance on stage or in Costa's film-opera and Zeffirelli's television-opera, it becomes apparent that the metareferential potential of the opera is differently expressed in each interpretation. The degree of metareferentiality of an opera, and especially of an opera on screen, hence depends primarily on the performance, which may strengthen or weaken potential metareflexive elements.

Opera is an artistic medium that can incorporate hetero-references as well as self-references. Hetero-references in opera point to reality outside the theater and the arts, for example by presenting stories or producing sounds that relate to the world. Self-references, on the other hand, do not connect with a reality outside, but with the world of art.

What makes the discussion of self-references in operas particularly appealing is the fact that operas are artifacts that combine several media or semiotic systems, which all have the potential to create hetero-references and self-references. Consequently, self-references in opera might be created by the operatic text, by the music, and/or by the sign systems of the theatrical presentation. In so doing, they become meaningful elements of an opera performance. This is equally true for the discussion of operas on film, but in addition to the media and semiotic elements relevant for a stage performance, the sign system of cinema, in particular that of the camera and editing, has the power to create new self-referential instances as well as to modify those of the operatic text and score.

As Werner Wolf has pointed out, self-references can be differentiated (see 2007 and his contribution to this volume). A first distinction concerns the function of self-reference. Self-references may merely apply on a formal level, without eliciting reflections on the medial status of a work. Examples in operas of this kind of non-self-reflexive self-references include references created, for instance, by rhythm or rhyme in the text or by repetitions of musical themes. Further examples are self-references such as mises en abyme which do not cause a cognitive reflection on the work of art if no additional self-referential statement is made or implied. The same is true for intramedial references, as in the case of open intermusical or intertextual references to other operas, or intermedial references, to literary texts, film, or the visual arts. If, for example, an opera performance includes a painting without specifically highlighting the relationship to that painting or to art works in general, the painting alone does not cause a cognitive reflection. All these examples certainly qualify as self-references, but they merely point to intracompositional, intramedial, or intermedial elements and do not entail additional metareferential significance if they are not otherwise marked and explicitly or implicitly made recognizable as metareferential forms of self-reflection[1].

On the other hand, if an opera includes or implies a self-referential statement, it has the potential to cause a cognitive reflection about the work itself or the arts and media in general. In order to elicit such a metareflection, self-referential elements must not only be made recognizable, but their successful communication furthermore depends on the capability and willingness of the recipient to identify the references. Only if the recipient initiates the cognitive process by actualizing the metareflection does the metareference fulfill its purpose. Consequently, in the case of opera, not only the librettist and composer are accountable for operatic metareflections, but also the conductor, stage director, singers, and others responsible for the performance, as well as ultimately the audience.

---

[1]   'Markers' are elements that signal the presence of a self-reference and thus make it recognizable for an attentive audience. When that is the case, it is more likely to categorize the self-reference as metareference. Jörg Helbig, who reflects on markers in the context of intermediality, distinguishes between "nichtmarkierter" ('unmarked'), "implizit markierter" ('implicitly marked'), and "expliziert markierter" ('explicitly marked') intermediality (2001: 135f.). This distinction is also valid for markers of metareference.

This paper examines opera as a plurimedial art form. Werner Wolf has defined the intermedial concept of 'plurimediality' as the presence of at least two distinct media on the 'surface' of a given work in at least one instance (cf. 2002: 22). In opera, this includes typically music, text, and scene or theatrical presentation. Opera may be discussed as 'medial combination' by considering the libretto and score separately, or as 'medial fusion' by looking at all combined semiotic elements of an opera performance on stage or, in our case, on film and television[2].

Central to the discussion of operatic metareferentiality is the performance aspect of opera since potentially metareflexive elements are usually actualized by the audience during the medial concretization of libretto and score. In order to examine how such metareflections might occur, this essay will first consider the opera *Pagliacci* as medial combination and analyze the metareferential qualities of libretto and score. Next, it will discuss two filmic versions of the opera: the 1948 film-opera directed by Mario Costa and the 1982 production for television by Franco Zeffirelli. The goal is to demonstrate how selected self-referential elements of libretto and score take on a metareflexive meaning if effectively presented in film. In addition, it will be shown that a filmic concretization of libretto and score can both diminish or increase metareferential qualities, for example by adding self-referential characteristics that are not part of the libretto and score or by suppressing or eliminating relevant elements. A film, like a performance on stage, can thus incorporate, for example, self-referential visual cues that are not part of the libretto's stage directions. If they imply self-referential statements, those elements might also initiate a cognitive metareflexive process in the audience and qualify as metareference. In the case of a film-opera or television-opera, filmic means can thus not only highlight or diminish operatic self-references but may also create new ones.

1. *Pagliacci* as a staged opera (1892)

Leoncavallo's opera *Pagliacci* has been frequently discussed as one of the prototypes of verismo opera and certainly contains many charac-

---

[2]   On the genre of 'film-opera' or on the phenomenon of opera on screen in general see Citron 2000 and Kuhn 2005.

teristic elements of the genre[3]. In addition, however, it is an excellent example for the analysis of operatic metareferences.

The opera's plot is a traditional story of love and jealousy ending in tragedy. Canio, the head of a traveling commedia dell'arte troupe, is married to Nedda, who is in love with the local Silvio. Canio finds out about Nedda's affair and kills his wife and Silvio during the performance of a commedia dell'arte play.

Considering the opera's text, it is evident that the story contains numerous hetero-references. The libretto unmistakably points to an event that took place in Montalto, a village that exists outside the theater and the world of the arts, and at least some instances of the story are based on true events[4]. In addition, intertextual relationships to other plays can be recognized[5]. Those ties, however, while certainly

---

[3]   The term 'verismo' has originally been used to describe the Italian literary movement which started around 1870 under the influence of French naturalism. Its main literary representatives are Giovanni Verga, Luigi Capuana, and Federico De Roberto. The term was adopted for Italian theater and describes a certain style of opera since 1890. Characteristic for this literary movement was a concern for lower classes and contemporary reality, especially of Southern Italy. The literature frequently emphasized local customs and adopted lower class idioms, an impersonal style of narration, as well as a true-to-life approach. While verismo operas share the focus on lower class characters with literature and theater and are often located in Southern Italian regions, the language of the libretti does not always depart from an elevated jargon. General stylistic elements of the verismo opera include an equal status of recitatives, solo pieces, and ensembles, the general absence of bel canto coloratura, an elevated importance of orchestral motifs, and the incorporation of local songs, dances, and other folkloristic elements (see Sansone 1992). For the relationship between *Pagliacci* and verismo cf. Dorsi/Rausa 2000: 499–508 and see Sansone 1989, Girardi 1993, and Guarniere Corazzol 1993.

[4]   According to Leoncavallo, the story is based on true events, specifically, a homicide that occurred in his hometown during his childhood. While it is true that a similar incident occurred indeed, significant differences exist between the events of Montalto in Calabria and the story of the libretto. For example, it is not true that a homicide occurred on August 15, the date the events in the opera take place, and that the real murderer was an actor belonging to a theater troupe. On 5 March 1865 at 4 a. m., Gaetano Scavello was murdered by two brothers after exiting the local theater. The reason for the murder was a quarrel about a woman. While the violent crime in Leoncavallo's hometown might have had an impact on the composer, most of the libretto is invented or based on other sources (see Lerario 1971).

[5]   Many similarities exist between *Pagliacci* and *La Femme de tabarin* (1887) by Catulle Mendès. After the first performance of *Pagliacci* in Paris in 1902, Mendès therefore even accused Leoncavallo of plagiarism, but did not further pursue the case

interesting for the genesis of the libretto, must be considered of low self-referential saliency, since the author himself made every attempt to conceal them and no marker within the opera highlights the relationship to other texts.

As far as the textual and musical structure is concerned, the opera is divided into a prologue and two acts, which are connected by a musical intermezzo. Within the narrative of the text, three different communication levels are distinguishable. The first level consists of the prologue, which is directed at the audience of the opera. The second level is formed by the commedia dell'arte troupe, their interaction with the villagers and Nedda's affair, which ends with the murders. The third level is created by the performance of the commedia presented within the second act of the opera by the troupe in front of a fictional village audience, in other words the story of Pagliaccio, Arlecchino, Columbina, and Taddeo, which ends abruptly with the murder of Nedda playing Columbina (see Girardi 1993).

The technique of beginning an opera with a prologue is as old as the art form itself[6]. In *Pagliacci*, the implied author communicates through the character Tonio alias Taddeo with his audience. After Tonio's greeting and self-presentation, he justifies the prologue by noting that it is intended to explain the function of commedia dell'arte elements in the opera: "Poiché in iscena ancor le antiche maschere mette l'autore, in parte ei vuol riprendere le vecchie usanze, e a voi di nuovo inviami!"[7] From the beginning of the prologue, the audience is thus confronted with a reflection on theatrical devices and traditions,

---

since similar pieces, such as the Spanish *Un drama nuevo* (1867) by Manuel Tamayo y Baus, existed before *La Femme de tabarin* (see Sansone 1989).

[6]   During the first days of opera, a prologue had to justify the phenomenon of opera itself as sung drama. Early examples of prologues in operas include *Dafne* (1598) or *Euridice* (1600) by Jacopo Peri. In the 19th century, a prologue sometimes provided background information to understand the plot, such as in Giuseppe Verdi's *Simon Boccanegra* (1857) or in Charles Gounod's *Roméo et Juliette* (1867) (see Carter 1992, Dalmonte 1982).

[7]   "Once again, the author wants to revive the ancient plays, partly to revive the ancient tradition, and we invite you!" Libretto citations and translation are quoted after Fisher, ed. (2002: 63–89; here 64). The prologue's text in *Pagliacci* explains the role of theatrical elements and devices. Comparable to the announcement of the different use of commedia dell'arte elements, the explicit distancing from the typical function of a prologue may potentially cause a reflection on such a device.

which on the textual level qualifies as an explicit metareferential statement.

The central theme of the prologue's text is the relationship between theater and life, or between reality and fiction, which is ultimately a reflection on the meaning of art in the world. According to the prologue, the opera *Pagliacci* attempts to paint a scene from life and is inspired by a true story: "No! No. L'autore ha cercato invece pingervi uno squarcio di vita. Egli ha per massima sol che l'artista è un uomo e che per gli uomini scrivere ei deve. Ed al vero ispiravasi!"[8]

This key idea, which refers to the relationship between reality and fiction, is a recurring theme within the following two acts. Since it is explicitly emphasized within the prologue, it has the potential to become a strong metareference within the opera.

Finally, the prologue reminds the audience that all actors are human beings – "poiché siam uomini / di carne e d'ossa"[9] – who have feelings, which is the last metareferential element of the prologue reflecting on the reality of actors within theater. Regarding the function of the prologue, it can therefore be concluded that its text contains explicit metareferential statements concerning the function of theatrical devices, such as commedia dell'arte elements or the role of the actors in theater, and the relationship between art and reality.

From a dramaturgical perspective, the prologue is antagonistic to the theatrical illusion, since an actor communicates the intentions of the implied author directly to the audience. This was likely a surprising element for the late-19th-century audience, who, after a symphonic prelude, probably expected the beginning of the stage performance. The music critic Eduard Hanslick, who attended early performances of the opera in Vienna, confirms this by evaluating the prologue correctly as an element that steals the illusion (cf. 1896/1987: 178). From a self-referential point of view, the performance Hanslick refers to was therefore successful in alerting the audience through an unconventional use of a theatrical device and has consequently elicited a metareflection.

---

[8]   "No! No. The author has tried to paint a picture of real life. He believes first that the artist is a man, and that he must write for men. And that truth has inspired him!" (Fisher, ed. 2002: 64) The phrase "squarcio di vita" (literally: 'a slice of life') refers to Emile Zola's theory of naturalism (cf. 1880/1989: 36).

[9]   "[…] because we are men / of flesh and bone" (Fisher, ed. 2002: 64).

A second element relevant for the discussion of metareferentiality in the operatic text is the commedia performed during the second act of the opera. According to the categorization of self-referential phenomena, narrative elements, such as mise en abyme, are in themselves a priori considered mere self-references without a metadimension (cf. Wolf 2007: 305). Nonetheless, in *Pagliacci* the play within the opera serves the function of communicating an implicit metareferential statement and thus in further highlighting the metacharacter of the opera. The commedia in *Pagliacci*'s second act can take on such a metafunction because the opera's text points several times in a metareferential manner to the relationship between theater and life which is exemplified in the play within the opera.

After explicitly highlighting the role of theater throughout the prologue, the first act contains further metareferential elements presented in particular through the main character, Canio. While the mere presence of characters representing actors does not produce a metareferential meaning, Canio's solo pieces that reflect on art are highly significant on a metatextual level. In the text of his cantabile "Un tal gioco" (Fisher, ed. 2002: 68), he distinguishes between life and stage and claims that life and stage are different. As example he proleptically compares the commedia dell'arte love triangle between Pagliaccio, Columbina, and Arlecchino with his personal situation and declares that if he were to surprise Nedda with a lover the story would finish differently than on stage, where Pagliaccio would calm down by beating up Arlecchino. At the end of the first act, he confirms this view in "Vesti la giubba" (ibid.: 79) by distinguishing between himself as Canio and his role as Pagliaccio as well as by pointing to the actor's duty to entertain the audience and to hide his real feelings. Canio thus opposes the idea of presenting reality on stage as declared in the prologue. Canio's thoughts on theater thus have a potential to trigger metareferential reflections in the recipient, since the prologue unmistakably alerted the audience to questions regarding the relationship between theater and life. Until the performance of the commedia, the audience is therefore confronted with two contradicting views: the first idea, pronounced in the prologue, is that life and stage are basically the same; the second, pronounced by the tenor of the opera, is that the realities of life and stage are different[10].

---

[10]   Konrad Dryden reads Canio's words as an echo of what Tonio declared in the prologue (cf. 2007: 217). Since Canio distinguishes between himself and his persona

The play performed within the second act of the opera, then, does not *explicitly* continue this discussion. The staging of the spectacle functions instead as an exemplification of the relationship between theater and life. The commedia thus demonstrates the contrast between the reality of the actors of the troupe and the sketch performed on stage. By contrasting the two realities, the opera therefore *implicitly* continues the discussion on reality and fiction and has a potential to stimulate a cognitive metareflection. Crucial for the triggering of such a reflection is the fictional audience which serves as a model for the real audience by commenting on the events happening on stage and asking whether what they are watching is real or a play[11].

Considering the mise en abyme within *Pagliacci*, it may therefore be concluded that although the commedia itself does not contain an explicit metareferential statement, it implicitly continues the reflections on reality and fiction initiated by the prologue and pursued by Canio in the first act on the diegetic level. The mise en abyme, therefore, functions as an intradiegetic capstone of the reflection on reality and fiction within the opera[12].

Significant for the discussion of potential metareferential elements is also the opera's ending. After Canio's double murder, the opera's text ends with the words, pronounced originally by Tonio[13] and tradi-

---

on stage, I read his words as contrasting with those pronounced in the prologue. Also Nedda in her duet with Tonio distinguishes between reality on and off stage, informing Tonio that he may tell her on stage (and thus implying not off stage) that he loves her: "Hai tempo a ridirmelo stasera, se brami! ... Stasera! Facendo le smorfie colà, colà, sulla / scena!" ("There's time to tell me tonight! ... Tonight! When you'll be acting the fool, up there, on stage!"; Fisher, ed. 2002: 71)

[11] On several occasions the crowd laughs during the first part of the commedia (cf. Fisher, ed. 2002: 83, 86). During the second part, after Canio pronounces that he is no longer playing the role of Pagliaccio ("No! Pagliaccio non son"; ibid.: 87), villagers comment on the effect the play has on them and how real it seems: "Comare, mi fa piangere! Par vera questa scena" ("Oh Lord, he's made me cry! The play is so true to life!"; ibid.: 87); "Fanno davvero? Seria è la cosa? ... Seria è la cosa e scura!" ("Is this reality? Is this serious? ... They must surely mean it!"; ibid.: 88).

[12] At the end of the commedia, the tension between the prologue's and Canio's points of view appears to be resolved in favor of the prologue. This impression, however, does change after the curtain falls and rises again. Then, on the extradiegetic level, the real theater audience realizes that all the actors, including those playing Nedda and Silvio, are alive.

[13] For an analysis of *Pagliacci*'s last words see Wright 1978. For a discussion on the particular significance of the character Tonio see Bini 1985.

tionally by Canio: "La commedia è finita!"[14] Considering the three different communication levels within the opera's text, this pronouncement has more than one meaning. To the fictional audience of the commedia dell'arte sketch, it announces the ending of the play. For the real audience of the opera, however, in addition to announcing the end of the play as well as the end of the opera, it refers back to the prologue. The meaning of the opera's last sentence within the context of the prologue's reflection about the relationship between theater and life can be understood as the declaration that the traditional comedy or the conventional form of theater is dead (cf. Bini 1985: 180), proclaiming instead implicitly the new form of theater presented through the opera *Pagliacci*.

Considering the opera's music, several additional metareferential elements are observable, but it must be emphasized that no metareferential statement is produced by the music alone[15]. In combination with the text, however, the music highlights certain characteristics and thus strengthens the metareflexive character of the opera so that it is appropriate to define *Pagliacci* as metaopera[16]. Among the musical self-references which in many cases take on a metareferential quality one can distinguish intermusical references and intra-compositional self-references.

The first type, intermusical references, involves musical citations or allusions to other compositions, which, since they point to other musical pieces, qualify as self-references. Perhaps the most famous one refers to Verdi's *Otello*, since the voice line of "Ridi Pagliaccio", one of the opera's main motifs, is almost identical to the voice line of Otello's "A terra! ... e piangi"[17].

---

[14] "The play is over!" (Fisher, ed. 2002: 89).

[15] Werner Wolf points out that the medium of music can only implicitly create metareferential awareness (see Wolf's contribution to this volume).

[16] For the concept of 'metaopera' and other examples cf. Frieder von Ammon's and Walter Bernhart's contributions to this volume.

[17] In both operas this line is crucial for the distinction between private and public role: Otello as political personality and Canio as actor (cf. Sansone 1989: 360–361, Girardi 1993: 69f.).

Example 1: "Ridi Pagliaccio", from Ruggero Leoncavallo, Pagliacci, *"Vesti la giubba", mm. 26–27.*

Example 2: "A terra! ... e piangi!", from Giuseppe Verdi, Otello, *Act 3, Scene 8, mm. 35–36.*

While this intermusical reference between *Pagliacci* and *Otello* is certainly compelling, also due to several parallels regarding the plot, such as the love triangle and the crime of passion, it has only low metareferential saliency because the relationship between the two operas is not otherwise made identifiable for the audience and no explicit or implicit metareferential statement is associated. The same is true for general stylistic and structural reference between *Pagliacci* and other operas, such as *Carmen* or *Cavalleria Rusticana* (cf. Giradi 1993: 65–67). Also intermusical references between the voice line of "Un nido di memorie" and Mendelssohn's 4th symphony, or between the Bell Chorus of the second scene and the instrumental work *España* by Chabrier are only mere self-references that point to other musical compositions without expressing or implying metareferential statements (see Girardi 1993, cf. Sansone 1989: 360)[18].

---

[18]   The same is true for the intermusical references to Mendelssohn's Piano Trio in D Minor and Beethoven's Piano Sonata in A Major, op. 101 of the duet between Nedda and Silvio (cf. Malach 2007: 41).

A different category of intermusical references consists of the adoption of historical musical forms, particularly during the performance of the commedia, which involve a deeper meaning by creating a musical contrast between the first and the second acts[19]. While the incorporation of historical forms, such as the 'minuetto' or the 'gavotta', itself does not create a clear metareferential statement either, it highlights the metaoperatic difference between the older form of theater and the newer form of *Pagliacci* explicitly and prominently thematized in the opera's text[20].

But the most important form of musical self-references with a metareferential potential are intra-compositional references in the form of recurring motifs and themes, which create paradigmatic connections within the opera and thus may aid trigger a metareflection in the audience. In the prelude, after the Pagliaccio motif (cf. *Example 1*), the violins play the theme connected with the love between Nedda and Silvio (see *Example 3*) followed by the motif associated with Canio's jealousy (see *Example 4*).

Example 3: 'Love motif', from Ruggero Leoncavallo, Pagliacci, *Prologue, mm. 80–82.*

---

[19]   Also Nedda's ballatella may be considered as a musical citation, since it follows the formal requisites of a song. It does not, however, imply a metareferential statement and its function is primarily to characterize Nedda.

[20]   These particular 18th-century musical numbers additionally point to a certain style of private performances, still popular in the late 19th century and familiar to the contemporary audience. Leoncavallo himself was active as pianist and had at least one gavotta, one sarabanda, and one minuet in his repertoire to entertain. The popularity of these forms in a contemporary non-theatrical context creates even further distance to their original function in the 18th century (cf. Piccardi 1993: 207–209).

Example 4: 'Jealousy motif', from Ruggero Leoncavallo, Pagliacci, *Prologue, mm. 89–91.*

These motifs can be heard several times during the first act. The love motif is particularly dominant during Nedda's and Silvio's long love scene, and the jealousy motif during Canio's cantabile "Un tal gioco", where the tenor compares Columbina's affair on stage with a hypothetical affair of Nedda[21]. These two motifs are then directly contrasted when Nedda and Silvio decide to escape at night and Canio surprises the lovers.

The use of the recurring motifs within the first act in order to characterize Canio's jealousy or to point to Nedda's and Silvio's love so far certainly qualifies as self-reference, but no metareferential statement is yet explicitly associated with it. Considering, however, the incorporation of these motifs in the second act, and particularly within the commedia, their metareferential relevance grows since they create ties between the separate communication levels of the opera.

The music of the commedia consists of separate numbers, including, for instance, a minuet, a serenade, and a duet between Arlecchino and Columbina. During this duet, which is mostly defined as "a tempo di gavotta", the motif representing the love between Nedda and Silvio appears at the moment when Columbina uses almost the same words with Arlecchino that Nedda used in the first act with Silvio: "A stanotte e per sempre tua sarò."[22] In addition, Canio's jealousy motif

---

[21]   During this solo piece the motif is accompanied by the words "Ma se Nedda sul serio sorprendessi, altramente finirebbe la storia, …" ("But if I should surprise Nedda like that in real life, the story would have a different ending, …"; Fisher, ed. 2002: 68). It then reappears at the beginning of Nedda's solo scene accompanied by the words "Qual fiamma avea nel guardo!" ("What fire there was in his eyes!"; ibid.: 69), which underlines that Nedda knows about Canio's jealousy.

[22]   "Till tonight: I'll be yours forever." (Fisher, ed. 2002: 76) The words expressed by Nedda during the commedia (playing Columbina) are only slightly different: "A stanotte. E per sempre io sarò tua." (Ibid.: 85) The meaning is certainly identical.

recurs during the following duet between Columbina and Pagliaccio and again before the assassination of Silvio. The motifs of the first act therefore reappear within the commedia and thus interrupt the traditional numbers, which works against the expectations of the fictional audience as well as the real audience. The recurring motifs thus create not only a link between the two narrative levels, the story of Canio, Nedda, and Silvio, and the story of Pagliaccio, Columbina, and Arlecchino, but by breaking with the commedia tradition, they further invite the audience to a cognitive metareflection[23].

While the creation of hetero-references is generally not considered a typical trait of instrumental music or the medium of music in general (cf. Wolf 2007: 303), it ought not to be considered unusual for verismo operas to produce imitations of sounds referring to the world outside the theater, and *Pagliacci* contains at least some instances of musical hetero-references. Examples include Nedda's ballatella, where the orchestra imitates the sound of birds, or the imitation of the sound of the cracking of the whip during Nedda's and Tonio's duet.

The score of the opera *Pagliacci*, therefore, contains musical hetero-references as well as self-references, which in most instances qualify as mere self-references without metareferential statements. In combination with the text, however, some recurring motifs assume a reflexive character, emphasizing the metareferential character of the opera by contrasting elements of the second and third communication levels.

2. Pagliacci on Film

After considering the opera as a plurimedial combination of words and music and studying the textual and musical self- as well as metareferences in the libretto and the score of *Pagliacci*, it is now time to reflect on the opera as a plurimedial fusion in order to determine how the self-referential elements discussed may be actualized in a performance, and in particular a filmed performance. Two prominent filmic

---

[23] Additional ties, although less obvious, can be found between the beginning of each act with the trumpet motif or the musical intermezzo and the voice line of "Un nido di memorie" of the prologue. Those references have certainly a reminiscing function and therefore highlight similarities and differences between the two acts, but they do not contain metareferential statements.

versions of the opera are the 1947 film-opera produced by Mario Costa as well as the 1982 television-opera by Franco Zeffirelli. While both films would certainly deserve an extended individual analysis, the following discussion has to limit itself to remarks about cinemato-graphic interpretation of the above discussed self-references.

The first self-referential element is the prologue, where, according to the stage directions, the audience is directly addressed and is thus confronted for the first time with the relationship between life and the-ater, or reality and fiction. Mario Costa's version is fairly traditional and presents Tito Gobbi as Tonio masked as a clown, entering a the-ater stage through a closed curtain. During the performance of the pro-logue the camera focuses exclusively on Tonio showing him in the center of the frame standing in front of the curtain[24]. The viewer of the film is consequently directly addressed by means of the camera. The setting of the prologue on an enclosed theater stage, while the rest of the film, including the images accompanying the prelude[25], takes place outside the theater, creates distance from the other parts of the film. Furthermore, the mask that Tonio wears is different from his Taddeo outfit in the second act. The filmic mise en scène, therefore, marks the prologue as a separate entity, which strengthens its potential of being recognized as a self-reflexive element by the audience and thus of eliciting the intended metareferential reflection about the relationship between life and theater. In addition it might alert the audience to pay attention to other potential metareferential elements in the following two acts.

Zeffirelli offers a different interpretation of the prologue by not vi-sually separating prelude and prologue and by not addressing the viewer of the film as directly as Costa's version does. From the start, Zeffirelli's television-opera shows a street theater, which has strong similarities to a circus tent and a cinema[26], where clowns attempt to

---

[24]   The only camera movement is zooming in and out of his face. No spectators are visible.

[25]   The first images of the film, accompanied by the prelude, show Tonio in normal street clothes preparing benches for the outdoor theater in which the performance of the play will take place in the second act.

[26]   The theater resembles a tent with sides that can easily be opened to let spectators in and out. They are decorated with writings (e. g. "ponte dei sospiri" ['bridge of sighs']) and various images, such as clowns or stars. The spot lighting the stage or the

express, through body gestures and miming, the meaning of the musical themes and motifs of the prelude[27]. Once the prologue begins, Tonio steps out in his Taddeo costume and performs in front of a fictional audience, mostly composed of children[28]. This interpretation changes the self-referential quality of the prologue and highlights the distinctiveness of this artistic product: Zeffirelli's interpretation for television of Leoncavallo's opera *Pagliacci*.

By opening this television-opera on a theater stage with clowns and a fictional audience, Zeffirelli highlights the metacharacter of the scene not only on the textual but additionally also on the visual level. Through the images the viewer is immediately confronted with a 'play within a play situation'. Television-operas are typically 'performance documentations' in that they record and broadcast actual stage performances of operas (see Kühnel 2001). In contrast to this, Zeffirelli's beginning distances this version of *Pagliacci* from the genre by clearly marking the audience as fictional instead of portraying a real audience watching a stage performance of the opera. In doing so, the film visually highlights the difference between live performance on stage and the filmic interpretation of an opera. This beginning might therefore be considered a successful metareferential statement and alert the audience of the film to the metareferential qualities of the work not only through Tonio's words, but especially through the filmic mise en scène.

The second metareferential element discussed above was the contrast between life and stage, or between reality and fiction, referred to several times during the first act. The play within the opera's second act then highlights this paradigm in form of a mise en abyme. Both

---

performers comes from projectors in the back of the theater. The projection of light onto the stage resembles the projection of a film in a movie cinema.

[27]   The presence of clowns has been interpreted as interfilmic reference to Fellini's films, such as *I Clowns* (1971) or *La strada* (1954) (see O'Connor 1984). The reference to cinema additionally highlights the intermedial relationship of the television-opera to spectacle in general and cinema in particular.

[28]   At the beginning of the prologue, the clowns disappear. They return when the text of the prologue refers to commedia dell'arte elements. At the line "Un nido di memorie" ('a nest of memories') Tonio takes off his wig. During the last part of the prologue, where the text reminds the audience to think about actors as real people, he enters the space of the fictional audience.

films closely follow the libretto, score, and stage directions, but due to different mise en scène and camera work the results are different.

Costa's film-opera focuses on the events on stage after defining an open air theater as the space where the action takes place. While the intratextual and intracompositional references between the commedia and the first act of the opera are musically and verbally presented, no additional visual ties are created with the prologue or the first act[29].

Zeffirelli's version, on the other hand, stresses the textual and musical connections between the first and the second parts of the opera by additionally emphasizing relevant moments with the camera. Since in this version the commedia is staged in the same space where the prologue was performed, and since the clowns that were present during the prelude and prologue are also shown, an important visual connection is created between the prologue and the beginning of the second act[30].

A significant difference between the two versions is the use of commedia dell'arte masks and the theatrical mise en scène of the play. In Costa's version, only Arlecchino and Pagliaccio wear recognizable costumes, while the other characters are hardly distinguishable from their appearance in the first act. Zeffirelli, on the other hand, creates a sensation of artificiality through heavy make-up and clearly distinguishable characteristic commedia dell'arte costumes, unnatural stage movements[31], and the inclusion of stage gags, such as a table that automatically moves down. By emphasizing the artificiality of the commedia dell'arte play, the contrast between the play and the world

---

[29] In one instance, the film changes the mode of the presentation by visualizing Arlecchino's serenade through a high-angle shot, which emphasizes the filmic nature of the work, but otherwise has no consequence for the metareferential quality of the interpretation.

[30] These visual cues also strengthen the intracompositional function of the sounds of the trumpets that open the first as well as the second act. Another important visual signal connecting events of the first and the second act is a repeated shot of a knife. A knife is used in the first act by Nedda in order to defend herself from Tonio's advances and to scare him away. At the end of the first act, Canio threatens Nedda also with a knife. Towards the end of the commedia it is Tonio who hands Canio the knife that will kill Nedda. In each of those instances the camera shows the knife in a close-up shot.

[31] This is made especially obvious during the duet between Columbina and Arlecchino, when the camera highlights the characters' simulation of eating without having food on their plates or kissing without touching each other.

of the troupe is increased. Zeffirelli also stresses the role of the fictional audience more than Costa does by frequently showing them in close-ups and having the murders take place in the seating area of the theater.

We therefore can conclude that the self-reflexive aspect of the mise en abyme is visually stronger in the Zeffirelli version than in the Costa version. Against the tradition probably started by Caruso or De Lucia of giving the last words of the opera to Canio, Tonio has the last word in the Zeffirelli version, which additionally fosters the link to the prologue[32].

Regarding the filmic interpretation of self- and metareferential elements of libretto and score, both versions include all musical and textual self- as well as metareferences. Their visual weight, however, is different. While the prologue creates a strong narrative break in Costa's film-opera, Zeffirelli uses additional visual elements to highlight its self-reflexive character. The self-reflexive character of the play and the opera's ending is stronger in Zeffirelli's version. Although it depends ultimately on the capability and willingness of the viewer that the metareferential quality of the opera is actualized, both film versions certainly offer the possibility of recognizing pertinent self-reflexive elements.

Both film versions also take the metadiscourse a step further by reflecting not only on the relationship between life and theater, but additionally on the medium used to present this opera. While Zeffirelli's version only points to other media or spectacle forms, such as the circus or the cinema[33], and thus distances itself from the genre of television-opera, Mario Costa's version implicitly highlights the different narrative possibilities of stage and screen.

After the prelude, the camera focuses on the opera stage, on which Tonio presents the prologue. This represents an 'explicit intermedial reference' (cf. Wolf 2002: 23–26) to the theater and thus creates a link between film and the older art form. In contrast to the conventions of

---

[32]   This closes the narrative circle opened by the last words of the prologue: "incominciate" ("let's begin"; Fisher, ed. 2002: 64). Regarding the significance of the last words (and its pronouncer) see Wright 1978.

[33]   Another intermedial reference is made during the first scene of the first act by focusing several times on a photographer taking pictures. The relationship between this television-opera and photography, though, remains only on the surface level, since no further medial self-reflection takes place.

theater, however, Tito Gobbi plays both baritone roles, Tonio as well as Silvio. While both roles are cinematographically clearly distinguishable through different costumes, the film's opening credits alert the audience to this curiosity, which on stage would be extremely difficult to realize. In film, on the other hand, due to editing, this is made possible[34].

Another example of emphasizing the filmic possibilities is the visualization of the intermezzo, for which Costa employs a visual flashback showing how Nedda was saved from starvation by the commedia dell'arte troupe, how Nedda and Canio fell in love, and how the two got married. While this flashback might distract from the contrast between the story of the first act and the commedia, it demonstrates the possibilities of the medium film to quickly change between space and time.

Mario Costa's film-opera therefore not only incorporates the meta-references of libretto and score of the opera, but elicits additional reflections about the different narrative potentials of opera and film by demonstrating that film has different possibilities in visually presenting opera than a stage performance.

3. Conclusion

While it is certainly possible to identify hetero-references as well as self- and metareferential elements by reading an opera libretto and score, their actualization takes place during a performance of the opera. This is equally true for a stage performance, a film-opera, or television-opera. Through the analysis of text and score of Leoncavallo's *Pagliacci*, this paper first identified several potential metareferences employed by the text and the score of the opera. Of particular significance in this regard are the opera's prologue and the contrast between the first and the second acts, i. e., between the reality of the actors and the play performed within the opera.

---

[34]   A similar phenomenon – although quite typical of Italian film-operas of the post-war period – is the separation of voice and physical interpretation of the characters. Nedda's role is thus divided between Onelia Fineschi (voice) and Gina Lollobrigida (physical interpretation). Afro Poli appears as Canio, lipsynching the voice of Galliano Masini.

Considering the interplay of the different media employed in Mario Costa's film-opera and Franco Zeffirelli's television-opera, it can be concluded that the metareferential potential of the opera is differently expressed in the two medial interpretations. While in both cases the self-reflexive quality of the opera is successfully communicated, individual metareferential aspects are weighted differently. Furthermore, both versions take advantage of the medial possibilities of film by creating additional self-reflections with cinematographic means. The degree of metareferentiality of an opera, and especially of an opera on screen, depends therefore not only on the aural and textual concretization of libretto and score, but also, and in particular, on the performance and visual presentation, which may strengthen or weaken potential self-reflexive elements.

References

Bini, Daniela (1985). "'... Ma quale 'commedia è finita'?' A Pirandellian Reading of Leoncavallo's *Pagliacci*". *Canadian Journal of Italian Studies* 8/31: 173–184.

Carter, Tim (1992). "Prologue". Stanley Sadie, ed. *New Grove Dictionary of Opera*. Vol. 3. London: Macmillan. 1142f.

Citron, Marcia (2000). *Opera on Screen*. New Haven, CT: Yale University Press.

Costa, Mario, dir. (1948). *Pagliacci*. Perf. Gina Lolobrigida (voice: Onelia Fineschi), Afro Poli (voice: Galliano Masini), Tito Gobbi. Rome Opera Orchestra and Chorus. Cond. Giuseppe Morelli. DVD. Bel Canto Society.

Dalmonte, Rossanna (1982). "Il prologo de *I Pagliacci*: Nota sul verismo in musica". *Musica/Realtà* 8: 105–114.

Dorsi, Fabrizio, Giuseppe Rausa (2000). *Storia dell'opera italiana*. Milano: Mondadori.

Dryden, Konrad (2007). *Leoncavallo: Life and Works*. Lanham, MD: Scarecrow Press.

Fisher, Burton D., ed. (2002). *Mascagni's* Cavalleria Rusticana / *Leoncavallo's* I Pagliacci. Opera Classics Library. Coral Gables: Opera Journey's Publishing.

Girardi, Michele (1993). "Il verismo musicale alla ricerca dei suoi tutori: Alcuni modelli di *Pagliacci* nel teatro musicale *Fin de Siècle*". Maehder/Guiot, eds. 61–70.

Guarnieri Corazzol, Adriana (1993). "Opera and Verismo: Regressive Points of View and the Artifice of Alienation". Trans. Roger Parker. *Cambridge Opera Journal* 5/1: 39–53.

Hanslick, Eduard (1896/1987). *"Der Bajazzo (Pagliacci)"*. Attila Csampai, Dietmar Holland, eds. *Pietro Mascagni,* Cavalleria Rusticana */ Ruggero Leoncavallo,* Der Bajazzo*: Texte, Materialien, Kommentare*. Reinbek: Rowohlt. 173–181.

Helbig, Jörg (2001). "Intermediales Erzählen: Baustein für eine Typologie intermedialer Erscheinungsformen in der Erzählliteratur am Beispiel der Sonatenform von Anthony Burgess' *A Clockwork Orange"*. Jörg Helbig, ed. *Erzählen und Erzähltheorie im 20. Jahrhundert: Festschrift für Wilhelm Füger*. Heidelberg: Winter. 131–152.

Kuhn, Bernhard (2005). *Die Oper im italienischen Film*. Fora: Studien zu Literatur und Sprache 9. Essen: Die Blaue Eule.

Kühnel, Jürgen (2001). "'Mimesis' und 'diegesis' – szenische Darstellung und filmische Erzählung: Zur Ästhetik der Oper in Film und Fernsehen". Peter Csobádi, et al., eds. *Das Musiktheater in den audiovisuellen Medien: '...ersichtlich gewordene Taten der Musik'. Vorträge und Gespräche des Salzburger Symposions 1999*. Anif: Müller-Speiser. 60–79.

Leoncavallo, Ruggero (1892/1963). *Pagliacci: Opera in Two Acts*. New York, NY: G. Schirmer.

Lerario, Teresa (1971). "Ruggero Leoncavallo e il soggetto dei *Pagliacci"*. *Chigiana: Rassegna annuale di studi musicologici* 26–27: 115–121.

Maehder, Jürgen, Lorenza Guiot, eds. (1993). *Ruggero Leoncavallo nel suo tempo: Atti del I Convegno internazionale di studi su Ruggero Leoncavallo*. Milano: Sonzogno.

Malach, Alan (2007). *The Autumn of Italian Opera: From Verismo to Modernism, 1890 – 1915*. Lebanon, NH: Northeastern University Press.

O'Connor, John J. (1984). "TV Weekend: Zeffirelli's *Pagliacci* from La Scala in 1982". *The New York Times*, 9 Sept. C 29.

Piccardi, Carlo (1993). "Pierrot – Pagliaccio: La maschera tra naturalismo e simbolismo". Maehder/Guiot, eds. 201–245.

Sansone, Matteo (1989). "The 'Verismo' of Ruggero Leoncavallo: A Source Study of *Pagliacci"*. *Music & Letters* 70/3: 342–362.

— (1992). "Verismo". Stanley Sadie, ed. *New Grove Dictionary of Opera*. Vol. 4. London: Macmillan. 954–957.

Wolf, Werner (2002). "Intermediality Revisited: Reflections on Word and Music Relations in the Context of a General Typology of Intermediality". Suzanne M. Lodato, Suzanne Aspden, Walter Bernhart, eds. *Word and Music Studies: Essays in Honor of Steven Paul Scher and on Cultural Identity and the Musical Stage.* Word and Music Studies 4. Amsterdam/New York, NY: Rodopi. 13–34.

— (2007). "Metafiction and Metamusic: Exploring the Limits of Metareference". Winfried Nöth, Nina Bishara, eds. *Self-Reference in the Media.* Approaches to Applied Semiotics 6. Berlin: de Gruyter. 303–324.

Wright, John (1978). "'La commedia è finita': An Examination of Leoncavallo's *Pagliacci*". *Italica* 55/2: 167–178.

Zeffirelli, Franco, dir. (1982). *Pagliacci.* Perf. Teresa Stratas, Plácido Domingo, Juan Pons. La Scala Orchestra and Chorus. Cond. Georges Prêtre. VHS. Unitel.

Zola, Emile (1880/1989). *Du Roman: sur Stendhal, Flaubert et les Goncourt.* Brussels: Editions Complexe.

Intermedial Reference as Metareference
Hans Christian Andersen's Musical Novels

Joachim Grage, Freiburg[1]

Metareference is a feature which is to be found in numerous texts by the Danish author Hans Christian Andersen, predominantly in the form of intertextual references. However, his two novels *Only a Fiddler* (1845) and *Lucky Peer* (1871) also contain intermedial references through which the works' metareferential character is established. These novels are characterised by their manifold references to music, which can also be understood as literary self-reference, as music is conceived of as a medium of narration in both texts. *Only a Fiddler* in particular suggests an analogy between literature and music which goes beyond merely considering both forms of language. The lack of social and economic recognition for the artist likewise refers to music as well as to literature. This very lack is articulated in the text and accompanied by counterexamples, while the differences between literature and music in terms of performance are not addressed thematically but are rather shown through the storyline. The direct communication between musician and audience during a performance is largely unachievable in literary communication, and the differences in the respective courses of education of musicians and poets are used to make narratable the education of an artist as the development in technical skill and craft.

1.

Instead of approaching the topic of metareference in literature and music systematically or through actual comparison, I would like to limit myself to an analysis of self-reflectivity in a specific group of literary texts in which the intermedial reference to music plays a significant role. In a paper on "Metafiction and Metamusic", Werner Wolf has already characterized "intermedial references, for instance the relation between literary texts and music embodied in verbal descriptions of musical compositions", as "self-reference in the broad sense" (2007: 305). In examining novels by Hans Christian Andersen, I would like

---

[1] Translated from German by Rett Rossi (Berlin), including all quotes unless indicated otherwise. – I would like to thank Rett Rossi and Janet Duke, Freiburg, for comments on the manuscript.

to pursue this and examine the contexts and conditions which engender metareferentiality in intermedial references to music, as well as the ways in which such references differ from purely intra-literary self-reference. After briefly looking at self-referentiality in other works by Andersen, I will base my argument primarily on the analysis of *Only a Fiddler* (1837) with a short digression to an earlier Andersen poem set to music by Robert Schumann.

2.

Hans Christian Andersen became internationally renowned first and foremost as an author of fairytales. However, his *Tales and Stories*, which he wrote incessantly from 1835 onward, constitute only a small part of his literary œuvre. While he gained world fame as a master of this particular genre, he also wrote six novels, numerous travel books, poems and plays. Already his first book, the humorous travelogue *A Walking Tour from Holmen's Canal to the Eastern Point of Amager in the Years 1828 and 1829* (Andersen 1829/1986), bears witness to Andersen's inclination for metareference. Following a path of a mere few miles, the journey described takes but a few hours, and not two years, as the title implies. In fact, it takes all of one single night: that of New Year's Eve, 1828. Being an uneventful expedition, it hardly provides the opportunity for narratorial hetero-reference which one would expect from a travelogue. Instead, the narrator elaborately describes who he writes the self-same travelogue. In so doing, he at the same time allows the book itself to have its say, as the subtitle of Chapter 6 announces:

> The book tells *the story of its childhood*, its *schooldays* at the bookbinder, its *release* to the Gyldendal Bookstore, *its first semester*, and finally its first excursion into the world. – The clock strikes 12.[2]

Such an approach displays all the signs of metareflexive narration, because the text not only discusses itself, but also reflects on itself and its mediality. Furthermore, Andersen ignites a firework of intertextual references, from the Bible to the authors of the German and Danish Romantic period, and thus simultaneously locates his text within the

---

[2]   "Bogen fortæller sin *Barndoms Historie,* sit *Skoleliv* hos Bogbinderen, *Dimission* til den Gyldendalske Boglade, *Rusaaret,* og endelig sin første Udflugt i Verden. – Klokken slaaer 12." (Andersen 1829/1986: 36)

context of contemporary culture and literature. The reader hence receives both the read as well as the instructions on how to use it: read me like a text by Ludwig Tieck or E. T. A. Hoffmann!

The novels that Andersen published after 1833 are less playful but continue the pronounced metareferential style. This already becomes clear from the subjects that Andersen deals with. The three novels from the 1830s, *The Improvisatore* (1833), *O. T.* (1835), and *Only a Fiddler* (1837)[3], are 'Bildungsromane' constantly discussing contemporary literary discourse: the first novel's title, refers to a poet as the protagonist. *The Improvisatore* tells the story of a Roman orphan who shows poetic talent early on and – against the opposition of a well-meaning patron – works his way up to being a celebrated improviser. He performs on stage and delivers verses that he spontaneously invents in response to the audience's suggestions. These poems for the most part deal with autobiographical events which the protagonist has experienced (and which have been told in the novel), a doubling which creates a remarkable self-reference within the novel and foregrounds details which moreover covertly refer to the author Andersen: the contemporary reader in the comparatively intimate city of Copenhagen knew that Andersen, too, came from impoverished circumstances and only managed to attain a secondary education with the help of rich benefactors. For the non-Danish reader this information is disclosed in the biographical preface of the German and English editions[4], or by way of Andersen's autobiography circulating at almost the same time as the novel[5].

Andersen's autobiographical motifs such as his origins in the lower social strata, the early loss of his father, and his yearning for the theatre as a place of self-realization are also discernible in *Only a*

---

[3]   Danish titles: *Improvisatoren; O. T.; Kun en Spillemand.*

[4]   See Frits (Le) Petit's biographical preface to the German edition of *A Walking Tour:* "Das Lebensmährchen des Dichters" (Le Petit 1846).

[5]   Andersen's autobiography was first published in 1847 as *Das Märchen meines Lebens ohne Dichtung* in the first two volumes of the German complete edition (Andersen 1847a). In the same year it was translated into English by Mary Howitt and published in London as *The True Story of My Life* (Andersen 1847b). The Danish edition was published eight years later: *Mit Livs Eventyr* (Andersen 1855). Mary Howitt had also translated the first three novels, published in London in 1845: *The Improvisatore, or, Life in Italy* (Andersen 1845a) and *Only a Fiddler! and O. T., or Life in Denmark* (Andersen 1845b).

Fiddler and in his last novel, *Lucky Peer,* published in 1870[6]. However, he chooses musicians as protagonists for each. The title itself,
Only a Fiddler, indicates that the hero does not achieve the goal he
has set himself in terms of his 'Bildung' (i. e., education and self-
cultivation)[7]. Christian, the son of a simple tailor, learns to play the
violin and unfolds a tremendous talent – perhaps even that of a genius.
Nevertheless, the support he receives is not sufficient to compensate
for his blemished origins. Although he has the makings for it, he is not
a celebrated virtuoso violinist like Niccolò Paganini or the Norwegian
Ole Bull, who was renowned throughout Europe. Instead, he is 'only a
fiddler', a musician who plays dance music at village weddings and
other parties and thus barely manages to eke out a living.

The opposite of this pessimistic novel is *Lucky Peer*, the story of
the incredible career of Peer, a boy born under a lucky star, in a mixture of 'Bildungsroman' and fairytale. Already as a child he stands out
due to a voice that is as clear as a bell and goes on to become a celebrated opera singer. Yet his career does not stop there: Peer even
writes an opera, a 'Gesamtkunstwerk' in the style of Richard Wagner,
based on the story of Aladdin and the Magic Lamp. As in the poems
recited in *The Improvisatore*, the hypodiegetic narrative level here,
too, reflects the intradiegetic level, that is, Peer's life story. Like
Aladdin, Peer, is lucky, which is emphasized by his singing the title
role himself at the opera's premiere. However, as if it were hubris to
let his own life dissolve into art, Andersen lets his character have a
stroke during the final applause and collapse dead on the open stage[8].

Whereas literary self-reference in *Lucky Peer* is primarily apparent
in the superposition of narrative levels, *Only a Fiddler* emphasizes
self-reference by exploring its own mediality in a remarkable way.
First of all, Andersen places one or two mottos before each of the
novel's 38 chapters – a total of 48 citations from German, Danish,
Swedish, and French literary works of the 18th and 19th centuries –
lines from plays, verses from poems, sentences from prose narratives,
but also texts from encyclopaedias, half of them in German. These

---

[6]   See Andersen 1870/2000. An English translation by Horace E. Scudder was
published in *Scribner's Monthly*.

[7]   For an analysis of the novel's position in the tradition of the 'Bildungsroman' cf.
de Mylius 1981: 122–163.

[8]   For a deeper analysis of the novel cf. de Mylius 1981: 210–225 and see Davidsen
1993.

intertextual mottos produce a frame of reference, which exhibits a peculiar ambiguity between self-reference and hetero-reference. The texts are simultaneously part of the ontologically real world of the author and reader and of the fictitious world in which all of them (except for the encyclopaedic excerpts) have the same fictional status as the story about the fiddler Christian. This is particularly obvious when Andersen cites, as a motto, an aphorism written in his autograph book by the Viennese author Ignaz Franz Castelli (cf. Andersen 1837/1988: 214). In the chapter that follows, Castelli metaleptically appears as a figure in the novel and interacts with the fictional character[9]. This is not meant to make the events more authentic, but rather to foreground the fictionality of the story. The reader witnesses how Andersen reciprocates the friendly entry in his autograph book. Besides, the mottos also serve to emphasize Andersen's knowledge of European literature.

Moreover the author allows his figures to act as if they knew that they are part of a fictional text: 'This is as in a novel!' Naomi, the story's second protagonist remarks about the life of artists who gain fame, 'but I want them to be unhappy at the end of their lives. It's so interesting!'[10] This is not exactly an 'ontological' metalepsis of the kind that is frequently employed in Romantic texts, but it does reflect the rules of the genre and the category of 'the interesting' which this epic form is based on. It is thus no wonder that the novel, in fact, has a sad and 'interesting' ending.

3.

It is, however, not only the self-reflexive relations between intra- and extra-textual elements in the semantic system of language, nor the intertextual references to literature in general that lend these novels their metareferential character. It is rather music that plays an important role as a sign system and object of intermedial reference[11].

---

[9] Cf. Andersen 1837/1988: 214–222. Andersen also has Franz Grillparzer appear.

[10] "'Det er som i en Roman!' sagde *Naomi,* 'men jeg vil have, at de skulle blive ulykkelige i Slutningen af deres Liv. Det er saa interessant!'" (Andersen 1937/1988: 130)

[11] The role of music as a medium that contrasts with literature in Andersen's works has not yet been examined systematically. Andersen's relationship to music in general has been treated by Hetsch 1930, Sørensen 2005, and Wenzel Andreasen 2005.

The medium, in which the artists in both novels try to develop and express themselves, is indeed not language but music. The fictional music, which is discussed in the text, is illustrated through comparisons to extra-textual music. A scene from *Only a Fiddler*, in which Christian hears how his godfather plays the violin, should serve as an example:

> Every ear that was open to sound stopped short. It was this melodic moaning that called forth the legend of *Paganini's* violin into the world, namely that he killed his mother and that her soul now trembled through the strings.
>
> Soon the sound blended into gentle melancholy; *the Amphion of the North, Ole Bull* called the same theme on his violin: "A Mother's Pain on the Death of her Child". His playing did not have the same perfection as both these contemporary masters in *Jubal's* art had, but it hinted at both, like the green branch in all of its details hints at the entire tree.[12]

Diegetic music is here set in relation to extra-textual reality by references to the contemporary star violinists Niccolò Paganini and Ole Bull. On the one hand this is done in order to describe the acoustic impression, but on the other hand it is done to semanticize the diegetic music and relate it to language. Playing the violin is linked to language twice: first through the 'melodic moaning' with the legend of the mother of the devil's violinist, Paganini, trembling through the strings, and then through the title of a composition by the Norwegian Ole Bull. In both cases music expresses matters that are not musical in themselves, and in both cases a concrete semantic content is assigned to it that can also be put into words. Music thus becomes a medium of expression that shares with language the potential for narration – music can not only express, but also tell: 'In its own way, music tells equally wonderful things as the godfather's tongue'[13]. A Romantic stereotype is thus invoked: the idea of music as language beyond language, as a language that does not need words, as the most direct

---

[12] "Ethvert for Tonerne aabnet Øre vilde have studset ved at høre derpaa. Det var denne melodiske Jamren, der fra *Paganinis* Violin skabte Sagnet, at han havde dræbt sin Moder, og at hendes Sjæl nu bævede gjennem Strængene.

Snart gik Tonen over i en blød Veemod, Nordens *Amphion: Ole Bull* kaldte det samme Thema paa sin Violin: 'En Moders Smerte ved Barnets Død'. Vel var det ikke denne Fuldendthed, som disse to, vor Tids Mestre i *Jubals* Kunst besidde, men det antydede begge, som den grønne Green i alle Enkeltheder antyder det hele Træ, den tilhører." (Andersen 1837/1988: 29f.)

[13] "Violinen fortalte paa sin Maade ligesaa forunderlige Ting, som Gudfaderens Tunge." (Andersen 1837/1988: 31)

medium of expression, which can bypass the rational mind and speaks directly to the human heart. This is also made clear elsewhere, when the grown-up Christian sits alone in his wretched garret and drives away the hunger and cold by playing his fiddle: '*Mendelssohn-Bartholdy* gave us the gift of a few musical compositions: "Lieder ohne Worte"; every kindred bosom will understand their lyrics in his soul'[14]. This is obviously an allusion to the Romantic concept of music. The songs without words need no interpreter, because the competent listener can intuitively and directly decipher musical semantics. What the verbal text thus evoked actually means remains, however, untold. Tied in with this example of Romantic music, the text continues:

> We could also add words to *Christian's* fiddle playing; may they be heard in the halls of the mighty, may in each century a true talent be saved from deprivation and hardship: Almighty! You grasp the works of the painter and sculptor, as these decorate your halls, but the utterances of the poets, the works of the musicians still seem a game to you; the richest tapestries of the spirit, which neither moths nor mould can consume, you do not understand, you first have to be told for a century of their divineness. *Do not allow the true talent to perish from earthly matters!* – May the words be heard, – in the same way *Christian's* fiddle playing was.[15]

The narrator understands the music the protagonist plays on his fiddle as a self-reflexive and metareferential comment which discusses the conditions of producing art and appeals to the listener. These statements are, however, based on the same conditions as is every metareflexive text. As Werner Wolf puts it: "[it] requires the actualization of such potentials by recipients who are willing and able to co-operate, for it is in the recipient that the essence of metareference, the eliciting of a medium awareness, takes place" (2007: 307). However, in the novel, those supposed to hear this message lack the correspond-

---

[14] "*Mendelssohn-Bartholdy* har givet os nogle musikalske Compositioner: 'Lieder ohne Worte'; ethvert beslægtet Bryst vil i sin Sjæl opfatte Texten til disse." (Andersen 1837/1988: 229)

[15] "*Christians* Violinspil kunne vi ogsaa underlægge Ord; gid de hørtes i de Mægtiges Sale, gid i hvert Aarhundrede dog eet sandt Talent frelstes fra Savn og Mangel: Du Mægtige! Du fatter Malerens og Billedhuggerens Værker, thi disse pynte hine Sale; men Digterens Frembringelser, Tonekunstnerens Værker ere Dig endnu en Leg; Aandens rigeste Tapeter, som ei Møl eller Rust kunne fortære, begriber Du ei ret, et Aarhundrede maa først have fortalt Dig om deres Guddommelighed. *Lad ei det sande Talent jordisk gaae til Grunde!* – Ordene blive hørte, – ja vist, som *Christians* Violinspil blev det." (Ibid.)

ing senses, or are not even compelled to listen, as Christian does not have the opportunity to perform in the halls of potential promoters, but is rather left to play in his attic room.

There is another interesting aspect to the quoted passage, though: it is made quite clear here that the reference to the semantic system of music within the literary text is to be understood as metareferential per se – the conditions for producing literature and music are differentiated from those of the visual arts. The text thus enters into an explicit media-reflexive discourse about the classic triad of the arts, whose phenomenological and semiotic differences were extensively addressed in contemporary discussions on aesthetics[16]. A distinction is made with regard to the social recognition and market value of the respective types of art. The narrator notes a divide between the representatives of the visual arts on the one hand and music and literature on the other. What is said about the semantics of music should therefore also apply to the semantics in which the text itself operates. Furthermore, one can understand this connection as an indication for this also applying to the entire novel: music is a metaphor for language. This has to be stated explicitly, because it is not necessarily obvious.

Upon taking a closer look, it becomes apparent that music is here instrumentalized in the interest of literature. First of all, it is obviously wrong that one needs a century of distance before being able to appropriately judge Christian's art. After all, his art manifests itself solely in the performative act of the recital. Christian is a performer, not a composer. In the days before appropriate storage media, his art – in contrast to literature that can be archived and memorized through writing and printing – is too transitory to survive a century. Secondly the novel itself provides evidence against the lack of social recognition for the virtuoso artists with the references to Paganini and Ole Bull. A few years later, Andersen himself described the celebrity hype about the pianist Franz Liszt, who had half of Europe lying ecstatically at his feet[17]. Thirdly, literature itself ultimately developed from

---

[16] The Danish participants in this discussion, who were all familiar with German Romanticism and idealistic philosophy, were Hans Christian Ørsted, Frederik Christian Sibbern, Johan Ludvig Heiberg, Søren Kierkegaard and others; cf. Koch 2004: 73–78, 138–145, 233–236. For Kierkegaard's theory of language and music see Grage 2005.

[17] Cf. the chapter "Lißt" in Andersen's travelogue *En Digters Bazar* from 1842 (Andersen 1826–1842/2006: 226–229). See also von Essen 2006.

occasional poetry, which served the purpose of representation, before becoming an autonomous art. In this process, literature's breaking away from patronage is a consequence of a literary-historical emancipation process.

Despite these obvious breaks in the narrative argument, the novel establishes a possibility for the word-artist's identification with the figure of the musician. He fails to achieve his artistic goal because he has not found the support and recognition due him. In that Andersen takes up a pattern upon which he had already based a poem several years earlier: "The Fiddler", written in 1831, translated into German in the same year by Adelbert von Chamisso ("Der Spielmann") and set to music a decade later by Robert Schumann (op. 40, n° 4):

The Fiddler

> In the little town there is much rejoicing,
> a wedding taking place with dance and revelry.
> For the happy man the wine sparkles so red,
> but the bride is as white as death.

> She is indeed dead to him she cannot forget,
> who is at the feast but not as the bridegroom:
> he stands amid the guests at the inn,
> playing his fiddle cheerfully enough.

> He caresses his fiddle, his hair turning grey,
> the strings vibrating shrill and loud.
> He presses it to his heart, regardless of whether
> it too shatters into a thousand pieces.

> It is horrible for one to die like this
> when his heart is young, still courting joy.
> I cannot and will not watch him longer!
> It might turn my head dizzy!

> Who told you to point a finger at me?
> O God, in Thy mercy preserve us all
> from being overcome with madness.
> I myself am a poor musician.[18]

---

[18]   Translated by Lionel Salter (see Andersen 1995), based on the German translation by Chamisso. Danish text: "I Landsbyen gaaer det saa lystigt til, / Der holdes et Bryllup med Dands og Spil; / Der drikkes Skaaler I Viin og Mjød, / Men Bruden ligner en pyntet Død. // Ja død hun er for sin Hjertenskjær, / Thi han er ikke som Brudgom her, / I Krogen han staaer med Sorgen sin, / Og spiller saa lystig paa Violin. // Han spiller til Lokkerne blive ham graae, / Han spiller saa Strængene briste maae, / Til Violinen, med Sorg og Gru, / Han trykker mod Hjertet reent itu. // Det er saa tungt, saa knusende tungt, / At døe mens Hjertet endnu er ungt! / Jeg mægter ei længer at see

The poem already connects the existence of a fiddler with an unful-filled love and deep desperation, which in the lyrical text (albeit not in the novel) ends in madness. The fiddler's identification with the poetic voice of the text's narrator also indicates that the media of language and music are considered to be interchangeable. The musician, who plays his fiddle until it shatters in his hands, turns out to be the doppelganger of the poetic voice – who at the end of the original Danish poem also indicates that he is a "Spillemand", i. e., a fiddler.

4.

The novel *Only a Fiddler* suggests an analogy between literature and music in that both lack social and economic recognition. This ob-scures the fact that they are subject to fundamentally different condi-tions of production and performativity. The social systems of music and literature exhibit clear differences which, however, do not go as far as to question their comparability in a fundamental way. It is these differences in particular that make it attractive to transfer a story about the conditions of the artist from the literary to the music system in the first place: in the latter, the artist's educational background can be much more vividly presented. I would like to consider the issue of performativity as one of the aforementioned differences first.

Christian is socially recognized as an artist during his perfor-mances; for instance, when, as a child, he appears at a social gathering of an earl, or later, when he plays the intermezzo at a private theatre performance. He receives attention from a group of people who give him direct feedback about his art through applauding him, encourag-ing him or giving him money as a form of recognition. Performing music thus differs fundamentally from the performativity of literature, which has a broad spectrum of forms, ranging from public to private readings or to quietly and solitarily indulging in a read. However, lit-erary reception usually takes place in the absence of the author, who is denied recognition in the immediate dialogue with the public, thus being'estranged' from his readers.

---

derpaa! / Jeg føler det gjennem mit Hoved gaae. // See Mændene holde ham fast i Favn – / – Men hvorfor nævne I mig ved Navn? / *Vor Herre* bevare Enhvers Forstand! / Jeg selv er en fattig Spillemand." (Andersen 1823–1829/2005: 222)

Furthermore, from a narratological point of view, the dialogue between the author and the reader is subject to conditions different from those of a musical performance. In literature, the reception of the artwork can be represented through scenic narration which simulates a particular concrete situation both with regard to time and space. In contrast to this it is significant that in the 'Bildungsroman', in which the main figure is a poet, Andersen chose an improviser, whose art is consummated at the moment of a theatrical performance in front of a large audience. Should one have instead wanted to mimetically represent writing and reading within a literary text, it would have demanded a larger degree of self-reflexivity. This, in turn, would require a very high degree of awareness and attentivenss from the reader. The intermedial metaphorization of literature through music is therefore quite suitable.

Moreover music has a requisite at hand in the form of an instrument – in this particular case the fiddle –, which symbolizes the musical profession per se and can therefore be integrated into the plot. Christian receiving a violin from his godfather marks the beginning of his musical career, while the fact that his stepfather later sells the instrument symbolizes the opposition which the genius has to stand against. And the fiddler of Andersen's earlier poem breaking his fiddle in pain quite graphically demonstrates the self-destructive strength of his music .

Finally, music's integration into the social system offers yet further possibilities for depicting the development of a poet. All in all, the metareference to music permits a clearer unfolding of a social component, since the musical genius depends upon lessons and musical education to a much greater extent than, for example, the improviser in Andersen's first novel. The improviser is self-taught in his art, in that he reads and later imitates what he has read. Christian, in contrast, has to take lessons in order to master the instrument. He has various teachers – first his godfather and then a professional music teacher, who introduces him to musical theory. The apparent directness of performed music requires a high degree of technical and theoretical proficiency. Andersen's text mainly illustrates competence in music theory through Christian's mastering the continuo. In order to acquire systematic proficiency in music, he thus has to brood over "*Törks* Generalbasschule" (which refers to Daniel Gottlob Türk's *Kurze Anweisung zum Generalbaßspielen*, published in 1791; cf.

Andersen 1837/1988: 134). Such an education focused purely on art cannot be presented in the education of a writer.

5.

The extent to which *Only a Fiddler* is a metanovel about writing under the premise of the aesthetics of genius was already acknowledged by a famous contemporary reader. In 1838, the Danish writer and philosopher Søren Kierkegaard dedicated his first book to an extensive discussion of this novel, cryptically called *From the Papers of One Still Living, Published Against His Will.* In particular, Kierkegaard submits Andersen's philosophy of life to a caustic critique and attacks his conception of a genius who requires support from his surroundings in order to develop. Kierkegaard reads the story of Christian as a poorly camouflaged autobiography. He did not know Andersen personally, but the book still leaves the impression that Christian is a self-portrait of the author. According to Kierkegaard, the same joyless battle that Andersen himself had fought repeats itself in his work. This leaves no room for a literary sublimation of one's own life nor for a distancing the author from the main character: 'When the hero dies, Andersen dies, too, and at most forces from the reader a sigh over them both as the final impression.'[19] Kierkegaard foresaw that Andersen would take this critique very much to heart and that it would cause him a great deal of pain. Attacking Andersen's work directly injures the author, since

> '[Andersen's] novels stand in so physical a relationship to him that their genesis is to be regarded more as an amputation than as a production. And it is well enough known that even if what is amputated is far away, one sometimes involuntarily feels a purely physical pain in it'.[20]

Would Kierkegaard agree with my thesis, that Andersen's musical novels are distinctly self-reflexive and metareferential? At first glance

---

[19] "[N]aar Helten døer, døer Andersen med og afnøder i det Høieste Læseren som sidste Indtryk et Suk over dem begge." (Kierkegaard 1997: 38)

[20] "[Andersens] Romaner staae i et saa physisk Forhold til ham selv, at deres Tilblivelse ikke er saa meget at ansee for en Produktion som for en Amputation af ham selv; og det veed man jo nok, at om det saaledes Amputerede end er langt borte, føler man stundom uvilkaarligt en reen physisk Smerte deri." (Kierkegaard 1997: 39f.)

this appears to be the case. One could speak of an extreme metareference when the author and his work completely dissolve into one another. Kierkegaard laments, however, that not a single reflexive instance can be identified, that there is a lack of conscious metareferentiality which would help transcend the concrete situation represented in the text. For Kierkegaard, self-reflection and metareference require 'sentimental poetry' sensu Schiller. From Kierkegaard's perspective, Andersen is a thoroughly naïve author, in whom life dissolves into work without the two ever having been separated in the first place. In my opinion, this is a very polemical but also understandable accusation insofar as Kierkegaard formulates an aesthetic critique of this indeed quite maudlin novel. However, he overlooks the complexity of the novel's metareference by means of intertextuality, intermediality and media reflexitivity, which I have tried to elaborate here.

References

Andersen, Hans Christian (1823–1829/2005). *H. C. Andersens samlede værker*. Vol. 7: *Digte I, 1823–1829*. Ed. Klaus P. Mortensen. Copenhagen: Gyldendal.

— (1826–1842/2006). *H. C. Andersens samlede værker*. Vol. 14: *Rejseskildringer I: 1826–1842*. Ed. Klaus P. Mortensen. Copenhagen: Gyldendal.

— (1829/1986). *Fodreise fra Holmens Canal til Østpynten af Amager i Aarene 1828 og 1829*. Tekstudgivelse, efterskrift og noter af Johan de Mylius. Danske Klassikere. Copenhagen: Borgen.

— (1837/1988). *Kun en Spillemand: Original Roman i tre Dele*. Tekstudgivelse, efterskrift og noter af Mogens Brøndsted. Danske Klassikere.Copenhagen: Borgen.

— (1845a). *The Improvisatore: or, Life in Italy*. Trans. Mary Howitt. 2 vols. London: Bentley.

— (1845b). *Only a Fiddler! and O. T. or, Life in Denmark*. Trans. Mary Howitt. 3 vols. London: Bentley.

— (1847a). *Gesammelte Werke*. Vols. 1 and 2: *Das Märchen meines Lebens*. Leipzig: Lorck.

— (1847b). *The True Story of My Life: A Sketch*. Trans. Mary Howitt. London: Longman, Brown, Green, and Longmans.

— (1855). *Mit Livs Eventyr*.Copenhagen: Reitzel.

— (1870/2000). *Lykke-Peer.* Tekstudgivelse, efterskrift og noter ved Erik Dal. Danske Klassikere. Copenhagen: Borgen.— (1871). *Lucky Peer.* Trans. Horace E. Scudder. *Scribner's Monthly* 1: 270–276, 391–398, 505–516, 625–639.

— (1995). "The Fiddler". Trans. Lionel Salter. Booklet to Robert Schumann. *Frauenliebe und Leben. 5 Lieder op. 40. 15 Lieder.* Anne Sofie von Otter, Bengt Forsberg. Hamburg: Deutsche Grammophon. 31.

Davidsen, Maria (1993). "På sporet af H. C. Andersens kunstkonception". *Synsvinkler* 5: 13–36.

de Mylius, Johan (1981). *Myte og roman: H. C. Andersens romaner mellem romantik og realisme: En traditionshistorisk undersøgelse.* Copenhagen: Gyldendal.

Grage, Joachim (2005). "Durch Musik zur Erkenntnis kommen? Kierkegaards ironische Musikästhetik". *Kierkegaard Yearbook:* 418–439.

Hetsch, Gustav (1930). *H. C. Andersen og musiken.* Copenhagen: Hagerup.

Kierkegaard, Søren (1997). *Søren Kierkegaards Skrifter.* Vol. 1: *Af en endnu Levendes Papirer. Om Begrebet Ironi.* Copenhagen: Gad.

Koch, Carl Henrik (2004). *Den danske idealisme: 1800–1880.* Den danske filosofis historie 3. Copenhagen: Gyldendal.

Le Petit, Frits (1846). "Das Lebensmährchen des Dichters". Hans Christian Andersen. *Abenteuer und Mährchen einer Neujahrsnacht, auf einer Fußreise nach Amack.* Trans. from Danish and biographical note of the author Frits Le Petit. Hamburg: Gobert. 1–80.

Sørensen, Inger (2005). *H. C. Andersen og komponisterne.* Copenhagen: Gyldendal.

von Essen, Gesa (2006). "'… wie eine melodische Agonie der Erscheinungswelt': Liszt-Paraphrasen aus der ersten Hälfte des 19. Jahrhunderts". Hans Georg von Arburg, ed. *Virtuosität: Kult und Krise der Artistik in Literatur und Kunst der Moderne.* Göttingen: Wallstein. 187–216.

Wenzel Andreasen, Mogens (2005). *H. C. Andersen og musikken.* Copenhagen: Bazar Forlag.

Wolf, Werner (2007). "Metafiction and Metamusic: Exploring the Limits of Metareference". Winfried Nöth, Nina Bishara, eds. *Self-Reference in the Media.* Approaches to Applied Semiotics 6. Berlin: de Gruyter. 303–324.

Notes on Contributors

Frieder von Ammon, born 1973, is Assistan Professor of New German Literature at the University of Munich. His main areas of research are poetry, satire, paratextuality and intermediality with a special focus on the relations between literature and music. Apart from a number of articles on contemporary, modern and early modern German literature as well as on music and film, his publications include *Ungastliche Gaben: Die 'Xenien' Goethes und Schillers und ihre literarische Rezeption von 1796 bis zur Gegenwart* (Tübingen 2005). He is co-editor of *Die Pluralisierung des Paratextes in der Frühen Neuzeit: Theorie, Formen, Funktionen* (Münster 2008) and of the series *Münchner Reden zur Poesie* (Munich 2005ff.). A collection of *Texte zur Musikästhetik* is forthcoming.

Walter Bernhart, a retired Professor of English Literature at the University of Graz, Austria, is the Director of the university's "Centre for Intermediality Studies in Graz (CIMIG)" and the founding and current President of "The International Association for Word and Music Studies (WMA)". His recent publications include "What Can Music Do to a Poem? New Intermedial Perspectives of Literary Studies" (2008) and "'Pour Out … Forgiveness Like a Wine': Can Music 'Say an Existence is Wrong'?" (2009). He is Executive Editor of "Word and Music Studies (WMS)" and "Studies in Intermediality (SIM)", and has (co)edited numerous individual volumes.

Peter Dayan is Professor of Word and Music Studies at the University of Edinburgh. He began academic life as a lecturer in French, and for fifteen years, his research concentrated on French literature in the 19th century (especially Mallarmé, Nerval, Lautréamont and Sand). His growing interest in the reasons for which literature describes itself as music, and music as poetry, led to his book *Music Writing Literature, from Sand via Debussy to Derrida* (Aldershot 2006). He subsequently began to wonder whether those reasons apply to intermedial references between the other arts too; his latest book (to be published by Ashgate in 2011), *Art as Music, Music as Poetry, Poetry as Art, from Whistler to Stravinsky*, attempts to show that painting presents itself as music or poetry in much the same way.

Joachim Grage is Professor of Scandinavian Literature and Culture at the University of Freiburg, Germany, after having been Junior Professor at the University of Göttingen from 2002 until 2008. He has conducted extensive research on the literary construction of music and intermedial aesthetics in Scandinavia between romanticism and modernism for several years and has also focused on the cultural transfer between the Nordic and German-speaking countries. In addition to a number of articles on these topics he has edited a volume entitled *Musik in der klassischen Moderne: Mediale Konzeptionen und intermediale Poetologien* (2006). Other fields of research include literary biographies and performance studies. He is also co-editor of the German edition of Søren Kierkegaard's works (*Deutsche Søren Kierkegaard Edition,* 2005ff.).

Michael Halliwell studied literature and music in South Africa and at the London Opera Centre. He studied with Otakar Kraus in London, and with Tito Gobbi in Florence. He was principal baritone for many years with the Netherlands Opera, the Nürnberg Opera, and the Hamburg State Opera. He is Vice-President and Editorial Board Member of The International Association for Word and Music Studies (WMA). At the University of Sydney Conservatorium of Music he has been Chair of Vocal Studies and Opera, Pro-Dean and Head of School, and Associate Dean (Research). He performs regularly in Australia and abroad. His book, *Opera and the Novel*, was published by Rodopi (Amsterdam/New York, NY) in January, 2005.

Bernhard Kuhn is Associate Professor of Italian Studies at Bucknell University (Lewisburg, PA). His current areas of research include Italian cinema, 19th- and 20th-century Italian culture, intermediality, and in particular the relationship between opera and cinema. He is the author of *Die Oper im italienischen Film* (2005) and of several articles concerning intermedial aspects of the relationship between stage media and film.

Robert Samuels is Lecturer in Music at The Open University in the UK. He studied at Robinson College, Cambridge, reading English and Music as an undergraduate (BA, 1985), and completing a PhD in music, supervised by Derrick Puffett. He worked at Lancaster University from 1989 to 1995 before moving to his current post. His work centres on music from the nineteenth and twentieth centuries, and is principally concerned with analytical theory, aesthetics, and the relationship between music and literature. He has written on Schubert, Schumann, Mahler, Cage, Boulez and Birtwistle amongst others. His book *Mahler's Sixth Symphony: A Study in Musical Semiotics* was published by CUP in 1995. A second book, *Novel and Symphony: A Study of Nineteenth-Century Genres*, is in preparation. He is a co-ordinator of the Literature and Music Research Group at the Open University. For more information see http://www.open.ac.uk/Arts/music/rspubs.shtml.

Simon Williams is Professor and Chair of the Department of Theater and Dance at the University of California, Santa Barbara. His primary areas of research are in the history of operatic performance, of Shakespearean performance, and of acting. His major publications include *German Actors of the Eighteenth and Nineteenth Centuries* (Greenwood 1985), *Shakespeare on the German Stage* (Cambridge 1990), *Richard Wagner and Festival Theatre* (Greenwood 1994), and *Wagner and the Romantic Hero* (Cambridge 2004). He was co-editor, with Maik Hamburger, of *A History of German Theatre* (Cambridge 2008) and is the chief editor of *The Cambridge World Encyclopedia of Stage Actors and Acting* (Cambridge, forthcoming). He is also an active critic and director of opera and spoken theatre.

Werner Wolf is Professor and Chair of English and General Literature at the University of Graz/Austria. His main areas of research are literary theory (concerning aesthetic illusion, narratology, and metafiction in particular), functions of literature, 18th- to 21st-century English fiction, 18th- and 20th-century drama, as well as intermediality studies (notably between literature and music as well as the visual arts). His extensive publications include *Ästhetische Illusion und Illusionsdurchbrechung in der Erzählkunst* (1993) and *The Musicalization of Fiction: A Study in the Theory and History of Intermediality* (1999). He is co-editor of volumes 1, 3 and 5 of the book series Word and Music Studies as well as of volumes 1 and 2 of the series Studies in Intermediality: *Framing Borders in Literature and Other Media* (2006) and *Description in Literature and Other Media* (2007). He is currently supervising a project funded by the Austrian Science Fund (FWF) on 'Metareference as a Transmedial Phenomenon', in the course of which he has edited *Metareference across Media: Theory and Case Studies* (2009) as vol. 4 of the Studies in Intermediality series. He is currently preparing the next volume in the same series: *The Metareferential Turn in Contemporary Arts and Media: Forms, Functions, Attempts at Explanation.*

Volume 1

Edited by Walter Berhart, Steven Paul Scher and Werner Wolf

Word and Music Studies. Defining the Field.

Proceedings of the First International Conference on
Word and Music Studies at Graz, 1997.

Amsterdam/Atlanta, GA, 1999. 352 pp.

ISBN: 978-90-420-0577-8   Paper € 33,-/US$ 46,-
ISBN: 978-90-420-0587-7   Bound € 95,-/US$ 133,-

Volume 2

Edited by Jean-Louis Cupers and Ulrich Weisstein

Musico-Poetics in Perspective.

Calvin S. Brown in Memoriam.

Amsterdam/Atlanta, GA, 2000. XVII, 313 pp.

ISBN: 978-90-420-1522-7   Paper € 23,-/US$ 32,-
ISBN: 978-90-420-1532-6   Bound € 68,-/US$ 95,-

Volume 3

Edited by Walter Bernhart and Werner Wolf

Essays on the Song Cycle and on Defining the Field.

Proceedings of the Second International Conference on Word
and Music Studies at Ann

Amsterdam/Atlanta, GA, 2001. XII, 253 pp.

ISBN: 978-90-420-1565-4   Paper € 23,-/US$ 32,-
ISBN: 978-90-420-1575-3   Bound € 57,-/US$ 80,-

Volume 4

Edited by Suzanne M. Lodato, Suzanne Aspden, and Walter

Word and Music Studies.

Essays in Honor of Steven Paul Scher and on
Cultural Identity and the Musical Stage.

Amsterdam/New York, NY, 2002. 324 pp.

ISBN: 978-90-420-0993-6   Paper € 35,-/US$ 49,-
ISBN: 978-90-420-1003-1   Bound € 75,-/US$ 105,-

Cultural Transfer through Translation

The Circulation of Enlightened Thought in Europe by Means of Translation

Edited by
Stefanie Stockhorst

Given that the dissemination of enlightened thought in Europe was mostly effected through translations, the present collection of essays focuses on how its cultural adaptation took place in various national contexts. For the first time, the theoretical model of 'cultural transfer' (Espagne/Werner) is applied to the eighteenth century: The intercultural dynamics of the Enlightenment become manifest in the transformation process between the original and target cultures, be it by way of acculturation, creative enhancement, or misunderstanding. Resulting in shifts of meaning, translations offer a key not just to contemporary translation practice but to the discursive network of the European Enlightenment in general. The case studies united here explore both how translations contributed to the transnational standardisation of certain key concepts, values and texts, and how they reflect national specifications of enlightened discourses. Hence, the volume contributes to Enlightenment studies, at least as much as to historical translation studies.

Amsterdam/New York NY, 2010. 343 pp.
(Internationale Forschungen zur Allgemeinen und Vergleichenden Literaturwissenschaft 131)
Paper € 69,-/ US$ 97,-
E-Book € 69,-/ US$ 97,-
ISBN: 978-90-420-2950-7
ISBN: 978-90-420-2951-4

USA/Canada:
248 East 44th Street, 2nd floor,
New York, NY 10017, USA.
Call Toll-free (US only): T: 1-800-225-3998
F: 1-800-853-3881
All other countries:
Tijnmuiden 7, 1046 AK Amsterdam, The Netherlands
Tel. +31-20-611 48 21 Fax +31-20-447 29 79
Please note that the exchange rate is subject to fluctuations

Orders@rodopi.nl—www.rodopi.nl

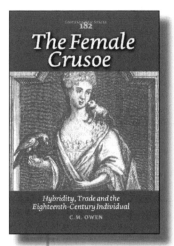

Solo Performances

Staging the Early Modern Self in England

Edited by
Ute Berns

In this volume an international cast of scholars explores conceptions of the self in the literature and culture of the Early Modern England. Drawing on theories of performativity and performance, some contributors revisit monological speech and the soliloquy — that quintessential solo performance — on the stage of Marlowe, Shakespeare and Jonson. Other authors move beyond the theatre as they investigate solo performances in different cultural locations, from the public stage of the pillory to the mental stage of the writing self. All contributors analyse corporeality, speech, writing and even silence as interrelated modes of self-enactment, whether they read solo performances as a way of inventing, authorizing or even pathologizing the self, or as a mode of fashioning sovereignty. The contributions trace how the performers appropriate specific discourses, whether religious, medical or political, and how they negotiate hierarchies of gender, rank or cultural difference. The articles cut across a variety of genres including plays and masques, religious tracts, diaries and journals, poems and even signatures. The collection links research on the inward and self-reflexive dimension of solo-performances with studies foregrounding the public and interactive dimension of performative self-fashioning. The articles collected here offer new perspectives on Early Modern subjectivity and will be of interest to all scholars and students of the Early Modern period.

Amsterdam/New York NY,
2010. 272 pp.
(Internationale Forschungen
zur Allgemeinen und
Vergleichenden
Literaturwissenschaft 132)
Paper €54,-/US$76,-
E-Book €54,-/US$76,-
ISBN: 978-90-420-2952-1
ISBN: 978-90-420-2953-8

USA/Canada:
248 East 44th Street, 2nd floor,
New York, NY 10017, USA.
Call Toll-free (US only): T: 1-800-225-3998
F: 1-800-853-3881
All other countries:
Tijnmuiden 7, 1046 AK Amsterdam, The Netherlands
Tel. +31-20-611 48 21 Fax +31-20-447 29 79
Please note that the exchange rate is subject to fluctuations

Exile in and from Czechoslovakia during the 1930s and 1940s

Edited by
Charmian Brinson
and Marian Malet

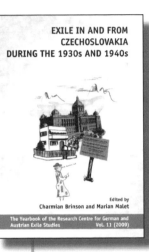

EXILE IN AND FROM
CZECHOSLOVAKIA
DURING THE 1930s AND 1940s

Edited by
Charmian Brinson and Marian Malet

The Yearbook of the Research Centre for German and
Austrian Exile Studies   Vol. 11 (2009)

This volume focuses on a previously under-researched area, namely exile in and from Czechoslovakia in the years prior to the Second World War as well as during the wartime and post-war periods. The study considers, firstly, the refugees from Germany and Austria who fled to Czechoslovakia during the 1930s; secondly, the refugees from Czechoslovakia, both German and Czech-speaking, who arrived in Britain in or around 1938 as refugees from Fascism; and thirdly, those who fled from Communism in 1948. From a variety of perspectives, the book examines the refugees' activities and achievements in a range of fields, both on a collective and an individual basis. The volume will be of interest to scholars and students of twentieth century history, politics and cultural studies as well as those involved in Central European Studies and Exile Studies. It will also appeal to a general readership with an interest in Britain and Europe in the 1930s and 1940s.

Amsterdam/New York, NY 2009. VI, 303 pp. (The Yearbook of the Research Centre for German and Austrian Exile Studies 11)
Paper €62,-/US$87,-
E-Book €62,-/US$87,-
ISBN: 978-90-420-2959-0
ISBN: 978-90-420-2960-6

USA/Canada:
248 East 44th Street, 2nd floor,
New York, NY 10017, USA.
Call Toll-free (US only): T: 1-800-225-3998
                          F: 1-800-853-3881
All other countries:
Tijnmuiden 7, 1046 AK Amsterdam, The Netherlands
Tel. +31-20-611 48 21 Fax +31-20-447 29 79
Please note that the exchange rate is subject to fluctuations

Orders @ rodopi.nl—www.rodopi.nl

Becoming Visible

Women's Presence in Late Nineteenth-Century America

Edited by
Janet Floyd,
Alison Easton, R. J. Ellis
and Lindsey Traub

This exciting collection of interdisciplinary essays explores the later decades of the nineteenth century in America — the immediate postbellum period, the Gilded Age, and the Progressive Era — as a time of critical change in the cultural visibility of women, as they made new kinds of appearances throughout American society.

The essays show how, across the USA, it was fundamentally women who drove changes in their visibility forward, in groups and as individuals. Their motivations, activities and understandings were essential to shaping the character of their present society and the nation's future.

The book establishes that these women's engagement with American society and culture cannot be simply understood in terms of the traditional polarities of inside/outside and private/public, since these frames do not fit the complexities of what was happening, be it women's occupation of geographic space, their new patterns of employment, their advocacy of working-class or ethnic rights, or their literary or cultural engagement with their milieux. Such women as Ida B. Wells, Mother Jones, Jane Addams, Rebecca Harding Davis, Willa Cather, Sarah Orne Jewett, Louisa May Alcott and Kate Douglas Wiggin all come under consideration in the light of these radical changes.

Amsterdam/New York, NY
2010. XI, 370 pp. (DQR
Studies in Literature 45)
Bound €76,-/US$106,-
E-Book €76,-/US$106,-
ISBN: 978-90-420-2977-4
ISBN: 978-90-420-2978-1

USA/Canada:
248 East 44th Street, 2nd floor,
New York, NY 10017, USA.
Call Toll-free (US only): T: 1-800-225-3998
                          F: 1-800-853-3881
All other countries:
Tijnmuiden 7, 1046 AK Amsterdam, The Netherlands
Tel. +31-20-611 48 21 Fax +31-20-447 29 79
Please note that the exchange rate is subject to fluctuations